Benevolent Aggression

Benevolent Aggression

The Necessary Impact of the Advanced Nations on Indigenous Peoples

RICHARD N. FARMER

DAVID McKAY COMPANY, INC.

New York

To Dick Hogue

With thanks for 583 argumentative lunches

PREFACE

The stink of poverty is everywhere—no one can quite get away any more. I've seen it in the Middle East, in Mexico, in Japan, in Europe, in California, and about ten blocks from where I now live in the center of mid-America. And it bothers me, as it bothers lots of people who keep running into it wherever they turn.

The enjoyment of affluence is everywhere too, at least out here in mid-America. You can go to the air-conditioned houses, sip the Scotch of the pleasant upper-middle-class types, watch their healthy kids grow up, chat with pleasant neighbors, work along side lots of nice, well-paid people, and enjoy life a bit. Maybe we're all a bunch of uptight, neurotic organization men, but at least we don't have to worry about being poor. As someone said, "Money may not be everything, but it sure as hell beats whatever comes in second."

But why are so many poor? And why are most poor typically so damn nasty, all hogwash aside about nobility, virtue, and all that? Why can't more, maybe all people, be well off in this confusing world? The problem has bothered me for as long as I can remember, and I've seen enough of it to put some of the pieces together to explain what's going on, and suggest what might be done.

My book is about the economic development of poor countries. It also takes a look at the economic development problems of poor subcultures in affluent countries, like the American ghetto. It tries to figure out how poor people all over can get rich faster.

Getting rich quicker is a pastime which has intrigued men for a long time, but only rather recently has the idea developed that a whole country could get rich quicker. Before World War II, some countries managed to grow, while others did not. If you are an American, you can anticipate a high income, even if you are poor, because the country has been growing at about 3 percent per year in income for a few hundred years. As a result, American per-capita income is now around $4,100 per year.

But lots of countries stagnated while the presently affluent ones were growing. In India, you could enjoy (or try to) an income of under $100 per year—and this fortyfold difference in per-capita income between countries is a key fact in all of modern life. The way we are going, the scenario for the year 2000 will be a small group of affluent countries steadily getting richer, surrounded by a world slum, containing two-thirds or three-quarters of the total world population, growing rich much more slowly, or worse, not growing at all.

If you happen to be one of the poor Americans, you also may find yourself out of the game by the year 2000—which is another reason to worry about wealth and poverty. The idea of a lot of poor, unproductive people out there, surrounding the affluent like you and me, is a somewhat disturbing thought. Some get ethically upset about it—most of our religions teach us that this is bad and that honest and honorable men should try to do something about it. Cynics may worry about revolution, wars, and other acts of desperate men who have no other options. And business types may be interested in better markets—you can't sell much of anything to a poor man, so if they get rich, business will improve.

Whatever our motives, the problems of poverty won't go away. When we drive into a modern downtown section of any American city, we pass through the decaying inner city, full of poverty and despair. When we go abroad, particularly to the third-world countries, we can see, feel, and smell poverty on all sides. It encroaches right to the edge of the rich enclaves foreigners typically inhabit. And if we know someone who worked in the Peace Corps or Vista, we also hear a lot about the plight of the poor.

We also hear a lot of theories about poverty: People are poor because some evil man wants it that way. Maybe—but given the ethical values in Western countries, unlikely. If my neighbor is rich, I am better off, both spiritually and economically.

If we don't like poverty, why is there so damn much of it? Why don't we do something about it? People try, but somehow, nothing works as it should. There are development plans, U.S. Commissions on every possible dimension of poverty, a local War on Poverty in the United States—and yet, people stay poor. Indeed, it sometimes seems that they are getting poorer. Why is this, and why can't we get more done than we do? Serious men and women, dedicated people, have done lots of serious thinking about poverty—yet most of the world is poor, and the way things are going, most will still be poor when you retire. We are moving ahead a bit, slowly but surely every year, yet we don't know how to do any better.

I have traveled, worked, and studied in quite a few poor countries, usually away from the foreign wealthy enclaves. This book reflects this experience. I suppose that I can qualify (dubiously) as an economic expert, since long ago I took some degrees in that field. But this is not a book for economic experts—it is for the concerned men and women who sometimes wonder why nothing ever works out as it should.

I have also done a lot of work in the American ghettos, and even more work with young black people from those ghettos, now at the university, with a foot in each culture. And I have watched the big poverty programs come and go, as stereotyped as a minuet. Big promises, big activities, and few results. Why?

In the end, it all boils down to a habit I picked up long ago, which is that of examining the unexamined premises on which so much of our social-science theory is based. Usually, something gets left out, or assumed away, whenever we spin out our theories of how to get a job done. This is fine, if our theories stay in books, but when some poor country tries them out, and spends billions to get them to work, then it becomes serious—as do the assumptions and underlying premises. So I propose to take a look at the backwoods and back rooms of the development process, trying to see what got left out, and what the results are. I also will try to figure out how it might all work out if these little bits and pieces got put in our models.

This book is not about the mainstream of economic development, although there are several chapters covering this material briefly. We are growing economically, and, believe it or not, we are actually getting a bit richer every year. The power of modern development theory is such that we can get almost any country to grow economically at a rate of from 2 to 6 percent a year compounded—which is very good, particularly if you are old enough to remember the Great Depression, when growth rates on occasion were *minus* 10 or 15 percent per year. My friends and colleagues who work very hard, both here and abroad, at the development process in a wide variety of environments, deserve a lot more credit than they usually get. The problem is not to condemn such men and women—the problem is to try to supplement their work, so that this whole messy problem can be resolved faster.

The difference is important: if all countries in the world grew at a rate of perhaps 25 percent a year, no one would be poor (by today's standards) by the year 2000. Unfortunately, we have no idea how to achieve such growth. There may be a way—there *must* be a way, if this planet is to stay glued together.

Another basic theme that runs through this book is that economic change is basically human change—that what we are doing is breaking up existing cultures and ramming something else down the throats of people who may not even be interested in change. But if we can get those people out there to make the right changes, we may be able to get our 25 percent growth rates. Much of what follows is about this point.

Prefaces are for thanks and acknowledgments, but virtually everyone I ever talked to or argued with gets into this book somehow. Just one special thanks is necessary—to S. S. Olayan, who gave me my first opportunity to see first hand lots of the things contained in this book. Mr. Olayan is a Saudi Arabian businessman, one of the cross-cultural types who are the real change agents in this world. He knows more about economic development (and lots of other things) than I could ever know, but he is far too busy changing things ever to write it down. Thanks again, Sulimon. I enjoyed the trip.

CONTENTS

CHAPTER I

. . . .

Change or Out

Who cares about economic development? A few people here and there. . . .

Sarah cares. It is hot, as usual, in the flattened-oil-can shacks on the edge of the city, facing the Arabian desert. Unlike American cities, this one is built inside out with the poor out where the suburbs might begin. Sarah nurses her youngest child, her seventh; five still survive. As is common in this Middle Eastern country, she is dressed in rags. Three of the children have some sort of rash; another has open sores. They move listlessly around the shack, since all of them are hungry. They are lucky, though—their father is working today, loading trucks down at the port. He might bring home two dollars, and they can eat tonight. Lots of people in this shack city haven't eaten today, and they might not eat tomorrow.

Sarah looks about fifty, though she is twenty-eight. She's sick too, but no one in the family would ever see a doctor, dentist, public-health official, or anyone else who might help. In this country, there is one doctor for every 6,000 people; one dentist for every 25,000; one optometrist for every 30,000. If you are unlucky enough to be sick, have rotting teeth, or need glasses, it's tough. Even if the country started today and pushed for thirty more years to get even basic social services available to all, they would never succeed, in part because the population is increasing over 3 percent per year, and officials have to run to stay even.

Sarah's shack has no electricity, toilets, running water, heating, nothing but four walls. There are no books, which doesn't matter, because no one around can read anyhow. Sarah's husband makes about $400 per year as a day laborer, scrounging jobs, carrying heavy loads by hand, burning himself out in the hot desert sun. But the family, facing passively yet one more day like the last one, really is lucky. There are a billion human beings on this planet who are poorer than they are.

Mr. Wilkins carefully pins up the ripped lining of his only suit before he leaves his neat English house to go to work. He is a clerk in an important business office in Manchester, a man with a good job, security, money. He makes $2,500 per year, which puts him and his family way up in the wealth league. Being born British, he has access to a free public-health and dental service, which seems these days to be staffed largely by Asians. Mr. Wilkins wants a car, but he can't afford it. He'd like to take his wife and two children to the seashore this summer, but that will have to wait until next year. His wife has wanted an automatic washer for years, but somehow the ever-tight budget doesn't quite stretch that far. And Mr. Wilkins is surrounded by the affluent society, which he never seems to be a part of. He knows it's affluent, since he reads about it every day in the paper. People are talking about zero population growth, pollution, and the need to cut back on consumption in order to achieve ecological balance. He wonders what he could cut back on—food? Never. House payments? Fat chance! Electricity? Hah! And his young son just missed getting accepted into the grammar school, which means that he will either have to pay $800 per year he doesn't have to send him to a public (in the United States, private) school, or kiss his son's chances for a decent education goodbye. Only 10 percent of English eighteen-year-olds get to the university, you know.

Mr. Wilkins sighs as he boards his train to take him to the city. If he could only figure out how to make a few more pounds, he would be all right. But how? What could a middle-aged man with only a grade school education do? Surrounded by the affluent society, Mr. Wilkins is feeling very poor. He doesn't know how lucky he is. Two and a half billion people are worse off than he is right now.

Johnny can't read as he sits idly in his third-grade class, possibly because he's hungry. The welfare check comes tomorrow, and funds are awfully short at home. Johnny is black, and he lives in a major American inner city. As a ghetto resident, he knows all about poverty, even though he's only ten. He's seen it every day of his life. Lord knows, his mother tries. It's hard to feed and clothe six kids on $400 a month, what with rent and food bills so high, but Johnny has neat jeans on, and he comes to school well scrubbed. After school, he can go home and watch the battered TV, seeing the affluent American world in action. In that world, anyone making less than $15,000 a year is not even considered. Working girls' apartments look like they might rent for $900 a month. But Johnny knows better because on the way home he can see the junkies, numbers boys, unemployed men, pushers, and all the rest. Johnny doesn't know how lucky he is. There are two and three quarter billion people in this world worse off than he is.

The author sits facing his $175 portable typewriter. Outside his $6,000 Oldsmobile sits. But he doesn't feel too rich despite his $IX,000 salary. He's got a daughter about to go to college, and across the table is a $600 dental bill for his thirteen-year-old. The kids all need new school clothes, and he knows about a hot stock he might buy if he could figure out how to get a few thousand clear of the endless round of taxes, bills, and payments. Just this morning, he debated with several other professors about zero-growth economies and the cost of pollution. Some argued that we simply had to slow down the economy to zero growth, since if we didn't, the country faced ecological collapse. The discussion quickly turned to whether or not we could afford both higher standards of living and pollution controls. Money doesn't count, some said, ignoring their own $15,000 to $25,000 a year. If we redistributed what we now have, we wouldn't need more. What we need is a better way of using what we already have!

Most of the world does not agree. Three-fourths of the way through the strange twentieth century, this world of ours has some really massive problems, from which no one can hide. They shape up about like this:

First, too many people are poor. If all world income were redistributed equally, your share would be $200 per year. There is a rich world, consisting of Western and Eastern Europe, North America, Japan, Australia and New Zealand, plus a few odd spots here and there. These affluent nations have about one-third of the world population, but possess over 80 percent of the world income and wealth. We do face a world maldistribution of income, as both our friends and our enemies in the poor world keep telling us. Poverty is relative—some of the supposedly affluent countries have less than one-fourth of the American average income. Many Americans on welfare get more income than the average citizen of Poland or Spain. But the Pole or Spaniard is perhaps ten times better off than the typical Pakistani or Indian.

One thing the poor want regardless of what the affluent want is more affluence. When your country has a per-capita annual income of under $400, when other countries like the United States run over $4,000, then there is only one major social and political question—namely, how to get rich faster. So we have had the Development Decade, which worked so-so, and we still have international agencies and national planning groups frantically trying to figure out how to get countries richer faster.

Second, world population is exploding. By the year 2000 there will be twice as many humans on this planet as there now are (if we're lucky—it could be more). And there are twice as many humans now as there were thirty-five years ago, in spite of famine, pestilence, and wars. Population is growing not because there are more births, but because there are fewer deaths. Death control, particularly infant-mortality control, is fairly easy; birth control, with its direct interference with the entire social fabric, is tough. All over the world, birth rates are gently dropping, but not nearly fast enough to prevent high population growth. And most of the problem is in the poorer countries, since wealthier ones, through years of change, have got their birth rates way down —often to less than half the rates in poorer countries.

With this population growth, we run to stand still economically. Doubling the population in under thirty years means that income will have to double as well, unless we have even more poverty. Because the poorer countries have the biggest population growths, they also are the ones that need the biggest income growth. It isn't working out this way. The poorer countries (or most of them) are doing modestly well in the income-growth race, averaging perhaps 4 to 5 percent per year in income gains. But 2 to 3 percent of this is immediately taken off the top by population growth. Meanwhile, in the affluent countries, economic growth runs from 3 to 10 percent per year, and averages perhaps 5 or 6. Only 1 percent comes off the top for new population, so the rich are getting richer while the poor get richer more slowly.

Third, it is becoming increasingly clear that this is spaceship earth. Everything is finite, and sooner or later you run out of key items. The world is running out of lots of things, and as income grows, so grows consumption of coal, oil, iron, and all the rest. Since the rich are getting richer, they are using up more than their share, often drawn from poorer countries. The United States, with 6 percent of the world's population, uses about one-third of the world's raw materials, and Japan and Western Europe, which are growing faster than the United States, are gaining. The one-third who are affluent are using perhaps 90 percent or more of the world's raw materials. If India were as wealthy as the United

States is, it wouldn't be, nor would the United States. That is, both countries, to say nothing of the others, would be unable to find enough raw materials and fuels to run both economies on the American standard. Toss in Red China and 800 million other consumers, and the game is ridiculous. It isn't going to happen.

Along with this consumption comes pollution. We are busily engaged in putting back into the atmosphere all the hydrocarbons that were deposited as coal and oil over hundreds of millions of years. As a result, in fifty, or maybe one hundred years, we may be back to a dinosaur climate or worse. And this statement ignores all the other nasty things industrialization does, such as ruin rivers and lakes and poison fish.

Finally, the world is on a compound growth curve where no one knows how to get off. Every fifteen years or so, we double the use of just about everything; we have to in order to get richer and maintain the ever-expanding population. While the world may be a spaceship, nations are not, and if nothing else, the rich of this world have all the good weapons systems to keep the poor in line. If you want to be the guy who keeps others in line, you'd better make sure you have the guns and bombs to do the job. Since guns and bombs normally come out of affluent societies, no one dares sit back and stagnate. If you did, moreover, what would happen to all those new people who have to be fed?

Even in the affluent countries, there is plenty of poverty, and this too is a problem. Some 30 million Americans are poor, some of them damn poor, and we would like to help them out of poverty. But getting them out of poverty involves only two possible alternatives: first, we redistribute income from the rich to the poor, something which has rarely happened, particularly in a country where the affluent are in the majority. The second option is to get richer, so that there is more to go around—and back we are on the growth track. If the United States with its $4,000 plus per-capita annual income still needs money and wealth to do the job, consider Spain, with its $800 per capita; or the Soviet Union, with its $1,000. Our reach exceeds our grasp; always we see the need for more income, more options, not less.

There is the problem in a nutshell. If we could get rich quicker, we could win the game, at least in this generation. Maybe we could control population, and maybe we could even work out ways of unpolluting the whole planet, but more affluence, more skills, more resources, and more money would make these jobs easier. The big question is, How can more wealth be created faster?

Some would argue that the game is already lost. A few countries may go down the drain, experiencing famine and pestilence, because no one can do anything. Bangladesh is a good candidate to be the first to have this dismal experience —possibly 10 or 15 million persons there may starve in the next few years, simply because no one knows how to prevent it. No one can sort out the political mess, the religious animosities, the uncontrolled birth rate, or the economic problems this country has. So, shrug your hands and forget the whole thing. Ten or fifteen million human beings is too big a number for anyone to comprehend.

But no man now alive can crawl into his shell because we are all a part of the interrelated whole. If Pakistanis starve, Americans also suffer, if only as a part of the same human race. If two-thirds of the world is rubbed in grinding poverty, then no man can be rich without some qualm of conscience about his good fate. There is no place to hide, because the whole world is a part of the problem.

Still further, others do care. For two generations now we have watched uneasily as political ideologies fought out their battles about how to organize the human society. Both sides took a simplistic version of the world. Follow Marx, and you live happily ever after, said some. If nothing else, existing Marxist states have demonstrated that there is no easy way to utopia through this system. Follow us, and you will be free, capitalist supporters cried; but there is no freedom at all in a country where per-capita incomes are under $200. Everyone is a slave to poverty, to wondering if they will even make it through next year, let alone in the long run.

Both sides in the cold war, noting that whatever happens will directly affect them, have offered material help and suggestions by the ton to the poorer countries. Nothing much seems to work very well, perhaps because our solutions are based on images of ourselves. We pass on some money, factories, or equipment to a poor country, and expect them to come out as well as if we did the job. We become economic and cultural imperialists, earnestly trying to show the ignorant heathen the way, and for some reason they call us economic imperialists and reject our advice, and often our personnel as well. The Russians are as bad as we are in this sense, if not worse, and their experience in manipulating "the heathen" has not been very good either.

Curiously, in spite of all the confusion, failures, and inept performances of the past thirty years, the world still plugs onward and upward in good style. Few ponder the fact that somehow we have managed to feed, clothe, and house twice as many people as we did thirty years ago, and somewhat better at that. World income is rising—but not fast enough to suit anyone. Somehow most countries manage to do a bit better than they did last year. Yet our reach always exceeds our grasp in the development game. For every problem solved, five pop up in its place. For every person who gains even modest affluence, a dozen poor seem to appear. For every peaceful settlement of a nasty international problem, a dozen fights seem to break out, using up precious resources for the belligerents. We not only run to stand still; we seemingly fall behind in our problem-solving. Everything is coming unstuck faster than we can put it together.

We Americans have had a peculiarly single-minded attitude toward the poor for a long time now, but most notably in the past twenty-five years. We like to help out the fellow in trouble. There was a cold war on; countries were in danger of being taken over by the Red Enemy. Hence it was important to make sure that they were not. Hence aid programs were tried. One worked very well indeed. The Marshall Plan got Western Europe going again after the war, and basically it was a very simple scheme. Just give the battered poor Europeans the necessary tools, machines, technical skills, and all the rest, and let them put it to productive use. It was done, and it worked. Western Europe did put the machines to productive use, and it took off on a growth curve never before seen in European affairs.

If this scheme worked, why not try it elsewhere? Since the mid-1950s, the United States has been aiding, in a modest way, many poorer countries. But this time, the aid hasn't worked as well as we would have liked. Money was spent, and the machines were sent, along with the technical advisers, but there was no great leap forward, no sudden surge to affluence. It all seemed to bog down in messy, inconclusive results. If something did work well, population increases quickly ate up the small gain. Americans responded by gradually losing interest. Foreign aid today is smaller as a percentage of American income than at any time since World War II.

Moreover, America had discovered poverty at home, as the poor moved in from the boondocks to the inner cities. After long years of neglect, a few riots and other unpleasantries convinced many Americans that there was plenty of antipoverty work to be done at home. Once again, images of the Marshall Plan appeared; once again massive sums were directed at the poor. And once again, nothing much happened. Small gains were quickly wiped out in small recessions. Programs full of noble goals bogged down in messy bureaucratic finagling, inept applications, and just plain bad planning. The poor are still with us, in spite of our good intentions, both at home and abroad.

Both at home and abroad, we were surprised to find that few were interested in becoming mini-WASPs, pale imitations of the real and virtuous thing, which we affluent know we are. Since we're rich, we know the proper behavior for getting and staying rich. But other unfortunates showed no

great interest in following this particular behavioral model.
Our own blacks, Chicanos, and Indians are quite happy with
their cultures, except that so far they have not been great
wealth-producing cultures. They would happily take our
money, but not our behavioral patterns. Neither would
Ghanese, Nigerians, or Indians. Most people like their own
culture and what it involves for them personally; to have
blundering and ignorant foreigners try to tell them how to
behave is just too much. Yet, those blundering foreigners are
so damn rich. . . .

Examination of the affluent of the world does suggest that
they behave quite differently from the poor, even when they
are in the same country. Because we are too polite nowadays
to suggest directly to someone that he should change his behavior, we normally talk about power plants and engineering technologies rather than behavioral change. It all comes
down to the same thing. If you're going to get rich the way
we did, you're going to have to behave the way we did—if
not, those nice mechanical toys just won't work right. Such
implications run through all aid programs, including ours
and the Soviets', and they are not well received.

This leads to an interesting dilemma for lots of thoughtful
affluent people. We observe poverty, and it upsets us. We
also observe behavior of the sort that is not going to make
people rich, now or ever. Like having ten children on a marginal peasant farm, or failing to respond to work disciplines
demanded by the new technologies, or failing to get the kind
narrow technical education that will enable a person to get
efficient hold of the tools of production, or insisting on
spending money on wakes and weddings instead of on productive things. We observe, sigh, and try earnestly to con-
vince our friends from the poorer cultures and countries that
they have to change, if they want in on the world's goodies.
Our own ethics say that this is not the way to behave, yet,
what else is there? All wealth is Western, in that only Western-oriented behavior leads to getting the goods produced.
So far no one has figured out how to do it any other way.

Our foreign friends are polite, but unconvinced. Indeed, they accuse us of trying to ram down their throats a behavioral pattern that even we find a bit disturbing. Often they can get quite nasty about it. But they too have problems. If they don't behave right, the goods may not get produced in sufficient amounts. So far, we have been right—but there may be some other way. Chairman Mao tried, and failed, but perhaps out there some place is *the* way.

The affluent liberal, observing the futility of so much of the development process, yearns to change things, yearns to get those birth rates down, to get others to behave right. He begins to want to play God. Maybe he can. How about world-enforced birth control, with only the elect being given licenses to have children? The present state of the arts in this field suggests that such things might soon be possible. How about some mind-bending drugs for a whole country, to lock them into line along the "correct" patterns? Such drugs may already be around. Playing God is fun, if you're God. Those who get manipulated, however, tend to object. But with the magnitude of the problem being what it is, and with the sheer desperation of inability to come up with easy and cheap answers, playing God is tempting indeed to those with the muscle and power to do it. It could happen sooner than most of us think. And if it does, more cultures will be busted up faster than most now feel possible. But what else have we got? Sitting back and worrying won't get us very far.

The hell of it is that no one has figured out how to get rich quick except those damned uptight Calvinist types (including the Russians and the Japanese, who may be out-Calvining the Calvinists). You work hard, plan ahead, get your big organizations put together properly, with lots of people in them doing little things correctly, and work your head off for fifty years or more. If people don't like the system, they starve, get tossed in jail, or stay poor. If you do all this, and if you get your machinery, power plants, mines, and factories in place, through more hard work, well then, maybe you can get rich too. And after you're affluent, you can play games with the greening of your country, or getting away from the harsh Calvinist discipline of work, more work, saving, putting off of pleasures, and punishment from God and man.

Since the affluent countries have had their fifty or hundred years of hard work, they can play this game, or at least the affluent ones in the countries can. The poor don't have much choice. Nor do the poor around the world, who already are living the idyllic life, but without good medicine, shelter, clothes, or anything else. They don't like it very much. This is not a good time for Americans to advise others to be up tight and work hard, putting off pleasures until next year, or even the next century. Yet no one has figured out any other way to do the job.

If we don't wreck the present system, it will collapse of its own weight anyhow, and sooner than most of us would like. But there are ways and ways of busting cultures. Some are painful, such as the way Americans busted the American Indian culture. You kill off enough people, and the culture collapses. Or you let population increase without income increases, and sooner or later mass famine takes care of your problem. Or maybe you try to create a mini-WASP society, a caricature of the United States, which no doubt would blow up shortly in contradiction and confusion.

There may be some good ways. One way, which no one seems to want very much, is somehow to get population increase down to zero, then cycle the system in the way it now runs forever. We've seen this model in action—it's the one that was used by most now-poor countries before 1950. Population increase stays low because death rates (mainly infant mortality) stays high. The trouble is, we now know how to keep death rates down, so we don't let people die. Maybe we could play God just a bit and get birth control going. Then the model would work again. The trouble is that cultures like this are put in zoos by the cultures that are going some place faster. Nothing much happens within the culture, so the ones who are getting ahead in the world run the place. Since they are steadily growing more knowledgeable and

more sophisticated (and maybe even more humane), they
take care not to bust open the old culture, letting it cycle
along merrily to nowhere. The greeners in America may
learn this to their dismay within ten or fifteen years. The
eighteenth-century imperialists just took this type of culture
over, and started a busting process which is still going on.
Maybe cycling is a dead end too. Most, if not all, poor countries think so, since no one in any poor country has suggested that this is the way to go.

Another culture-busting model is where a country uses its
own strengths to get some place it wants to go. So far,
though many have tried, no one has succeeded, because, as
we mentioned above, everything along these lines ends up
looking very Western. If you go some place, you need Western technology, Western organization, and Western education to get there from here. Moreover, there is an emulation
effect which is hard to beat. Poor countries, observing the affluent, can hardly resist trying to do what comes naturally in
the West. Not only are weapons systems, technology, and education all on the West's side, but also all the prestige in this
world. A man from Switzerland, Sweden, or even the United
States is the one to watch, since he comes from the right culture. Few elites in any country have the guts to strike out
into unknown ground. As a result, we see pale imitations of
the West everywhere. Thank the Lord for this, at times—
who wants to ride on anyone's airplane which is maintained
in a mystical manner, rather than the way Boeing says it
should be maintained? And if airplanes fly successfully only
by Western rules, it is easy enough to conclude that everything else should run by Western rules too. So the main
model of change everywhere is some Western one, or some
copy of some Western one, like Japan.

All of this is very painful to the natives. Americans can see
the pain very visibly among American minorities. Behave
like us, we say, and you can be rich too. And sure enough,
the blacks and Chicanos who get through the Western mainstream universities manage to do pretty well. But this

doesn't mean that they like what they've done. Black power, black pride, and all the rest are in one sense a reaction to the painful choice of being yourself or trying to copy the man. Around the world, lots of people are trying to decide whether or not to copy the man, be he a Russian, American, or Japanese. And whatever the man is, he isn't exactly what most people have in mind as a behavioral model.

Countries that have opted to follow the Western model quickly get involved in all sorts of mysterious things, like big, impersonal bureaucratic organizations designed to do the world's work. After all, General Motors is big, efficient, and the very model of what a productive, high-wealth producer is and should be. But somehow, a lot gets lost in translation. Instead of General Motors, far too many of these pale copies run as though they were managed by Charlie Chaplin in one of his wilder movies. Indeed, so striking is this phenomenon that we have had great debate over the management gap in recent years. Somehow, Westerners know the mysteries of how to get a big organization functioning. If only these mysteries could be revealed, then others could get rich fast too. Since they don't, maybe we have been following the wrong model in the poor countries for quite a while. Note the analogy: the United States has big organizations, and it is rich. Therefore, if I have big organizations, I'll be rich too. But focus on the big in the West may miss a key point, namely, that most organizations in the West were pretty small until very recently. Maybe there is another, as yet unexplored, model for growth, taken from history, about how to grow fast with small things—organizations which another culture can handle better.

This one is hard to sell to our friends from poor countries. They feel that only the best will do, and who can top General Motors? Small means poor, lousy, inept, incompetent, and all the rest. Yet, after several decades of trying the big, things aren't working out too well. Maybe we had better reconsider our premises and see if the small might work somewhat better than the inept big we have tried for so long.

The biggest culture buster of all was Chairman Mao. He

tried to rearrange the whole of China along lines unknown in the West. The goal was to beat the West in a non-Western way. So the Great Leap Forward was tried. It didn't work, and now China is slowly coming back down from Cloud Nine. The promise was there. Maybe, out of this experience, might come something that could work. It's worth a look. Cultures, including ours, are going to get blasted all over the place in the next thirty years. Given the problem, there isn't any choice. It will get done—the hard way or the easy way —and our problem is to figure out the easy way. In the end, it all comes down to individuals, who typically are a messy bunch, particularly in terms of our own nice values. They insist on doing things their way. And as cultures change, people in them change too, and not always for the better. Sometimes, they have no choice—a starving man just starves, if his society can't somehow get him food. Sometimes they do have choices, and the problem is getting them to behave the way they should, given the cultural, economic, and political problems at hand. And here we get into reward-and-punishment systems, which are value-laden all the way. How do we manipulate rewards and punishments to get what we want? Play God once more?

The mainstream West is now liberal, humanitarian, and permissive, for better or worse, and our friends in poor countries, whose ethics are at least as good as ours, find this attractive. After all, they want the best for their people too. But how do you get rapid change in people without pushing them around a bit? Examination of Western history suggests that no one knew—so people got pushed around a lot. All of this pushing was inhumane, but it got the job done. Now poorer countries are reluctant to push, but they have to figure out some alternatives. If people don't change, the society will collapse through weight of increasing numbers, if nothing else. So, back to the drawing-boards to figure out some behavioral manipulation which is both effective and humane. If you can't figure this one out, nothing much else will happen.

The human-behavior problem interlocks with the organizational one, since some kinds of organizations, large or small, good or bad, will be trying to get people locked into the proper work patterns and responses. If they are not, the organizations won't work, income won't be generated, and we're back to square one.

So this is what we are going to consider. We begin with a problem: if we don't grow economically, we're in for deep, deep trouble of the fatal kind, like mass famine. Moreover, we all would like to do a bit better than just sit where we now are—we would like to get richer, both collectively and individually. To do this, we are going to have to restructure our economic, social, and political systems in ways that will produce the goods better. We already have some good economic and political ideas about what has to be done, although even here some of the more widely accepted premises merit study, since they could be wrong. But we have no idea really about how to bust up cultures in a way which guarantees that they can be perpetually reformed along creative, constructive lines. Culture-busting just happens. Maybe it needn't have to be this way. Moreover, culture-busting to date has not been all that constructive, as any American Indian can testify.

Those who think that whatever is can cycle nicely forevermore, with perhaps a few marginal changes at the fringes to straighten things out, are doomed to disappointment, since the magnitude of the world development problem we face virtually guarantees that it won't work out this way. Examination of any culture of any Western affluent country also suggests that along this road to affluence lies the debris of old cultures that just didn't work out. Even at the present end of the road, the United States, the cultural outcomes are not all that exciting to lots of people. Yet they happened, and they will happen again. The idea here is to try to figure out how to make the changes as easily as possible. What other choice have we got? None really. We could play God, and build a totalitarian state unlike what anyone has yet seen. We might figure out how to get world birth control, and then cycle whatever exists at that time, letting the poor stink in their own poverty forevermore. At least this way we might survive. Or we might just wait for the whole house of cards to fall apart and collapse. Somehow, the options don't look all that attractive.

We could also just let our poor foreign friends figure it out for themselves. They might do a lot better at it than the affluent, whose advice record is not so good. But then again, perhaps the affluent, sadder but wiser in their affluence, can offer some wisdom, can show where the false turns are. At least it's worth a try. And lurking in the background is the uneasy thought that even the most affluent have some really sticky poverty problems at home as well, which also involve some massive culture busting if they are to be solved. Anyone who has observed the United States in the past decade is keenly aware that cultural change is here too, not just out there someplace for someone else. Maybe the whole damn system is inherently unstable; maybe in the end the world blows up no matter what we try to do. But it's worth a try. Maybe we can see if there are not some things overlooked here and there about culture-busting which might prove useful along the line into the future. Nothing much we've tried recently seems to work; perhaps we can take another look and see if we've missed something.

. . . .

CHAPTER 11

The Development Mainstream

Americans, like everyone else, look nostalgically back on the past, seeing a simpler, more satisfying life, where individuals could be fulfilled. Almost any evening on television we can see the endless Westerns, formal as opera, with all the stereotypes we have come to accept. Rarely stated or even implied, however, is that when we see the Westerns we also are looking at the stark face of agrarian poverty. The flickering tube reflects what many countries are today—agricultural, animal-powered, and very poor.

At the time the Western yarns were actually happening, most of the United States was already well along in its industrial push. It was, in the east, the America of the robber barons, of tremendous growth in railways and steel and other heavy industries, of the transformation of the land into an industrial empire. Although it was crude, materialistic, and messy, the result was that the United States accelerated its development push, to the point where a Western, instead of being something which is really happening over the next hill, is now a reflection of our romantic never-never land, where justice is sure and swift and the land is pure.

Lots of other countries never got off the ground. American Westerns are very popular on Saudi Arabian TV, because they are only mildly distorted versions of what was going on only a few decades ago, out in the trackless deserts. Because while we built steel mills and railroads and sweated immigrant labor, many countries cycled endlessly in their traditional ways, never changing much, never worrying much about industrialization or other modernization. Sons lived exactly as their fathers did, and all was well. Without much communication from the outside, it didn't seem to matter.

Europe, prodded by fears of war and threats of neighbors, also got into the industrialization game early. Indeed England started the whole thing, somewhere between 1750 and 1800, and began a vigorous advance that carried the country into the twentieth century as the wealthiest country per capita in the world. But in the twentieth century, World Wars I and II drained off the wealth of most European states, pushing them back, far below the Americans. Only now does it appear that some countries, such as West Germany, France, Sweden, and Switzerland, might finally catch up in income terms.

In the East, Stalin's Soviet Union started the heavy-industry push in 1928 with a new Five-Year Plan, and the Soviets have been in the modernization and industrialization race ever since, held back for five brutal years by World War II. The rest of Eastern Europe also belongs to the affluent class, although close to the bottom of it, as various countries have struggled to get ahead in the world for a long time, with the pace attempted to be quickened in the communist postwar period.

Toss in Japan, which got into the modern world in the 1870s in a systematic way, Australia, New Zealand, Canada, and the white part of South Africa, and you have the countries that began industrialization and modernization early and who now are considered affluent. No latecomer who began this process after 1940 is yet in the affluent category. It takes more than will power to get into the big leagues in economic terms.

Outsiders, observing this development through all of the twentieth century, gradually became convinced that the only way to move was to follow the lead of the various affluent countries. There were lots of reasons for coming to this conclusion. Latin America in the 1930s, largely independent but poverty-stricken, perceived early that no one cared about poor countries. They had neither troops nor moral suasion, nor influence, nor pride among the nations of the world. No one cares about Paraguay or Ecuador, but lots of people are interested in Sweden or Norway. Why? Who has the income and cash? Moreover, moral critics of poor societies constantly pointed to social injustice, noting evil, suffering, and degradation for the poor. And in a country with per-capita incomes hovering around the $100-per-year level, virtually everyone was poor. If a country wanted to build hospitals, schools, or churches, more real income could help. If income was to go to the poor, having a growing pot to distribute avoided many nasty social confrontations, as well as allowing more to be distributed.

Ex-colonial countries had seen enough of the power which comes from wealth to be impressed. It was the wealth of Europe that gave the guns to the imperial troops to take Africa and Southeast Asia in the first place. Hence if one was to be proudly independent, wealth counted. Moreover, he quickly found that being independent wasn't enough. Eating crow as a colony of some European power was replaced by eating crow at international gatherings, because no one much cares about the opinions of the poor. And of course the leaders of such countries were as moral as anyone, and they badly wanted all the welfare that churches, mosques, schools, health services, and all the rest that wealth would bring. They witnessed the impressive power of the Soviet Union in world affairs, and later they saw the influence West Germany and Japan could obtain with little more than a fast income-growth rate.

So everyone, by 1955, was very interested in economic growth, and many had already experimented extensively with various ways of getting rich as quickly as possible. But development in the 1950s was a nebulous thing, involving crude copying of the more obvious success economies in North America and Europe. America had power plants: therefore build some for your country. England had steel mills: therefore, add a steel mill to your capital stock. Russia had railroads: hence railroads had to be built to lay claim to first-class power status. It was all rather simple minded, and sometimes effective.

The power of compound-interest rates begins to enter the equation about the same time. Only in 1936 had measurements and definitions of national income become useful, when Lord Keynes evolved his macro-economic theories for quite different purposes; only during World War II was income measured even in advanced countries with any degree of precision. Then scholars observed that a growing country might expect to gain perhaps 3 or 4 percent income per capita per year. If this could be done, income would double per capita in about twenty-two years at 3 percent—or in sixteen years at 4 percent. In 1950, if you had $100 income per capita, by 1966, it would be $200; by 1982, $400, by 1998, $800. An eightfold increase in a single lifespan was impressive, since even in 1950 many countries had incomes only one-tenth or less of the affluent countries. The magic of compounding had been working steadily in the United States and Europe for a century or more, and they were far ahead.

Perhaps with planning and a big push, a country could do better. Wartime examples, where pressures were really on in affluent countries, suggested that 10 or even 15 percent annual per-capita income increases might be achieved. Advances in economic thinking, experiences in the communist world with planning, rapid borrowing of technology from developed countries, and the will to achieve in poor countries could be combined to achieve such rapid growth rates. At 10 percent, incomes double in seven years; at 15 percent, incomes double in under five. At these rates, the catching-up process could be successful. The $100-per-capita country of 1950 could be a $3,000-per-capita country in 1972, perhaps as high, or even higher, than income levels in the 1950 wealthy countries. The newly rich countries would have their schools, their mechanized armies, their health systems, and all would be well.

By 1972, the actual gap between rich and poor had widened. The rich were now perhaps ten to thirty times as well off as the poor, and they were pulling away in income terms. By 1972, it seems that we have two worlds—one affluent and getting more so, yet still concerned about its own lack of resources and local poor; and another poor world, a sort of perpetual slum, where virtually everyone is poor, and is quite likely to remain so for as long as we can foresee. These poor do get richer, but with agonizing slowness, doubling income every fifty years or so, instead of every five or ten. What went wrong?

It wasn't for lack of trying. Most poor countries by the mid-1950s had set economic development as their major goal, and most wealthy countries agreed, to the point of helping out with billions of dollars of aid of all sorts. In spite of the cold war, the capital assets were built up in the poor countries, and steel mills, railroads, and industries were started. Most poor countries tried to plan their economies rationally, and planning ministries tried to set priorities and work out the development strategies rationally. Development economics became a major industry in most countries, including the United States, and every university worthy of the name tried to develop better theory and practical applications of theory. And in an absolute sense, all of this worked. The rich countries did not have enervating depressions which brought incomes down (older people can remember between the two world wars that the problem in the then-affluent countries was to get back to 1929, not to move on to higher ground; nothing of this sort has happened in any rich country since World War II). Poor countries did grow, and a few of them did well. There is probably not a single country in the world where per-capita income is actually lower now than it was in 1950. But inching ahead is not what everyone had in mind. A great leap forward was envisioned (and even tried in Red China). Somehow it never came off.

What went wrong really is the whole concept of economic development. It works, but it doesn't work well, because it talks about the wrong things.

The Development Mainstream

In the early days before 1965 (this field changes very fast), the economic-development problem was seen as purely economic, with perhaps a bit of technology and political science tossed in for good measure. The development idea was simple. It was noted that rich countries got rich by investing in capital equipment of all sorts. If some one (a private firm or the state) invested a million dollars in a factory, then this factory could produce products and add to income. Typically, from $200,000 to $300,000 of extra income might come out of such a plant. This income increment to capital investment could be measured (here from 3.33 to 5 to 1). If the rich could do it, the poor could too. Invest a million, and add the $300,000 to per-capita income.

Where did the million come from? People making $100 a year are not big savers—they can't be, or they would starve to death. If you are going to invest, someone has to save— that is, refrain from current consumption. Rich countries can do this easily, but poor ones cannot. Here is where aid and foreign loans come in. If a poor country can borrow foreign currency, it can get its factories without sweating savings out of its population. And if this process works, people gradually become richer, and they save more, in part because they can afford to.

Americans tend to forget that when the cowboys were roaming the western plains, Englishmen were financing a lot of American investment in exactly this way. Few cowboys (or their city counterparts) were wealthy enough to save very much, and a weak central government could not do too much either. Hence foreign aid, in the form of long-term capital-development loans, assisted the development process. Even fewer people remember that from time to time American firms (and even American state governments) defaulted on repayments. All morality and justice is not on one side.

The question of what to invest in initially appears obvious. After all, a poor country has more to do than any reasonable amount of funds available can do. Yet the decision is critical. Suppose that each million invested yields $200,000 per year in one poor country, while in the second, each million invested yields $300,000. Here the second country is investing in higher payout investments. Whatever it is doing, people are willing to buy the outputs from the new investments at higher prices, or the factories, mines, etc., are more productive per unit of capital. And the result will be that the second country will grow much faster than the first, get richer more quickly, be able to save more (and hence invest more) faster, and keep on growing more rapidly. In short, the productivity of new capital becomes a key point.

It really doesn't matter if the investor is a private firm, a state railroad, or an agricultural cooperative, since the key point is to achieve high payouts. But each of these investors thinks it needs more capital than there is available. Who gets it?

At this point, politics, good old business administration, social attitudes, and sound economics enter the picture. Someone has to decide. Some countries, like America long ago, let the market decide—the one who gets the cash in free competition makes the investment. Most modern poor countries (along with all the communist ones) let planners decide. They laboriously calculate costs and benefits for the society and make the decision. Very often this decision is related to a national Five-Year Plan, which lays out priorities for the whole country. And, as often as not, the planners are wrong. If they are wrong, payouts are lower, and growth slows. It is tough enough to figure out returns on a small company, let alone a whole country.

The Investment Strategies

Countries contemplating a surge of dynamic growth find many models around. Countries as diverse as the United States, the U.S.S.R., England, France, Switzerland, Sweden, Denmark, and Japan have already done the job. Which model looks good to follow?

This problem is really the "Invest in what?" question. A country can, to follow various now-affluent countries, try investing heavily in social overhead capital projects, such as railways, ports, electric-power systems, telephones, roads, irrigation and flood-control projects, and similar items. The advantage here is that such facilities are critical to any development—if a country has little electric power or transportation, nothing much else can happen. An economic infrastructure has to be built, often at very great cost, since such projects are typically very capital intensive.

Here also we encounter the tricky concept of profit for whom. Public utilities may not make much money in themselves, but their existence may make lots of other things very profitable. Hence a small firm able to lock into an electric-power system finds many things possible which it simply could not do without the power system. The retail store with a telephone that works (rare in the less affluent countries) has a major advantage over one without this facility. There clearly is some kind of total profit for the society involved in these investments, in addition to the usual profit (if any) for the firm involved in providing the social overheads. Consideration of this point has led many persons to believe that such facilities should show little if any profit—which in turn suggests some form of state ownership. And indeed, in most poorer countries, the big, expensive public utilities are almost always owned by the state. They are also capital intensive, expensive, and take a long time to pay out. It is not unusual to find that a big power project will take a decade or more to come into full production. In the meantime, capital is sunk into the project which is paying off nothing, and the country stays poor. Most poor countries are investing a third or more of their total available capital, including foreign aid, in such social overhead capital facilities. They almost have to, given their needs for such facilities to get on with the rest of the job.

A second attractive investment option is that of industry. Here we find heavy industry, which consists of such capital-intensive projects as steel mills, heavy-machinery establishments, and similar enterprises. The investment per worker tends to be high, as do the skill levels needed by workers. Heavy industry, in many quarters, appears to be the guts of industrialization and modernization. No major power ever became one in our century without massive expansion of this sector. The smoke-belching steel mills and all the rest appear to be the essence of progress. But once again, along with the social overheads, the capital requirements are enormous, and no poor country can afford more than a fraction of what it needs or thinks it needs in this sector. That minor point about worker and managerial skills also can be a major problem. Even when the mills are actually built, they rarely operate at anywhere near the efficiency level of the mills in the advanced countries, so such heavy industry investments tend to be a drag on, rather than a boost to, poor economies. But this fact does not stop anyone from dreaming.

The other side of the industrial coin is light industry, where modest investments lead quickly to output and income. Textiles, toys, light manufacturing, furniture, and innumerable other items involving relatively little capital are included here. Most now-rich countries (including the United States) got started in such industries, which get into operation quicker, sometimes require fewer skills, and often pay off rather better than heavy industry. But they hardly are dramatic. The idea of a few dozen natives laboring with simple lathes or punch presses in some hole-in-the-wall factory is not exactly anyone's idea of the modern society. Yet wherever such light industry gets started, it typically works reasonably well. Light industry also has major advantages in being fast to get going, and in saving foreign exchange. Why import someone else's textiles with scarce foreign exchange, when with relatively little time and effort, you can do this job yourself?

Agriculture is still another option for focusing scarce investment funds. Until very recently (around 1965–67), few poor countries paid much attention to agriculture, since most of their people were already peasants, and the idea of investing in what the country was already doing seemed somewhat absurd. But as the gradual realization dawned that there was no way to get everyone (or even the majority) into industry within a century or so, and as populations steadily increased, the need for better agricultural practices became steadily more apparent. Now, countries are actively toying with the idea of working much more in agriculture than they initially did, and some are even planning for further expansion along these lines. After all, affluent Denmark and New Zealand offer attractive models for many small countries.

An attractive investment option for anyone is in health and welfare. Poor people are sick, uneducated, and needy all the time. What better thing to do than to try to get them into better shape? This idea is furthered by the thought that such investments, while not considered business-type projects, actually could have a high payout for the country, if sickness, absenteeism, and educational deficiencies could be remedied. A real difficulty here is that such activities are typically high skill, labor intensive, and often even capital intensive, and the very things poor countries don't have are lots of skilled doctors, teachers, psychologists, health therapists, dentists, and hospital administrators to start and keep a good social system going. Also the money required for good schools, hospitals, and clinics can be staggering—far beyond the abilities of any poor country to afford. But the propaganda pictures from anywhere suggest where our values are, and what other countries expect us to like. We see the spanking new hospital, the fine modern school, the healthy, happy kids, and all the rest. This is what the world is supposed to be about. If there is only one good school in the country, and 85 percent of the kids don't attend any kind of school—well, dreams can beat reality any time.

A final investment possibility is in mining or petroleum. If a country has some good deposits of ores or oil, developing them can quickly lead to higher incomes, huge gains in foreign sales, meaning lots of foreign exchange to buy foreign equipment, and rapidly increasing wealth. As with heavy industry any sizable mineral development is very capital intensive, and few poor countries have either the money or the skills to exploit such a deposit properly. They have to rely on foreign help, which creates its own problems. And of course not every poor country is lucky enough to have the right kinds of minerals in the right place.

Since everything is wrong with most poor countries, there is a tendency to try to do everything at once. Discussions with American liberals (not economists), who are used to much higher levels of affluence than what we are talking about, suggest the problem. Their usual response, on being exposed to the problem, is to want to do *everything,* simultaneously and immediately. Why not? The harsh fact of resource limitation seldom enters their thinking. Educate the kids, build the steel mills, start a railroad, get some textile factories going, build the clinics and hospitals—and get it done by next Monday morning. Revolutionaries in the poor countries (out of power) frequently talk the same way. The reason we are poor is that some evil people (typically Americans, or maybe some other affluent foreigners) have exploited us and held us back. Therefore, let's go! When the revolutionaries get into power, from the right or left, they are as confused as the rest of us by what to do first, second, and third. It seems that with one doctor for every 20,000 people, one engineer for every 40,000, one teacher for every 5,000, somehow, nothing can get going as fast as it should.

One of the critical problems of all development is the strategy of what to do and when. If everything is wrong, not everything can be cured right away. But where do you start? This whole problem is complicated by the overwhelming presence of the successful wealthy countries, who can easily do things which are impossible in poor ones. Hence the United States can afford Medicare, reasonable pensions for old people, laws against child labor, and minimum wages, to say nothing of enforcing safe and reasonably pleasant working conditions for most workers. Although such things are often expensive and difficult to come by, a poor country, seeing these humane goals, tends to want them too. A good pension scheme, however, can mean that scarce funds are consumed by the elderly, not invested in new factories or other productive assets which earn income for younger people. Insisting on high safety standards costs money, which means that other workers will not have jobs. When per-capita incomes are below $200 per year, such nasty problems constantly arise. Yet we all want a good, decent, humane world, so we all push for the latest models of niceness and reform. How to pay for it seems trivial, given the obvious needs. But paying may turn out to be the critical problem in the end. The hard facts of the matter are that there is never enough money or real resources to go around, so tough decisions have to be made.

The West, including the United States in its day, solved this problem rather simply. Workers and farmers had the savings sweated out of them, through long hours of work under poor working conditions at low pay. The surplus they generated was invested by bloated capitalists to get still more production. In the Soviet Union, the workers and peasants had the savings sweated out of them, through long hours of poor working conditions at low pay. The surplus they generated was invested by bloated commissars to get still more production. There isn't any other way to do the job that anyone knows, yet every poor country is haunted by the fact that such sweatings are now seen as evil, immoral, and so on. What else is there?

Public and Private: Open and Closed

Investment and human-resource development strategies also involve detailed considerations of who owns what and how much foreign influence should be allowed. The public private debate is as old as Marxism. Since Karl Marx started writing, there have been many proponents of the public sector as being critical and perhaps the only one. Here, the state owns everything—or as much as seems possible—and still gets the job done. Since Marxism, in all its guises, is also attached to deep and powerful statements about the rights of man, freedom, ethical concern, and all that, it tends to be an attractive philosophy for a poor country. Where there are poor money markets, an avaricious landholding class, ex-colonial influences, and general lack of direction in the economy, state ownership tends to be attractive. Few poor countries, whatever their political persuasion, are completely attracted to capitalistic systems. The lack of a large capital supply from private sources alone leads reactionary states such as Saudi Arabia and Ethiopia to own airlines and railroads; more liberal or radical states often own much of the modern industrial sector. Some, such as Cuba and Albania, own it all.

If ownership of assets were all there was to development, this issue would have been settled long ago in favor of the Marxists. But unfortunately (or fortunately, depending on your politics), there is much more to the problem than this. Ownership in itself gives power to one group or another; but it does not automatically lead to income, output, health, and happiness. Indeed, it may do just the reverse. On the other hand, the private-ownership strategy normally works

well only in less capital-intensive situations, such as light industry. Poor countries typically just don't have enough ready
cash to provide major sums of capital for anything in the private sector. If private ownership is large, it is very likely to
be foreign capital, investing in mines, oilfields, and other activities which will yield rapid increases in wealth. This
truism leads directly to the problem of whether or not to
allow foreigners to dominate the local economy. Many now-
poor countries were recently colonies of some other now-affluent country—and the idea of letting wealthy foreigners
back in is not all that appealing. But they have the cash, and
many very poor countries of twenty years ago are now quite
affluent because they did let the foreign devils in. This decision can be a real trauma for a poor country's leadership,
since the name of the game is to get rich—and total isolation
rarely, if ever, gets the job done. No poor country has the
technical skills and resources to develop its own minerals
and oilfields properly, to say nothing of being able to market
them efficiently in richer countries. If foreign capital doesn't
do the job, then it won't get done for a while—maybe fifty
years—and in the meantime, the country stays poor.

The various poor countries confronted with this dilemma
directly, in that they have a very good mineral asset, have
usually gone international and signed a concession agreement with the detested Western company. But a few (India,
Brazil) have resisted. The problem here gets back very directly to capital formation. If a country is very poor, where
can it find the necessary capital to get something developed?
The usual answer is that it cannot. Hence the pressure to let
the devils in.

Minerals are only one part of the problem. For other
types of investments, the more normal pattern is to keep rich
foreigners out as much as possible. The heavy industries
(which few Western firms would care to invest in anyhow)
are all locally owned, as are light industries, social overheads, and educational facilities. In only a handful of industrial projects, where a Western affluent firm's knowhow is

critical, are the rich let in to do the job. All countries (including the affluent Western ones) have various barriers to letting foreigners do the job—which is what nationalism is about, in one sense. What is the point if your own people, your own country, cannot do the job and reap the rewards itself? Hence the typical stance is for a semiclosed situation to prevail, with lots of state ownership and investment in many sectors.

Here again we encounter the strategy of development in full flower. What to do? When to do it? Who does it? and Who owns it? are the key questions. But no matter how these questions are decided, the problem is always the same—the country is desperately poor, and the way to get less poor is to get some more income. The way to get income is to accumulate some income-generating assets. How is this done? This *is* the development problem. And doing this job right is what every nation is trying to do.

Income, the Fine Things in Life, and Redistribution

Until 1950 or so, most thinking about economic reform concerned income redistribution, rather than income growth. In a very real sense, people could not do arithmetic—they figured that if the millionaire's money were given to the poor, everyone would be rich. But giving fifty millionaires' incomes to fifty million people would not make much difference, except perhaps in some ethical sense. Everyone being one dollar a year better off is nice, but hardly earth-shaking.

Hence when economists started thinking and measuring income for the country, rather than just wistfully observing the few visible very rich, attention began to be focused on income growth, rather than on income redistribution. If income increased 5 percent, then everyone, from the avaricious millionaire to the poorest peasant, would be 5 percent better off as a result. And if national income doubled in ten years, then everyone would be twice as well off, without going through the agonies of revolutionary income redistribution at all. Needless to say, this idea was attractive to the top half of the income recipients, since it got a potentially painful problem off their back. Right now in the United States, if your family makes much over $10,000 a year, you would be liable to a 100 percent tax on the excess, if total equality in income distribution were to be followed. In India, the typical family would face a 100 percent income tax after perhaps $400. Since everyone who can read or has any skill at all is usually above these lines, the idea of total redistribution (or typically even partial redistribution) is not all that appealing. Much better to double income in the next ten years, and take your chances on getting your share.

Hence modern theory focuses on growth and development. There are still lots of radicals, even in the United States, who would simply redistribute everything. But those countries which have tried massive redistributions (the U.S.S.R., Cuba, Red China) have not made their case. Such radical changes just don't seem to work very well, if some notion of maximizing human welfare is your goal. Indeed, it is now likely that the Soviet Union has a worse real-income distribution than the United States. After various early experiments showed that human-motivation problems with fairly equal incomes were pretty tough, the Soviets went back to inequality. To a lesser extent, Red China did the same after its experiments with Red Guards and the Great Leap Forward.

Economists invented economic development, and their own ideas about what to maximize were accepted early. The fundamental measure is Gross National Product (GNP), which is basically the total income produced by everyone in the country, including state firms and other organizations. There are plenty of conceptual problems associated with measuring the GNP, but it does serve as a good measure of what is going on within any country. Nevertheless there are very real problems associated with cross-cultural comparisons

—you would starve to death in Chicago on an Indian peasant's cash income, but he seems to survive, and maybe even prospers.

Noneconomists are always bothered a bit by this single-minded focus on money and income. Why not worry more about really important things, like education, welfare, and happiness? Well, one major reason why GNP per capita is so widely used is that there is a fairly high correlation between income and all these things—except maybe happiness, which seems to elude even good philosophers. A country with a high GNP typically has not only income, but lots of skilled people; social overheads; reasonably good schools; fairly adequate medical facilities; and all the other items associated with the good life. It may also have high levels of suicide, juvenile delinquency, social ills of all sorts, and maybe even less happiness, but so far no one has been able to create a welfare index which would do the job as well as income does.

There is a mousetrap here for the unwary. If you really believe that some things are beyond price, then they require infinite resources. Hence a country can get into genuine trouble investing its resources (all of them) in something too valuable to be priced or measured. If you really feel that churches are too important to be considered in vulgar price terms, you get eighteenth-century Mexico—full of beautiful churches, attended presumably by sick peasants, their teeth rotting out, dying at age twenty-five, their kids illiterate, and all the rest. If you really believe that empire and conquest are more important than anything else, then you get 1940 Japan, where peasants and workers existed on subsistence levels, while all resources got put into armaments. If you really feel that all medical care and all human life has an infinite price, then you leave the resource allocation decision to others, and you get 1972 United States, where ghetto infant mortality rates are only a bit *below* those in very poor countries, while unused kidney machines and expensive cobalt guns wait, underutilized, for middle-class people.

We have to pick our strategy to use our resources. And income considerations, investment payoffs, and price-system allocations are a good way to do the job. This simple point bothers humane people. It seems obscene to let people suffer, one way or the other, because resources are limited. Why not do it all at once? Because the world is poor, that's why. It is now, and it always has been. We see affluence around us —yet it would take fifty years of American income, all invested, to give the 550 million Indians the same rather modest income level Americans now have. It would take all of Western Europe's income for fifty years, totally invested, to give Africa the level of income Western Europe now has. There is just no easy way to do this job although too many sincere people think there is.

Related to this point is what might be called the absolutist-solution theory, which is very common in the United States today, particularly among intellectuals. No matter what is going on anywhere, something is wrong—not a new observation or an incorrect one. But the proposed solutions are new and frightening. Fix it absolutely, 100 percent, and do it next week, even if you kill everyone to solve the problem. Hence, if ghetto kids can't read (nor can a billion other kids from the poor countries, for that matter), restructure the world to make them read, no matter what the cost or what the results. There is some utopia out there, if only we can get rid of evil men and do it right. . . . Ralph Nader, in his more dramatic moments, tends to this sort of absolutist solution, as do many others. But it is highly unlikely that such solutions exist, and if they were tried, the cure might be worse than the disease. If you like total quick solutions, quit reading now—there aren't any in this book, because no one has the slightest idea of how to resolve the current desperate problems of poor countries, including the people in the countries themselves.

In short, the problem is to figure out, in a very cold-blooded way, how to trade off one kind of thing against another, with the ultimate goal of improving, however slightly, the human condition. The development strategies which countries follow are in effect their solutions. They want to get rich, because by so doing they will solve some of their problems. But they cannot do this all at once, and to do so requires investment strategies, sectoral strategies, and human-resource development strategies. Our basic argument is that these may not always be the right ones—that something better could be tried. And maybe something could be accomplished.

The Nature of the Poor Human Condition

Poor countries have deeper problems than the rich on the state of the human condition, since so many nasty things that can happen to people happen more often in poor countries. This is why they are poor. Here are some of the common characteristics of poverty, taking as examples the very poorest countries in the world:

1. People die earlier. Death rates in poor countries, at about twenty per thousand per year, are twice the average of rich countries with per capita incomes over $2,000 per year. No one ever has an abcessed tooth, cancer, or an inflamed appendix on an American Western TV show, but one can ponder just what the sufferer might have done. He would do what many citizens of poor countries now do—die.

2. Many more babies are born per thousand of population (from 30 to 55), and more die young (from one-tenth to one-half of all babies will die before their first birthday). In rich countries, the birth rate is around 15 to 20 per thousand population per year, and infant mortality is much, much lower.

3. The population of poor countries is always much less educated than the rich. The adult literacy rate ranges from 15 to 55 percent, as compared to 90 percent or better for every affluent country, and of course the affluent citizens have spent many more years in school as well.

4. Most citizens of poor countries work in agriculture or mining, usually using primitive equipment and techniques. Sixty to 65 percent of workers will be in such jobs, as compared to 5 to 10 percent in affluent countries. And the job of an American miner or farmer would be considered a political one by almost any poor country worker. Since capital is scarce, most jobs are done the hard way, with animal or muscle power. Anyone old enough to remember (perhaps with nostalgia) digging ditches or tunnels by hand, or plowing with horses, knows how physically tough this can be. Why not buy tractors? Well, you need a factory, which takes capital, which isn't available.

5. Young people don't get to attend school as often. In really poor countries, as few as 15 percent of the persons five to sixteen will be in school; in slightly wealthier ones, this percentage may go up to 55. But wealthier countries have over 90 percent of their young people in school, learning how to be productive adults.

6. Social services of all sorts are poor or nonexistent. Simple things like police and fire protection are not always available; old people do not have pensions (who could afford them?); medical facilities are painfully inadequate; workers may not get unemployment benefits; and training facilities of all sorts are inadequate. Without enough income or skilled people to staff such services they exist only on paper, for a very few, or not at all.

7. The typical poor-country culture is traditional and non-Western in orientation, revolving around the village, clan, or tribe. Tradition, not science, logic, and technology, governs most affairs. The extended family life-style is very common, since the only way to survive is with the family. This system often is accompanied by nepotism in rather extreme forms—your relative is definitionally preferred to outsiders, no matter how competent the nonrelative. Genetic inheritance systems, for jobs as well as wealth, are common.

8. Politics are violent, obscure, and often very shaky as various factions (often assisted by friends in more affluent

countries) struggle for power. Marxism, religious romanti-
cism, military dictatorships, democratic socialism, and even
theocracy try to gain adherents and power. The politician
who serves out his appointed term is something of a wonder
—it is not at all uncommon to find that there have been perhaps twenty governments in thirty years. Related to both
this point and the previous one about nepotism, the public
services are often extremely ill-managed. The wrong people,
underpaid and unskilled, struggle with problems of public
health, workers' pensions, and fire and sewer services, often
with few results.

9. Underemployment and unemployment is endemic.
Americans get upset if our unemployment rate goes above 5
percent, but in many poor countries unemployment is over
20 percent, and underemployment (typically in under-
worked agricultural jobs and petty services) runs the total
above 40 percent. Virtually every poor country seems to have
endless battalions of unskilled workers available for almost
any unskilled job. Curiously, skilled people are in very short
supply. Doctors, engineers, chemists, and good managers are
not to be found. But it is not curious if you ponder the implications of the educational picture discussed above.

10. Most poor countries have a balance-of-payments crisis
all the time. That is, they cannot earn enough by selling
goods to foreigners to pay for needed imports from the affluent countries. Their exports of raw materials, food, and minerals are rarely large enough to earn money to pay for machinery, food, capital goods, and all the rest needed from the
West. Poor countries rarely trade with each other much
because each produces raw materials of some sort. They
need industrial goods, and only affluent countries produce
them.

In short, everyone, with very few exceptions, is in very
tough shape. By the standards of any West European country or the United States, their condition is desperate. No one
likes this, and it is easy to try to find some devils to blame.
But finding devils won't get a couple of million kids into

school next week; it won't get the doctors necessary to lower the death rate; and it won't somehow, by magic, get women (or men) to practice birth control. All of these things have to be done the hard way, taking lots of time and patience. They also have to be done the expensive way, since no one knows any cheap and easy method of changing the human condition rapidly. Yet it is tempting to pass laws, give out dreamlike propaganda, and spend scarce funds on a handful of citizens, to suggest that everything is well, that this poor country is just as good as any of those rich countries who have already done these things.

This approach is the emulation effect in action. Instead of trying to invest in new ways of doing the job, it is easier and more attractive to do it the way poorer-country leaders see it being done in wealthy countries. Hence investments are made in esoteric machine tools, jet aircraft, the most advanced steel mills, and all the rest. The leaders ignore things now-rich countries did fifty or even one hundred years ago. The result can be an enclave system, where a handful of people live like those in wealthier countries, while most citizens suffer in poverty as old as man.

A further problem is that the initial economic-development formulation omitted lots of things. Since the early theorists were economists, they naturally worried about economics and technology. This is kind of sanitary—if you talk about capital/outputs ratios, income growth, and similar matters, you don't have to worry about such nasty things as people's behavior, political instabilities, and other sensitive matters. A computer or jet aircraft seems ethically neutral, in that anyone can use it, and hence we can all talk about it without getting personally upset. But because some key points were omitted, the development process didn't work out as well as most people had hoped. Here are some of the key things that were never talked about much until very recently:

1. Management is unimportant and irrelevant, and hence is not considered as a valid part of the planning process.

Economists assume competence in management, which is a good assumption for an affluent, educated country like the United States or West Germany. But it is a dangerous assumption in a country where perhaps half or more of the adults are illiterate. As big companies found their place, somehow people turned up who understood marketing, finance, production, how to organize large numbers of workers into productive groups, and all the rest. It was never quite clear where these supercitizens would come from, but they were expected to appear fully trained and ready to go.

Increasingly, as various countries and firms, both publicly and privately owned, got into deep trouble because management was inept, more attention has been paid to this point, and now most American business schools have many foreign students from poorer countries diligently studying this complex subject. But in the 1950s, and indeed well into the 1960s, this point was dismissed as trivial and easily solved.

But management in complex organizations does count— and these new copies of Western technology are typically complex organizations. If there is any single reason why the United States does have more income per capita than any other country, it probably is that American managers are somewhat better on the average than persons in other countries. Growing realization of this fact has led recently to much more attention being paid to management than in the past, but we can still find many who will argue that this one is irrelevant. Incidentally, the main reason the United States has so many internal problems is that the country still does not have enough really good managers to go around. If we could somehow manage our poverty programs better, or if our own black enterprises could obtain superior management, then we would be in much better shape.

2. Economies of scale go on forever: that is, the higher the level of production in a given firm or plant, the lower the unit costs. If this point is true, then bigness means cheapness, and even the smallest country should build big and bold. Here economists and others were mesmerized by the

likes of Henry Ford and U.S. Steel. Bigness sometimes does
mean low costs—but not always. There are many sectors
where bigness just means inefficiency and confusion, and efforts to get large can just cause more problems than they
solve.

Which sectors? Just look at the ones in the West which are
characterized by small firms, and in the East by great difficulties in planning. Virtually all light industry, motor truck-
ing, furniture manufacture, a lot of retailing, and much
much more, falls into this category.

This point gets back to the first point. Sectors which can
operate with small-scale firms do not need big management.
The boss and his few workers can somehow manage to keep
things going, and even compete with big firms. But this is not
what most people think about when they consider the dy-
namics of development. The idea of some mama-papa store
opening does not match the drama of a new jet aircraft or
petrochemical factory. Hence small things tend to be ignored.

3. White-collar work is always superior to blue-collar
work. Here is the ghost of endless ancient class wars, with
the notion of the scribe as superior to the peasant buried
deep within the idea. If this is true, it follows that any
white-collar, clerical job has to be better paid than any blue-
collar, working-with-the-hands job. This belief, fairly common in most developing countries, can play hell with sup-
ply-demand relationships in labor markets, educational
systems, and many other things. It also leads to the depress-
ingly familiar poor-country scene of battalions of office workers doing little, while the boys who get the real work done
are few and scorned—to say nothing of underpaid. And
somehow the clerks can rarely be original or start something
new, whereas an occasional bright blue-collar man, when
given the proper encouragement, can start his own little
shop, making something or other.

4. Production management is the key to everything. Here
is the ghost of Frederick Taylor. Firms and countries start-

ing the industrialization process are naturally enough intrigued with production, since production must be done right before anything else can happen. But it is not the whole story, by a long shot. Those Russian warehouses full of unsalable goods bear mute testimony to the need to be a complete manager, with a complete managerial staff, before an economy can function reasonably well. Few really believe this, until disaster hits them.

5. Planning an economy is easy. Many early economic development specialists noted that all one has to do is get a few good men together in the Ministry of Planning, figure out a rough input-output table for the economy, and tell everybody else what to do. Within five years, all will be well. Nowadays one wonders how many economic plans come remotely close to their stated objectives. Certainly rates of growth in most countries suggest that failures far outweigh successes. In addition to random shocks, such as external events, we also find the impossible task of dealing with billions of prices and costs even in small countries. Aggregate economic planning is fun, but it hardly works well in practice—perhaps because most of it is based on the four premises noted above.

6. Population control is either irrelevant or easy. Until the mid-1950s, no one worried much about population growth, since death rates were still very high in most poor countries. Although birth rates were high too, population grew very slowly. But death control is easier than birth control, and by 1960 the income gains of poorer countries were largely being eaten up by population increases. Now this *is* considered a critical problem, but in the past it was not.

7. Agriculture can take care of itself. Since agriculture was employing a steadily smaller percentage of people in the wealthy part of the world, and since it seemed to get done without much attention, poor countries concentrated on industrialization. The primitive agricultural sectors were generating exports to pay for capital imports, but they were stagnating. Moreover, population increases were beginning

to eat up export surpluses. Once again, this error has been recognized, but twenty years of neglect have taken a toll in many countries. Here again we find the enclave idea—it is better to invest the $10 million on one modern plant, employing perhaps 500 workers enjoying conditions few are accustomed to, than to put the money into some local roads, warehouses, or plows which would benefit agriculture and lots of people a little.

8. Educational and behavioral problems are not serious and hence can be ignored. By some mysterious process, illiterates could become aircraft mechanics, and peasants could adjust easily to industrial discipline. In short, the whole culture-busting notion was ignored, largely because no one liked to admit that whatever passed for good behavior in a poorer country could be wrong for an affluent one.

Poor countries have always stressed education, and they-(and their friends from affluent countries) always talk about the need to "modernize" the people as well as the economy. Once again, the action took the form of blind copying of affluent countries, rather than careful thinking about how to do it locally. If America had great universities, then each poor country had to have some, even if this type of education yielded yet another enclave in a poor country. It is not accidental that university students in poor countries are typically very revolutionary. They are men and women who are out of joint with their countries and their times, and they know it. But they do not know how to get back in step, and their pathetic revolutionary programs would only lead to more emulation of the affluent East or West, with even fewer visible productive results than their countries now have.

9. Everything has a humanistic, liberal Western orientation, even though such humanistic ideals are unrealizable in any meaningful time-span. Here walks the ghosts of the English Fabian socialists, since many leaders of many now-poor countries studied in England under such men and women. Indeed, the early leadership of India was probably

better suited to run 1935 England than 1955 India, given
their education and training. These leaders believe evil
abounds; workers are exploited; peasants cannot get their
fair share of income. Hence pass a law, reform society, take
over the means of production, so that fairness will prevail.

The fact remains that no matter how you slice a $100-per-
capita income, there still is only $100 per capita in the
society—which is not enough. And worse, such social reform
is painful, since those being reformed tend to object. En-
ergies and abilities best suited to increasing production are
sidetracked into sterile debates about who shares in what
way the pathetically small wealth now available. Any country can pass a law giving more to workers and peasants and
less to the rich, but if there is very little income around,
such laws won't work very well. Any country can pass a law
granting free medical care to all, but if there is only one doctor per 10 thousand persons, the law does not give the shots
or provide the examinations.

To sum it all up, we get about what we would expect:
grandiose plans with huge projects, rarely realized properly;
big work forces in capital-intensive situations wildly unreal-
istic for the existing labor/capital cost situation at hand;
inept or idiotic marketing of the little product which finally
is produced; and administrative hierarchies of tremendous
complexity and little productivity. In short, nothing works
well. Worse, such activities show waste in amounts which are
criminal for the poor countries concerned. Instead of vast
new industrial complexes, they have half-finished factories.
Instead of large outputs from the latest technical capital
equipment, they have unused machinery, excess capacity,
and broken-down equipment.

Increasingly, thoughtful people are beginning to see these
usually overlooked problems, and there is much debate, confusion, and argument about all of them. But by now we have
twenty years of ideological development in the economic
mainstream to say nothing of the theological lock-ins about
Marxism and capitalism, which tie people into various

thought patterns. It is hard to get any middle-aged person to change his views, even if the outcomes he realizes are not exactly what was expected.

So, the results are mixed. Poor countries have grown, but rich ones have done better. Population growth, the unexpected development, has eaten up much of the gains so laboriously made. Agriculture is in tough shape everywhere, yet most people are peasants. And because countries have to sell abroad in order to buy the machines for development, agricultural stagnation has also meant that exports have lagged behind needs, leading to balance-of-payments problems and the need for more foreign aid and loans than most countries could readily obtain, from either East or West.

The needed behavioral changes required to get development moving have not occurred fast enough, and most peasants, along with many others in newly expanding cities, are decidedly not modernized, preferring instead age-old ways of behavior—which are perfectly fine unless you want to restructure entire countries to get rich. Those who have changed more often than not are stuck in enclaves of modernization, in small pockets here and there where their impact is slight.

And now, we have a long-term crisis. The image of two worlds, one rich and affluent, the other poor and miserable and falling behind, is not exactly appealing. Nor does it make economic development in the past twenty-five years any real success story. So, back to the drawing boards to prepare for something new that might even work.

And what might that be? Well, try the idea of getting perhaps 20 percent income growth per year in the poorer countries, while the rich ones grow at 5 or 6 percent. By the turn of the century, the poor will be closing in very fast on the rich, and the world could be in somewhat better balance than it now is. A few countries (Japan, South Korea, Hong Kong, Taiwan) have managed to get 10 to 12 percent annual growth for a decade—perhaps we can figure out how to do better than that. No one ever has, but nothing else seems to answer our problems.

One possible other way is for the rich to give voluntarily to the poor. Western Europe, the Eastern communist countries, and North America might give 10 to 30 percent of their income voluntarily to the poor. Some radicals have suggested just this, although it is a bit difficult to figure out, given modern nation-states and their attitudes, just how it could be done. Few rich have ever given away their incomes, and it does not appear likely in the foreseeable future. Indeed, aid from the rich to the poor has trended downward for a decade. The United Nations has called for grants totaling 1 percent of the GNP of the wealthy to the poor, but only a few countries, not including the United States, have even met this modest quota in recent years. It appears as if we will have to do it the hard way, and it further appears that we will have to do it in a quite different way from what is now being tried.

. . . .

CHAPTER III

Wakes and Weddings

When you're very young, you rarely see what you are look-ing at. I wandered down many Mexico City streets in 1949, trying to take in all I could. Among common things to be seen, particularly in the poorer sections of the city, were the coffin shops. Two or three men would be working in an open-front shop, diligently manufacturing cheap pine cof-fins. Many, maybe most, were children's sizes, particularly very small ones for the babies. And, if you hung around such neighborhoods for more than a few hours, you could see a funeral procession too. Sad mourners, a pair of pallbearers, and the little coffin up on their shoulders, marched along the crowded streets, while an occasional bystander crossed herself. In those day, lots of kids died young in Mexico and many other countries. I was looking at the tail end of the old infant mortality problem from another age, another world, and I didn't know it. I know it now, and I would never want to see it again. Now the infant-coffin business is in decline. You look long and hard before you see this particular specta-cle nowadays. The Mexicans have their shots, their clinics, their midwives, their clean water, and the other simple things that keep babies alive. Who would want it otherwise?

Yet the absence of the small coffins has created another kind
of revolutionary world. Population increases have done more
to change the nature of the world economic game than anything else. Indeed, there isn't even a second factor which
comes close. If this problem isn't solved soon, there may well
be no tomorrow.

It all began simply enough. In 1800, Dr. Jenner, an English physician and scientist, discovered that a small inocula-
tion could prevent smallpox. Within a decade, inoculations
were common, and the first of the deadly preventable diseases was on its way out. The rush of scientific discovery in
the nineteenth century led to one medical triumph after another, culminating finally in the late 1950s with the polio
vaccine. At the same time, discoveries which lead to realiza-
tions that dirt carried bacteria and viruses led to sanitary
practices in all types of medical care, and deadly infections
began to disappear.

You can see this easily enough in any nineteenth-century
churchyard. There lies John Smith—and wives one, two,
and even three. And there beside the wives lie the children
—aged one, five, eleven. The American pattern until this
century was one of many children, wives dying in childbirth
and its aftermath, and grieving widowers. But each year of
the nineteenth century brought a bit more medical and public-health progress, and each year the death rate inched
downward. At the same time, the birth rate began its downward spin, for reasons as yet not clearly understood, but it
happened in all developing countries. For a century these
two rates drifted downward together, until now in any advanced, affluent country, we find birth rates of between 13
and 20 per thousand population, and death rates of 7 to 12
per thousand. The difference between these two rates, with
minor adjustments for immigration and emigration, is the
rich country's population growth rate, which typically ranges
from ½ to 1 percent per year. At this level, population will
double every seventy-five to 150 years.

In the poor countries, the pattern is very different. Birth

rates until now have stayed high—in the range of 35 to 50 per thousand per year. Until twenty-five years ago, death rates stayed right up there too, so that population growth was under 1 percent, and those coffin shops did good business. As there is a humane streak in most of us, practically nobody likes to see people succumbing to preventable diseases. So the Presbyterians, Baptists, and Methodists collected their pennies in Sunday school, as did members of many other denominations, to send medical missionaries out to heal "the heathen." This image now survives in the hospital ship *Hope*. We know how and what better thing to do than cure the sick, prevent disease, keep mothers from dying in the agonies of childbirth? Anyone reading the Scriptures of any major (or minor) faith could not fail to heed the plea. In all great religions, human life is sacred. The Presbyterian medical missionary carefully showing African midwives how to wash up before attending a birth did not see himself as a world revolutionary, except perhaps in the sight of God, but he was. No culture, no matter how strange or poor, likes to see its children dying, and this sort of death control remains the easiest cross-cultural sale ever made.

And even after missionaries became relatively less important, the World Health Organization, along with medical and public-health specialists from every affluent country, carried on the campaigns. The World Health Organization could spray DDT on malarial swamps around an entire country for a pittance, and even if the country could not afford it, France, Britain, the Soviet Union, the United States or the United Nations could easily pick up the small tab. Death rates dropped dramatically. From perhaps 40 to 50 per thousand they would drop to around 15 to 20 per thousand within five or ten years. The affluent countries had to get their death rates down slowly and painfully over a century or more, because they didn't know how to do otherwise; now a poor country can do it in a tenth that time.

Birth rates stayed up. If, ten years ago, half the babies died, and if the country, like most poor ones, had no unemployment insurance, no social security, and no other welfare programs, the wise peasant had many sons. Not only did his entire cultural situation emphasize this as a duty, but it also protected him in old age. If six out of seven of his children survived, perhaps because of those mysterious needles the health man stuck in them, then God was kind. After all, he was the only survivor of five sons his father had had.

Spray the malarial swamps anywhere in the subtropics and knock five points off the death rate. Train the midwives properly, and infant mortality drops by 30 to 75 percent. Inoculate the kids against the usual communicable diseases, and another five points comes off the rate. Clean up village water supplies, and down the death rate comes some more. Even before one begins to talk about any sort of sophisticated medicine, you have a 12 to 15 per thousand death rate, as compared to 40 or 50 earlier. And it can all be done, even in the most primitive countries, in under ten years.

It has been done, and the difference between birth and death rates is now from 2 to 4 percent per year in virtually every now-poor country. And the magic of compounding begins to work again. At 2 percent, population doubles in thirty-seven years; at 4 percent, in sixteen years. Our happy peasant with his five healthy sons may begin to have some second thoughts about his luck as he ponders how to divide his four-acre farm. Until this generation, there was no problem —always before, there were about as many people around as in the past generation. But now what? With luck, one or two of his sons might have a year or even two of elementary schooling, painfully acquired at the new school in the village. So off to the city they go, to seek their fortune. They are joined by thousands of other number two, three, and four sons, equally unlucky, equally uneducated, to scramble for the jobs which always seem so hard to get. The government is building many factories, following models from the United States and Europe, but somehow only those with high school educations can get in the door. It seems that complex machinery requires more training than these displaced peasants have.

So here we find two worlds again. There is a rich one, where birth and death rates are low, and where population grows slowly. In the United States at present rates, it will take about 75 years to double the population—and the birth rate is still dropping. In some European countries, such as Sweden and England, it will take 150 years to double the population. These affluent countries, all scare talk to the contrary, can easily handle this kind of population growth. But the poor countries—that other world—cannot. Here populations double every fifteen to thirty years, and there is no surplus wealth. If the country does an excellent economic job and manages to get 6 percent income increases every year, as much as 4 percent of this increase is taken by the new population. Moreover, the same 6 percent in an affluent country nets out to 5 percent per capita. So income in the poor country *per capita* doubles every thirty-five years or so, while in the affluent country income doubles every ten or twelve years, starting from a much higher base. This problem has nothing to do with political ideologies. Poor communist countries look demographically just like poor capitalist ones; affluent communist countries have the same pattern of low birth and death rates as their affluent capitalist counterparts.

But the problem is worse than this. Very high net growth rates lead very quickly to a younging population. After fifteen years or so of 4 percent growth rates, half the population is fifteen years of age or under. Where do the teachers, parents, and health personnel to handle the young come from in such a population mix? They don't, particularly if the country is poor to begin with. Hence one sees the young animals in any large city in any part of the poor world. These are the kids who are literally left to survive by their wits. They have few or no family connections; they do not attend school; they do not have even the minimal housing and clothing necessary for animal comfort. You can see them hustling, as bootblacks, newspaper vendors, prostitutes, and other minor-service sellers. Services are supposed to be the sign of affluence in a country, but many poor countries have more petty services available per capita than most affluent ones have. In short, family life disintegrates under such population conditions, independent of the moral values of the population. The kids swamp the system. Remember that most of these kids come from abject poverty, and their families simply cannot handle them. In earlier generations, they were dead. Now they haunt every country with a population problem.

As people are literally forced off the fixed supply of land in poorer countries into the cities, we see another peculiar phenomenon. It could be called the inside-out city. In the United States, the most affluent people live in the suburbs where there is room to stretch out and space for cars. But in poorer countries without many cars, even for the upper-middle classes, the affluent live where our ghettos are, close to the city center, while the poor live in what we would see as desirable suburbs. Marginal improvements in transportation, sewage, and water supplies, plus the terrific population growth, have made such urban development possible. There are cities in Asia few Americans have ever heard of with well over a million citizens—many of whom sleep on the sidewalk or in shacks on the outskirts. Because the big projects normally associated with economic development do not use much unskilled labor, it is also common to find unemployment rates ranging up to 25 percent, with underemployment going above 50 percent. No one knows how to handle the new population.

While this is going on in poor countries, the affluent countries are experiencing an aging population. Now, the most common American age is ten; in twenty years it will be thirty, because more babies were born ten years ago than ever before or since in this country's history. As fewer babies are born, average age rises. So here is another difference—as poor countries become younger, rich countries get older. If radicalism is related to age, we can expect a cautious, conservative Europe, Japan, and North America arrayed against a radical, impatient, and dynamic third world within a decade.

Anyone who expects that some traditional culture, including the American one, can withstand the sorts of attacks these demographic facts will cause is very optimistic. Indeed, take any traditional culture, give it effective death control, wait thirty years—and that culture will be destroyed. Four percent net population change will wipe out the culture as efficiently, if not more so, than any other shock which could be imagined. All traditional societies are literally based on static or near-static populations—which is not surprising, in view of the fact that every culture since the dawn of time, excepting this past fifty years, *has* been a static population culture.

Static population tribal cultures also tend to develop values that sanctify any human life. The threatened tribe can survive by both keeping people alive and outbreeding enemies. But now we find that death control can explode the static, traditional culture in population within a mere twenty years. Unless the economic system is changed rapidly, the whole system comes unstuck. And that is what culture busting is all about. Accept death control, and your culture has no choice. And, given the inclination to save every human life if at all possible, death control will be accepted.

There are essentially five basic ways to solve this problem in a century. One is to give up death control, and let people die. This seems a bit nasty, but already governments like ours have indicated that unless poor countries start thinking about population controls, they can expect no aid. Run a population doubling every sixteen years out a half century to see why. If we gave aid to a country like this, they *could* outbreed us. Note the irony of the problem. In 1880, people died of typhus, and no one knew what to do; in 1955, kids died of polio, and no one knew what to do. These were acts of God, and we prayed. Now we do know what to do. If we deliberately withdraw our knowledge from people who will die of preventable diseases, what kind of God-playing are we doing? Few of us even like to think about this problem, so the possibilities of changing our death controls are ignored.

Major wars have been suggested as good death controls although the human race has yet to experience a war which reduced population just from casualties incurred. World Wars I and II now show up as minor blips of population increase slowdowns, as world population rose right through each conflict. Perhaps some atomic catastrophe could do the job, but few would think seriously of this answer.

Mass famine also might solve the problem. If present population-growth trends continue, we will have over 7 billion people in the world by 2000; and by 2030, 14 billion. Sooner or later, something may give, particularly since most of these people will be in poor countries with laggard agricultural technology. Indeed, we will probably see the first mass famine in a long time within the next decade—try Bangladesh as a most likely locale. We might fight off this one, but as population grows geometrically, it will be only a matter of time.

Another possibility is to decrease the birth rate. After all, this is exactly what the now-affluent countries have done, so it is not impossible. The problem is that the rich countries took a century to do what has to be done in the poor countries in ten or twenty years. Nevertheless, the whole panoply of devices and propaganda can be used—coils, pills, condoms, loops, and abortion. And many countries, including India and Red China (which between them have over one-third of the world's population) have begun such campaigns. They work, too—India's birth rate has slowly dropped from around 50 per thousand in 1947 to perhaps 35 per thousand now. But the key question is whether or not such tactics will work fast enough. So far, the evidence is not encouraging.

Only one country has managed to get its birth rate down rapidly—Japan. In the late 1940s, concerned about stagnant postwar economic conditions and the real possibility that Japan could never ever expand beyond its small islands, the government authorized legal abortions. Smaller families were officially encouraged and abortions were available everywhere at low cost. The results were phenomenal.

Within five years, the birth rate had been halved, and Japan now has a rate of about 15 per thousand, below some other affluent Western countries. Ironically, Japan's great postwar economic boom peaked just as half the previous number of eighteen-year-olds began to come on the labor market. The irony of a major Asian country with a labor shortage emerged for the first time. Now Japanese thinkers are pondering the possibility of increasing the birth rate again.

If the poor countries don't practice birth control, it is possible that someone else will. It is not too difficult to imagine moving birth control from individual pills to water or air supplies. If this were done, we could convert pregnancy from an act which normally happens to one which happens only as a positive act—like getting a pill which allows pregnancy. If those poor out there insist on breeding, perhaps we rich can fight them by making sure they don't have kids. When the next Vietnam comes along, in about 1980, America simply sprays the air in the nasty enemy country, and says, "Go do your thing, boys. Conquer anyone you want. One hitch —as long as you don't behave, no children will be born in your country." Then sit back and wait—wait ten, twenty, thirty years. They'll come around, because no kids is as bad as too many kids. Is such a war more or less moral than any other, with B-52s, napalm, and all the rest? If you don't think that this population problem isn't culture-busting reconsider. This one is dynamite under the whole human race.

The final way to beat the problem is to get economic production up faster than population rises. Right now, the rich countries can do this without much strain, and all are. But the poor have problems, since the increase needed is so great. For a decade or two, we probably have no choice.

One major breakthrough in just the past few years is the so-called green revolution. What happened is that after twenty or more years of hard work and careful scientific experimentation, high-yield strains of wheat and rice have been developed which can produce up to three or four times as much output per acre as conventional strains. These new strains require much better agricultural management, mainly in the form of proper application of fertilizers and water, but they work. They also are used so widely within three years that there is another production revolution throughout Southeast Asia. Countries that had food deficits now have surpluses, and general famine seems to have been put off for about thirty years. (Consider again the potent arithmetic of 3 or 4 percent population growth to see why such productivity gains last such a short time.)

Then we find another culture-busting problem. Those clever and educated farmers who use the new strains now have triple incomes—which they use to buy land from illiterates who don't understand the new techniques. This is encouraged by governments worried about food problems. Why leave scarce land in the hands of those who can't produce? More people are pushed off the land, into those exploding inside-out cities, since only about one-third as many agrarian laborers are needed. Moreover, the successful farmer can now perhaps afford to buy a small tractor, to displace still more peasants. And the cycle of culture-busting keeps right on going.

So here's a nasty mess. The poor countries have an agricultural revolution, a younging population, and growing numbers to worry about. The rich don't really have much of a population problem, except that they will steadily become a smaller minority, given their low population growth relative to the poor. They can handle the population problem at home, but they just might be tempted to fight a population war abroad. And to complicate the problem, two major theologies, communism and Catholicism, are dubious about the ethics of birth control.

No one wants to accept the implications of abandoning death control, yet it is very hard to get effective birth control in any reasonable time. Experience to date in poor countries suggests that this can be done, but only much more slowly than anyone would like. And in many poor countries, communists argue that birth control is a capitalist, war-mongering, imperialist plot by mad-dog foreigners, while the Catholic church down the street also preaches against such heresies. He who ignores the numbers has to live with them.

Figure out how to handle this one, and the game is won. You would be the first to do so. No one really has handled population growth very well, which is not surprising, since it is a very new problem. The Catholics and the communists show signs of coming unstuck on this issue, and not a few poor-country governments *have* fallen apart over this question. This one is also the cultural time bomb. None of us now has the proper culture and values to deal with this question, since it has been around so short a time. We have inherited values acceptable to other worlds, other ages, and we can't often even consider this one. But it will change us all forevermore.

CHAPTER IV

. . . .

Culture Busting on a Global Scale

There was no revolution visible, as I watched Othman set the valve train of the Cummins diesel. Or was there? It was 110° in the quiet Saudi Arabian shop where I watched him follow the chalked instructions on the blackboard alongside his work. Othman was carefully following the complex set of instructions about dwell, valve settings, and other stuff I never did understand. Othman didn't understand it either, four years ago. He was illiterate at thirty—a bright young Sudani who went to Mecca, as all good Muslims do, got stranded for lack of cash, and then drifted into the oilfields in search of work. My predecessor had put him to work as a mechanic's helper in 1957, and now in 1965 he was top mechanic in the diesel section.

Illiterates don't set valve timings for diesel engines, no place, not ever. This is a skilled job, a disciplined job, a job requiring a kind of feel for machinery and technical knowledge few of us would ever have. Othman had the feel—he came from a village of blacksmiths in the far-off Sudan. In 1960, he learned to read, taught in a class of four by my wife. The textbook was the Cummins repair manual for one of their fuel pumps. If guys are learning to *do,* they might as

well get the right vocabulary. Othman never learned a great
deal—just enough to know the numbers, follow the simple
descriptions in the manuals. That, plus ten years' experience, plus the feel for machinery all good mechanics have,
got him to this point, puzzling over a torque-wrench setting
in a quiet Saudi shop on a hot day in June, getting the engine right so it would run another 150,000 miles without
being torn down or tearing itself up. He walked over,
chalked a note of his torque setting, puzzled out the instructions for the next step, smiled at me, and went back to work.
Fifteen dollars a day, four kids in school, a decent house, and
a craftsman's job—it was a long, long way from that village
in the Sudan, where a young man might, with luck, get to
earn $200 per year as a simple blacksmith. No revolution?
Hogwash! This was where the revolution was, not out there
in the streets.

It comes down to this: all cultures are going to get busted,
and the most painful busting is going to happen in the
poorer countries and subcultures. Once a culture or country
accepts death control, all else follows. Population expands;
unless the economic base gets changed very fast to cover the
increase, someone starves sooner or later. Just give the kids
some shots, train a few midwives, and clean up the water
supply—all feasible options even in very poor cultures—and
wait thirty years. The population will at least double on the
same economic base, and trouble is certain. Now, how do
you increase production? The Western way is the only one
we know that works. So get your power plants, your irrigation systems, your fertilizers, your factories, and all the rest
—and in the process change men and women to be able to
handle these new tools. That's the rub—the kind of person
who can figure out what to do in a power plant or fertilizer
warehouse is not going to be anything but a Western man.
No other kind can do it.

Cultures also get busted up because they typically want to
get the economic goodies, as soon as they figure out what
they are. Young American romantics can sigh and dream for
the commune or village life, uncomplicated by worldly

goods, but the vast majority of the human race is, let's face it, materialistic. They want in the mainstream just as fast as they can get there, and typically faster than their economic system can get them there. If getting the goods involves major structural changes in culture and human behavior, then leaders start figuring out how to manipulate people so they will be the right kinds.

Also the idealist dreams of one peaceful world, but realists everywhere have noted that all the weapons systems are on the Western side. No one ever flew a jet fighter with an illiterate peasant pilot; no culture ever fixed its machine guns with prayer rugs; no machine-gun factories ever produced anything in a traditional village economy. And those with guns use them, sooner or later. If you feel that your country belongs in this world, and should fight to stay here, you had better start thinking very seriously about changing behavior very fast. You need the disciplined, educated soldiers, the arms, and the organization to keep the enemy away.

The trouble is that you don't train a peasant from a traditional economy up to a jet mechanic or a power-plant technician or whatever and expect nothing else in his life will be changed. Everything will be. And the more of these types you get, the more remote the traditional culture will be. You may not like it, but there isn't any other option.

Richer countries, including the United States, are also going through a process of dynamic social and cultural change. Once you step on the growth treadmill, there is no place to go but up, and each additional move up brings about still more demands for still more change and growth. Western Europe discovers daily, to its surprise, that it has American cultural tendencies; the Soviets fight off the heresies of the affluent West daily; and modern Tokyo somehow looks more like a European city than something Eastern. Everyone is on the same growth treadmill. And as incomes keep going up and up, we somehow find still more ways to spend until our whole cultural fix is different from what it used to be.

Some say, stop! Consider the pollution, the shifting values, the drugs, the delinquency, the total vacuousness of American (or anyone else's) life. So let's stop—and within three years, we would break the American culture wide open. Why? Consider three straight years of stagnant American income. We start with about 6 percent unemployment; add about 1 percent more for the net increase per year in the labor force. Then add about 4 percent more unemployment to the total for the annual increase in worker productivity. At the end of year one, we have 11 percent unemployment. In year two, we get another 4 percent productivity gain, plus another 1 percent addition to the work force. Unemployment goes to 16 percent. At the end of year three, unemployment is 21 percent—and ponder the plight of any politician trying to get elected on *that* record. We could, maybe, completely restructure the role of work and who does it—but as we said at the beginning, your culture is destroyed whether you like it or not.

Other cultures tend to be swamped by the dominant one because the interactions between them are so easy these days. Marco Polo took a couple of years to get to China; now you can go there within a few days. And when you go, you take along a lot of excess cultural baggage. The clothes you wear, the stuff you drink (from Scotch to Coca-Cola to clean water), the way you act, the watch you wear—all are grist for any local mill. The cultural artifacts Westerners take for granted are real bombs for most cultures, threatening to blow them sky-high any moment. Here are a few of the real bombs:

1. An ordinary truck looks safe, and even reactionary regimes buy them all the time. After all, they do cut movement costs by 50 to 80 percent, depending on how good or bad the roads are. But that movement cost cut means revolution. It means that peasants can get into the major urban markets with produce—and suddenly they are not self-sufficient peasants any more, but truck gardeners worrying about market prices. Trucks mean that goods too expensive to be shipped anywhere before can now be imported or exported.

They mean that a whole new social class has to be formed to repair them—traditional cultures do not have mechanics, or men trained in the art of carburetors, fuel pumps, and brake-shoes. Where do these fellows fit into the traditional cultures? It depends; they are a new class. For example: Where does my friend Othman fit into his world? No one knows, but he sure makes more money than anyone in his social set ever made before. And he is a disturbing factor in a place where few disturbing factors have appeared for millennia. Moreover, it will stick, as his sons go on to something that the traditional culture never knew.

Trucks mean that cities explode, because underemployed peasants forced off the land by population growth and agricultural technology changes can ride the loads into town free, and get fed easily when they get there. They mean mobility of a sort only dreamed of in traditional cultures. Trucks mean a new class of entrepreneurs and promoters, seeking out new markets, expanding into old ones—or maybe a whole new government controlling state-owned firms, full of thousands of paper-pushers. They mean a new concept of police action. They mean that the military now has new mobility to work with against ancient enemies.

They only cost a few thousand dollars apiece, and even poor countries can use them to replace animals, so why not? Loose a few trucks in a culture with death control; sit back and watch it dissolve.

2. Transistor radios are another harmless gadget. Even some poor countries, like Taiwan, can make them now for three or four dollars. They aren't the best receivers in the world, but then in most places there are only a few radio stations to listen to anyway. Any family making even a few hundred dollars a year can afford the set and its batteries. And you don't need a billion-dollar power system to keep them going—just a factory in Hong Kong or some place. The price is low enough for even the poor.

So they are sold by the tens of millions all over the world, and a few people have some noise in their lives for the first time. Nice deal. But it's also a revolutionary deal. The transistor radio opens the door for the first time for a couple of billion people (unlike the United States, one per village is enough—all can listen). They hear educational programs, political polemics, entertainment, religious education, and all the rest, for the first time in their lives. They even hear soap operas in some places, complete with commercials. What does an illiterate Burmese peasant think about all this? Whatever it is, he's a different man forever. It is as if our own ancestors, locked in mid-nineteenth-century isolation in the Kansas prairies, could suddenly tune in on everything in the world—and it happens immediately, not after fifty years of isolation. Your enemies try propaganda from the next country; the Russians and Americans get in on the act with their broadcasts; and the local government preaches the virtues of the nation-state, education, and health and welfare. Confusing, but changing and revolutionary, no matter what comes out of the little black box.

3. Take an ordinary, harmless factory, producing almost anything, and you have another revolution on your hands. We've had them around for 150 years, but when they come into a traditional culture, they're dynamite. For the first time, people have to learn to live by the clock—factories run on time schedules unique to the Western world. The ex-peasants have to learn to live with the five-day, forty-hour week, with disciplined tasks, with new kinds of thinking to be done. Save your pity for the endless, monotonous toil— life in the traditional village was pretty dull, too, but this type of work is very different. And consider the technicians, the managers, the clerks, all doing jobs no one ever thought of in a traditional society. New roles are created, new status symbols form, new classes plug into the traditional system. And all this links up to the trucks talked about earlier, with shipping schedules and payment dates, and all the marketing links no one ever thought of before. After five years of this, no one can even remember what traditional life was like—

and no one wants to, because life *was* nasty, brutish, and short in the not-so-good old days.

My friend Othman always showed up early for work—but only after the first six months. It took him that long to get locked into this strange new world of clocks and time. After that, he was brainwashed, another kind of man. Moreover, he really liked his work—he had more fun doing his thing out there in the shop than most workers I've seen. After all, he was a master craftsman, and he knew he was good. And the clocks and time and precision were a part of him now, seven years after he came out of his village. He was never going back, nor was his culture.

4. Consider a burp gun, one of the more common exports from the affluent to the less fortunate, often as gifts for one revolutionary group or the other. With a few of these, warfare is different forevermore. Actually, the side that learns to maintain the things first and get more bullets will win. These simple things involve a whole new way of thinking about the world—they involve the world of precise cause and effect, of complex logistics to get the bullets to the right place, of planning, organizing, and controlling the system. And if you don't learn fast, you lose, which is incentive enough to get on with the process. Here there is no choice at all for any culture or subculture. If you don't learn, your destiny is not your own. Someone else, perhaps your hated neighbors, will call the tunes. Whole regions of the poor world, such as all the Arab states, have learned this the hard way in the past thirty years. You modernize, change, break up your traditional culture—or else.

5. Consider something really complicated and modern, such as a jet aircraft. As fighter or transport, this equipment works *right,* or else you don't have it for long. If you don't have your share, you're not even considered a part of world civilization, so countries beg, borrow, buy, or steal the things. But the jet aloft is the tip of the iceberg. Behind the plane are battalions of carefully trained maintenance special-

ists, electronics technicians, dispatchers, route planners, traf-
fic-control experts, and on and on, all of whom must have a
totally modern approach to their work. There is no mysti-
cism here. You do the job the Western mainstream way, or it
doesn't get done.

To get this kind of human resources into the game, be
prepared to restructure your educational system along Western lines, avidly follow all the latest technical developments,
listen to the earnest technical salesmen from Boeing, and
keep pushing as hard as you can into the twenty-first century. There is no other way to do the job. And if you don't
succeed, someone else will, and in the end will absorb your
culture.

There are many more examples of these innocent Western
artifacts which are bombs blowing up local cultures every
day. Lots of people don't like it, but what else is there? Perhaps a gentle greening of America or some other land, where
happy new peasants can forever cycle their lives in bucolic
splendor. The hitch is that those who get the burp guns,
trucks, and jets will decide whether the rustics live or die.
That's the way the world is. And because virtually all countries, including the most backward, have seen this point so
very clearly, all scramble to bust up their own cultures before someone else does it for them. Those which are a little
laggard wait for the next coup, and the new regime's fum-
bling efforts to get into the mainstream before it's too late.

Military and political imperialism have gone out of style,
but cultural imperialism, and maybe economic imperialism
too, are still around. The traditional cultures have little to
offer the West except handicrafts, poverty, and perhaps a
fuzzy image of the life of the noble savage. The West has it
all. Any time an American official merely shows up acting
normally, he practices cultural imperialism. The cigarettes
he smokes, the clothes he wears, the car he drives, and even
the almost imperceptible twitch of his nostrils as he smells
some good old-fashioned poverty convey his distaste and contempt for whatever is going on in the local scene. Americans

needn't feel too bad about this; Russians, Englishmen, Frenchmen, and even Japanese do the same—anyone, that is, who is in on the brave new world of affluence, reason, and fast-growth economics. The rich have always rubbed it in the faces of the poor—the only difference now is that entire nations do it to other nations. "If you were just well-behaved, rational, intelligent people like us," they all say, "you too could be respected and envied." The poor know better than to argue—they've seen it all before. And as the poor countries gain independence and some control over their own destinies, guess where they start heading. Maybe it's wrong, but that's the way the world is.

There may well be economic imperialism too. The things the world wants are the trucks, transistors, TV sets, machine tools, and all the other paraphernalia from the affluent countries. Since poor countries cannot produce these goods, they are stuck with what is left, namely, raw materials, minerals, petroleum, and agricultural products—in short, the low end of the value scale. If they could produce the goods, then they could get in the game too. And to do this, all the poor countries have to do is be exactly like the rich, economically and culturally. So, back to square one, and on to the total modernization and industrialization of the economy. In the process, the local culture dissolves.

The poor rarely like the rich, so it is common these days to find that these poor cultures also hate our guts. The ugly American is being joined by the ugly Russian, the ugly Japanese, alongside fading images of the ugly Englishman. There is little discrimination in most quarters. If you're rich, you are wrong, and besides, you probably got rich by exploiting and squeezing the blood out of the now-poor countries a long time ago, in the slave trade, by colonial exploitation, illegal mineral land grabs, or whatever. But hate turns to love as the poor eye those gadgets, the military power, the prestige, and the wealth of the hated ones. What can they do to be like the rich?

The rich, like rich everywhere and in every time, feel a

bit guilty. Besides, they have the cash and knowledge to help out. So they do. And one characteristic of our era is a bewildering expansion of everyone's aid programs and the increase in loans to poor countries. It never seems to be enough, but a crafty poor country can obtain quite a bit of help from the rich if it plays its cards right. Of course, it has to put up with all those uglies wandering around and giving advice better suited for the homeland than the poor country. But something is better than nothing. The aid goes on. Unfortunately, more and more local citizens are exposed to the temptations of the rich world, and they begin to get ideas that maybe they too could be rich if only they could get their own country and culture restructured.

What other way is there? In modern times, only Red China tried to modernize in a non-Western way. They called it the Great Leap Forward. Here, the idea was to short-circuit the torturous learning process which every other country had been through. Instead of getting youngsters to go to college for five years to learn metallurgy, they would set up a backyard furnace and produce steel with illiterate workers chanting the thoughts of Mao. Instead of highly skilled architects and engineers building high rise buildings, peasants would do the job. Instead of keeping kids in school, they were sent out to educate their elders in the positive virtues of the new China.

It didn't work. Indeed, it nearly finished off China, and now the country is back in the race with the rest of the poor, trying to figure out how to be more like the West as quickly as possible. If you want your engines to run right, find yourself an Othman, not a mystic. The sad fact is that there is no other way to get the economic job done. If you want economic progress, you need Western educational patterns, Western technology, Western values, Western military systems, and Western thinking. And don't forget, if you don't buy all this, then you better eliminate death control and let the babies die—because you really have no other choice.

So the non-Western dream fades. There was a time, maybe

only fifteen or twenty years ago, when poets, philosophers, and dreamers could ponder some non-Western kind of world —perhaps in the image of Rousseau or Walden, where happy peasants wandered in idyllic happiness across the green fields. The sad fact is that this image was based on a ghastly mortality rate, particularly for children. Many died so that the survivors could enjoy. Now the kids don't die— and the dream is ended. Broken along with it are all the cultures that tried to set up some endless cycle of births, marriages, and deaths, based on very low-production animal-powered cultures. It is easy enough for any Westerner to nod and say, "Of course." After all, it isn't our culture that's getting busted up, and while ours changes pretty fast, we've become accustomed to change. We can handle it, or so we think. It's the other guy that has to change his spots, restructure his thinking and life-style, and generally accept someone else's view of what the world is all about. This sort of change is as painful to any person as any change can be, and it is not too surprising that in the countries which have the most changing to do there is war, revolution, social unrest, retrogression, and dismay. For such people the world really is out of joint.

And if they don't change? They will starve, or stay very, very poor at best. They will be tolerated, like animals in some zoo, and maybe they can build a lively little tourist industry (run by Western-oriented foreigners, of course) to stare at the natives in their natural habitat. And if their neighbors start developing faster than they do, maybe they should study carefully what happened to the American Indians, who could not change fast enough to get into the modern world. Affluent cultures are kind, in their own curious way. There may be space some place for a reservation where such curious cultures can be observed. And the natives will be harmless, because the zookeepers will have all the guns.

Maybe in the end the nonchangers will prove they are right. At least the early, non-Western cultures were ecologically harmless, and they could survive for millennia without fouling the environment too much (but remember that some Middle Eastern early cultures wrecked their environment because they did not understand enough about pasturing sheep and goats, and hence ruined the topsoil). Maybe we will have ecological collapse, and the American Indians, the Australian Bushmen, and the Pygmies will inherit the earth. But this present century points in quite a different direction. So, we bust up cultures—including our own.

When I read the papers about the most recent revolution in some far-off poor country, I keep thinking back to Othman, with his kids in school, his neat small house, his TV set, his habit of being a very good Muslim and practicing his religion like any sober, conservative citizen should in the world he lives in. I keep thinking about his company, which somehow can fix things to run when no one else out there can. And I keep pondering what running trucks mean in a desert world, where it used to take weeks to get anywhere. Othman is apolitical—he'll fix a truck for anyone, regardless of race, color, creed, or political persuasion. He'll never spend time in jail as a subversive, like some other friends of mine, who stand on street corners and shout slogans, or pass out illegal pamphlets about revolution and social reform. But I wonder who the real revolutionaries are in the long run. I'll put my bet on Othman.

CHAPTER **V**

· ·

The Liberal Dilemma

So the United States decides to help Uguland out with an aid program. Our motives are usually mixed—perhaps Uguland is at the perimeter of the communist countries, and it would be nice if this poor place stayed out from under the Red spell. Perhaps we feel that it is useful to help poor countries who try to help themselves, or maybe it's that the country, with its growing population, could use some surplus agricultural commodities our own farmers have produced in response to domestic price-support policies. Maybe the Ugulanders themselves are good gamesmen, always balancing precariously on the edge of going capitalist or communist, but somehow staying in the middle most of the time, accepting loans and aid from anyone nice enough to offer them. In any case, the aid gets under way. This time it's a large electric-power complex—dams, distribution systems, the works. Lord knows, the Ugulanders need more power, since their electric consumption per capita is about one-twentieth that in Western Europe, and most people and families, to say nothing of industry, have to do without.

In this case, the reasons for aid are even stronger than usual, since various United Nations study groups have sug-

gested that power is a major national concern in Uguland,
and the World Bank also has agreed to grant a loan to tie
into the project. World Bank loans are only granted after extensive study of the real need of the project, along with
projections as to how easily the country can eventually pay
off the loan. Even the Soviets are in the game a bit, with
promises to help out on some railroad building necessary to
complete the project. The Uguland political leaders are of
course all for this project, since it will get them into the
world mainstream of power users, income producers. They
will become men of substance. In short, the world elites
along with the local ones are convinced that this is what is
needed. So, the work begins.

No one asked the typical Ugulander if he liked this idea,
since it never occurred to anyone. The typical Ugulander is
an illiterate villager, as he has been for a few thousand years.
Uguland culture was well developed when the Roman Empire was in flower, when northern Europe was barbarian.
Somehow it slipped into a static agrarian pattern of villages
producing at the subsistence level, cycling generation after
generation in the same old way. But it definitely is, and was,
a viable culture. There are religious monuments, palaces,
and numerous other artifacts to prove it. Radical American
students would (and do) like the old culture just fine—it
looks like the greening of America, with the happy children
playing gentle games around the small villages. Ugulanders
haven't bothered anyone for a thousand years, and if left
alone, they won't bother anyone for another thousand. And,
if anybody bothered to ask, perhaps most of the villagers
would say that their world is just fine—why change? The social roles are simple and well understood; everyone knows
his place. Life flows gently on in a mellow blend of births,
marriages, plantings, harvests, and deaths.

Of course, this sort of life has nothing to do with the development mainstream. The Uguland elite are aware of their
weaknesses—after all, the country was a colonial territory of
a major European power for over 150 years, and it only be-

came independent in 1958. Its present prime minister spent eight years in various jails for agitating for independence, and he knows very well how impotent a country can be when faced with the armed might of even a modest modern Western power. He and other elitists in Uguland have visited the United Nations, and they know very well what is considered important by other countries. No one there cares much about gentle villagers, handicrafts, or other evidence of proud and ancient civilizations. He also knows that his neighbors are modernizing very fast, and already their army is significantly superior to his. They can do it because their wealth and political contacts allow them to get the best in modern guns.

The prime minister also knows about population explosions. He is aware, as his sleek Mercedes traverses his capital, of the tremendous new urbanization which is occurring as peasants are forced off the land by both population pressure and agricultural improvements. He knows that his basic raw-material exports of cotton, coffee, and sisal are stagnating in world markets, and that he cannot realistically expect to expand his critical supplies of hard currencies very much in the next decade. He knows that his newly developed white-collar class wants as many Mercedes (or even Fiats), radios, TV sets, modern apartments, and all the rest of modern Western civilization as it can get, and it wants them now. And he is painfully aware, in spite of his own great efforts to make it different, that over 70 percent of his people are illiterate.

Given all this, and much more, why not try to get into the world mainstream? The bright young economists just returned from the United States and England have the plan set up, and while he finds their enthusiastic discussion of input-output matrices, capital ratios, and cost-benefit analysis confusing, he knows that it all adds up to modernization as fast as possible. Everyone who can read and who has any aspirations at all wants the Western package, so why not? Perhaps it will cut decades off the development push; perhaps

Uguland can hold its head high in the United Nations before he retires in a decade or so. As father of his country, it
is only right that he should be the one who pushed modernization to its practical limits. Besides, the AID people from
America are innocent enough. They would like to push
some pro-American propaganda along with their aid, but
they do not really try too hard. The World Bank people certainly are innocuous politically, being a group of financiers
and technicians, seemingly only interested in the practical
aspects of the project. And even the Russians look harmless.
Like the Americans, they push their propaganda, but without much effect, and their technicians tend to hide away in
separate compounds, bothering no one. The prime minister
has seen plenty of blatant imperialism in his time, but compared to the old days, these people are innocents indeed. Political and economic imperialism seem a part of the remote
past.

On the other side of this fence, the relatively sincere AID
mission, the Soviet technical delegation, and the World
Bank group see it about the same way. Many of these dedicated men and women got into this business because they
did want to help poor people and poor countries; what better way to do it than to lend one's expertise to Uguland,
which so clearly needs it? Oh, there will be an occasional
CIA man in the crowd (or his Soviet counterpart), and a few
characters will be in the game for money, women, or other
dubious reasons, but for the most part, one sees only sincere
people performing a set of complex tasks they perceive as
being critical to world stability, peace, and development.

So with the blessings of all and the questioning of none,
cultural imperialism charges on. The project begins, and all
these sincere people start blasting apart Uguland's traditional culture. As the project is out in the boondocks, various natives have to be recruited for simple tasks, such as
manual labor, driving trucks, and handling materials. And
at this point, the complaints begin. Somehow, these crazy
Ugulanders just don't understand anything! They don't

show up on time, material is stolen, and the wastage rate for equipment is frightening. Timekeeping clerks can't really read or figure, foremen don't control, and everything bogs down in molasses. The poor contractor brings in more foreigners than he thought he would have to (at wage rates five to ten times the local rate), and his maintenance bills skyrocket.

The natives rather like the fuss. After all, the pay rates are twenty times what anyone ever got before, and it's fun to see what foreigners really do. Besides, they have a new clinic for workers, and everyone quickly realizes that they can send their wife and kids there for shots. Within five weeks, everyone has a transistor radio to listen to, and wives get new clothes. Some of the clever young men are driving trucks now, and a few villagers who had long since gone to the city now show up again as mechanics or greasemen or personnel clerks. No one in the village is quite sure what status these people have, but they do have money, and they do seem to be very confident of their new-found opportunities. Who wants to work forever in local fields, when you can go to the city, become a driver, and maybe even own your own truck someday, as Ahmed now does? Or work in the shops, as Khalil does, making so much money? Or even better, be a clerk in the air-conditioned office, like Samir? All of these people have the good life, do they not?

Villagers also watch with great curiosity and interest the life-styles of Americans and Europeans who are on the project. They seem to drink a lot, but they also have such healthy, happy children, and their living quarters would make a prince drool with envy, even out here in the bush. Air-conditioning, cars, short-wave radios, good clothes, the works. The bosses yell a lot, but they seem to be pleasant enough otherwise, and the wives are very helpful some of the time, to say nothing of presenting an image of a sort of woman no one has ever seen before—particularly the villagers' wives.

When, after two or three years, the power system is finished, the foreigners go home leaving a whole new set of role-players in the neighborhood. There are power engineers, distribution-system maintenance personnel, line maintenance men, system installers, and all the rest of the technicians needed to operate, at even modest efficiency, such a system. At first, many of these people will be foreign, but the prime minister was smart enough to insist on a major training component for the new system, so gradually the key jobs get taken over by Ugulanders.

Where do these people fit into the local culture? No one knows, because they never existed before. They are obviously important, well paid, and very strange people, insisting on rational work standards never heard of in Uguland before. Their orientation and training is totally Western, and they too often view with total contempt the pathetic village life-style, so irrelevant to modern conditions. Because they tend to get paid on some Western-oriented scale, rather than a local one, their incomes are far above the local culture, and their ability to consume properly, get the best wives, live in the finest houses, and generally be powerful and clever people is noticed widely by young aspirants to the good life.

So another culture gets busted up by men of good will, men of considerable personal charm and capability. No one really planned it that way. The older imperialisms are rightfully passé, but new ones keep popping up. Who played God? The United Nations did; the World Bank did; the American AID people did; and the Soviets did. Anyone else who gave aid, loaned technical personnel, or provided funds did too. And if the eventual result is a schizophrenic Uguland, torn between the traditional and the West, frustrated because somehow the power system did not lead to endless income increase, peace, happiness, and prosperity, well, that's Uguland's problem. On to the next project! Hell, even the Uguland government was all for the project. No one pushed anything on anyone. As a matter of fact, the problem is to decide who gets the next project, not to force people to buy the development ideas.

The planners and thinkers and world politicians, sitting in their nice offices in the mainstream parts of the world, thinking about power curves, population growth, income changes, and all the rest, know what the problems are. They know that things have to change, and fast, if the world is to hang together. They know all about the new countries' governments, faced with expectations revolutions, pressures for rapid change, and static villages out in the hinterlands. They know what to do about it, and they know that the leaders and elites in the third world will buy anything that looks as though it might get them where the affluent countries now are. So they plan and figure and promote, with great success. Their only problem is where to get still more resources to get still more change under way.

But they're playing God, all the same.

Peasants have been manipulated for a long time by lots of people. Maybe it is a credit to the peasants that they manage to resist the manipulation as often as they do. But somehow, this new-style manipulation, this business of doing what's good for you, whether you like it or not, is not even questioned very much. No one is running in guns (well, not too many), or sending in the Marines; no one is practicing old-fashioned imperialism (except the Soviet Union); and no one is adding new political colonies to their strings. Yet this new variety of imperialism is turning out to be manipulation on a scale old-fashioned imperialists could only dream of. It's bothersome to liberal Western traditions. Systematic manipulation of someone else doesn't quite fit the usual notions of what should be done about the world. But if we don't manipulate, what else have we? Famine, pestilence, and kids dead even though we know what to do about it—to say nothing of stinking poverty which any good technician should know how to clean up in a reasonable length of time.

We're beginning to run into some real dilemmas here. In the finest liberal traditions, human life is sacred, and we must do what we can to protect every human being. And we know a lot about this in the West. So, what do we do— practice death control on a massive scale, which leads to population explosion, which leads to famine? Of course not. Then feed the poor—and somehow the idea of half the world on the dole is not too appealing. So development follows, and the Ugulands of this world get their power plants and all the rest. And in the process, their cultural heritage is blown sky-high. We didn't really mean to do that, but then again, maybe we did. What kind of freedom is the kind that comes from foreigners fixing the game so that your particular kinds of freedom are going to be limited to the Western idea of what it is? Once that power-plant project gets started, it doesn't take too much insight to see exactly what will happen to the local culture, so the manipulative aspects of it should be clear. But rarely does anyone raise this nasty question. You know that family relationships, personal dignity, tribal customs, and all the rest will change very drastically, and you also know that this will be painful for those involved in it. Yet, there is no choice. Or is there? Lord knows, the radical young Americans are not exactly satisfied with the end result we are so diligently trying to achieve for the Ugulanders of this world.

In the end we always find ourselves in the same spot. If you're so smart, why aren't you rich? The West is rich, ergo, the West is good. Therefore, get there from here as quickly as possible, and the way to do this is to manipulate whole populations, whole cultures. Give them transistor radios, trucks, and death control, and wait a while. You can break up any traditional culture that way, and maybe, if you're lucky, you can control the outcome so it will lead to a richer society. Play God, because you know the answers. It is an easy route from a few bothersome doubts about what is going on to the plans, the loans, the efforts to help the Ugulanders help themselves. They want it, we can provide it. If we play God a little, well, lots of people have before, and for a lot less noble purposes. And lots of people are going to play God in the future. We've barely begun the economic development pushes in whole continents (Africa). Lots of peasants and tribesmen have to have their thinking and behavior straightened out before the turn of the next century, or it may be too late.

We've got to stop population growth in the poor countries the way it has slowed in the affluent ones, so maybe some coercion here will be necessary. At the very least, the kinds of behavioral manipulation used on American TV advertising and so detested by liberals will have to be used. At worst, population control may be some form of war. But one way or the other, it will be controlled. And it may happen by letting some countries have mass famines, because we just don't want to accept the idea that any irresponsibly breeding groups can get away with it. It's a long way from the medical missionaries and the pathetic ads in *The New Republic* about kids with bloated bellies, but it may come. We've got to curtail a lot of individual freedoms, too. Certainly the freedom to breed is going to have to be cut; how about freedom of movement in an overly urbanized world? Maybe the only way to run a shaky poor country is with a military dictatorship of the left or right. Anyhow, the old image of democracy is fading fast for the poor. Who can really expect some form of democracy in a country where half or more of the adult population is illiterate?

Another aspect from the other side of the coin is bothersome. At the moment we see the affluent third of the world using up about 90 percent of the exhaustible resources of the world—how fair is this, if you buy the idea that wealth is great, and that the primitive cultures should be busted? By the time they get rich, there may not be much around to get or stay rich on. Perhaps the rich should start thinking about preserving something for the poor—except everyone knows that they won't. The idea of some sort of world slum, even after you bust up all the cultures and try to get them rich, where the rich one-third gets most of the wealth, while the two-thirds struggles in poverty, is not too appealing to most liberals. If you toss in the racist angle, and note that except for a hundred million Japanese, all the rich are white and all the poor are not, the problems can get even stickier.

We've come a long way from the sincere and concerned medical missionaries, worried about illness and death in the backwoods. Wherever you turn, you come up with sticky issues that no one can even think about, let alone resolve. So, we go ahead on the mainstream path, which appears about like this:

1. People are poor, and we know how to start curing poverty, so let's go. This one gets right at culture-busting, but the problem is studiously ignored.

2. Cure the population problem with manipulation of people's breeding rights. The way to do this is to get them to use contraceptives themselves. Page Madison Avenue— they know all about behavioral manipulation—or do they?

3. Try to bring human resources to their fullest potential as quickly as possible. This one gets back to Point 1, since you can't run a Western-type state without highly skilled and brainwashed people, so on with education, Western style.

4. Accept any poor country's government they decide to have, unless it's overtly racist. Anyone can play, from the extreme right to the extreme left.

5. Accept a deeply felt mainstream Western ethical system about the dignity of man, the sacredness of life, and so on, even though in practice things may not quite work out this way. If they don't, oh well, maybe next time.

It all adds up to culture-busting, often without much interest in the problems, except to cheer when it happens fast. It also adds up to a kind of cultural arrogance on the part of the West which makes one pause. I'm right—you're wrong. Maybe—but that isn't exactly what the old-fashioned liberals had in mind. But, as we said before, what else have we got?

If you buy the necessity of busting up cultures, there is another problem. How do you bust them up efficiently? We don't want American Indian-type results. We want to get the traditional cultures going along, say, the Japanese pattern.

So far, our culture-busting efforts haven't produced all those good results in most cases. Cultures, after all, are resistant to change, particularly if they have been around for a millennium or two. There must be a better way to do the job.

. . . .

CHAPTER VI

The American Ghetto as a Developing Country

I was out in Los Angeles with a Latin American friend, just after the Watts riots. José had never been to the United States before, and he wanted to see Watts. The riots had received a big play in his local papers when they broke. So, we got the car and took off.

"Is it safe?" José asked. "I mean, the pictures showed terrible things . . ."

"Oh, I think so," I said, thinking about the movie we once went to by accident in the area. The kids were as wriggly as any I've ever seen, but aside from that, no one much cared about a white face or two in the crowd. A lot had happened since, but maybe not that much.

"Well, where is it?" José asked.

"We're right in the middle of it," I said.

José looked around, bewildered, at the shabby 1910 frame houses. Some were pretty beat up, others were very neat. There were trash and papers here and there.

"In my country," José said, "this would be an upper-middle-class neighborhood. Look at all the space! And each family has a house."

"Some are doubled up—maybe tripled, José. Incomes are very low—maybe under two thousand a year."

José glanced at me, and I realized I had said the wrong thing. As a young professor at home, he made only $2,500. "Oh. Well, I suppose that that is low in North America."

"It's damn low, José. Low enough to riot about. And then there is the unemployment, the lack of skills, the transportation problem, and all the rest."

"Just like home, Dick, eh? An underdeveloped country."

"Yeah, José, an underdeveloped country. All the signs, and the symptoms, all the problems . . ."

"But not quite so bad, Dick, not quite so bad." José gazed moodily out at the old buildings, the small houses, the trash in the streets, the lounging men, the swarms of kids. "But maybe you are right. Maybe it is the same . . ."

Poor countries are far away for most Americans, and earnest discussions of what to do about them often seem very academic and unreal. But there is a poor country easily within range of most of us, called the ghetto, which has many of the typical characteristics of any poor country.

Income per capita is significantly lower than in the mainstream community surrounding it, while birth rates and infant-mortality figures are above the national average. Educational standards are lower, while most indices of human welfare also are lower, such as incidence of various diseases, average lifespan, and general physical condition of the inhabitants. Virtually any measure of income or welfare suggests that the ghetto is indeed a poor country. If we looked at American Indian reservations, Chicano ghettos in the Southwest, or even the white poor in Appalachia, we would find similar dismal statistics, for virtually any American poor group shares the subculture of poverty. But the black ghetto is the vivid poor country, because it is near us all.

The black ghetto also has a lively subculture, which few white Americans care much about or even understand— except when white America borrows some interesting part of it, such as its music. And the ghetto has its brain drains, its concerned citizens worrying about economic development, and foreigners (we whites) ready to give whatever aid and foreign assistance is feasible or proper. And, like so many other experiences in helping out poor countries, we find that getting rid of poverty is much harder than anyone initially thought when the question first came up, not too many years ago.

Actually the black ghetto is relatively new as a major subculture, dating back only to World War II, when millions of southern Negroes began their trek north, searching for jobs and a better deal than they were getting in southern states. The transition was from agrarian southern poverty to urban northern poverty. Millions of Negroes have been in the north for a century or more, but the really major jump in black populations in the inner city came after 1940. This shift coincided nicely with the major shift of whites to the suburbs—in effect, the older housing in the inner city was abandoned, and blacks filled it up. When the working whites left, the jobs went too—to the suburbs, where modern, low-lying plants could be much more efficient. Firms these days need access to trucks and electric power, not to railroads. It is cheaper to find land out in the open spaces, near a freeway, than to try to operate in a multistory plant in the crowded inner city. And as the big plants left, all the small service-oriented jobs left too—the little typewriter-repair shops, tool-and-die operations, and all the rest.

Jobs also got transferred overseas. In the old days, immigrant girls were sweated in the inner-city lofts making buttonholes or skirts; the jobs were rough, the hours long, the pay short. We also did a lot of light industry in the inner city, like making toys, kitchenware, and so on. But with freer trade, plus immigration restrictions, we increasingly get this material from abroad. The sweated labor in such industries is now in Hong Kong, South Korea, and Taiwan. Everything is relative—a job at two bits an hour would appall most Americans, but a Taiwanese peasant used to two bits a day would consider this a step up. Of course, we feel that if an American does this sort of labor-intensive work, he should get at least two dollars an hour for it. But as long as someone

is willing to do it for two bits, the jobs go overseas. If we restricted trade enough to bring the jobs home, they wouldn't
be here anyhow, in that the costs at two dollars an hour
would be so high as to preclude too much consumption. So
the latest city arrivals, the blacks, are stuck—the old housing
is there, but the jobs aren't.

When black discovery and the war on poverty first began
in the early 1960s, the response of the mainstream was predictable. Whenever Americans (or any other affluent Western-oriented people) get new ideas about economic development for someone who is outside their mainstream culture
and economic system, they inevitably respond in about the
same way as they have historically. What we did was about
like this:

First, we poured in money, by the hundreds of millions,
and later by the billions. The money never goes as far as one
would want—the problem, by the time it is recognized, is
usually too big for a few billion dollars to make a dent. But
slum renewals were started, and old shacks were torn down
to be replaced, eventually, by high-rise buildings. Money was
spent on planning and transportation. A bewildering variety
of programs were started to solve or study inner-city problems. As is typical of such programs, the start-up times are
rather long, often years, so big announcements of such programs lead to expectations of change which don't happen for
a long time. Inevitably, there is discouragement. The shacks
torn down were lived in, and poor people had to find new
cheap quarters. Maybe four or five years later they might
have a chance to get into the new high-rise apartment building. In the meantime, their housing standards declined. A
new rapid transit system may take five or ten years to get
into operation—meantime, there may be less transportation,
rather than more.

Second, new agencies were set up specifically to handle the
problems of the inner cities. Model Cities, Community Action Programs, and all the rest were established and given
the charge to do various useful things. Large numbers of

people were hired to perform these tasks. Since these organizations are mainly typical modern organizations, those hired were not the very poor (except in a marginal way), but rather nice serious middle-class types—administrators, typists, accountants, receptionists, and all the rest. Many of these were drawn from the affluent mainstream, not the black poor. Blacks with proper social, technical, and administrative skills were of course hired, but these people are not typically the hard-core poor.

These new agencies, with their broad mandates for change, began activities with a flourish. Big programs were announced—and then quietly faded away. Intense persons very concerned about poverty problems and racism came to power and tried to get the poor blacks into the game. Somehow they rarely succeeded with the very poor. Where real efforts to get the poor in on decision-making were tried, the program often collapsed or was scaled down after money leaked away. Political efforts to gain power frightened the middle-class whites and resistance developed. In short, the programs were long on promise and short on real performance.

Human-resource development of a technical sort was also tried. Programs to create adult literacy flourished; technical training abounded; various manpower programs tried to figure out how to get various hard-core types usefully employed. Nursery schools were started, along with Head Start programs, to get the kids out of the cycle of poverty and despair. All of this turned out to be much more expensive than initially expected, in part because any sort of human-resource development tends to be skilled-labor intensive, and few professionals are so dedicated that they will work for less in the ghetto. If a good teacher is worth $10,000 per year in the mainstream, then that will tend to be the price in the ghetto. And asking for one hundred such teachers yields a budget of a million a year for this item alone. A hundred skilled professionals will hardly make a dent in the problem in one city, let alone the entire country.

As these other programs got under way, black nationalism in many forms began to develop rapidly. The Black Panthers and the Black Muslims are only two of many such movements in this direction. We also began to encourage black capitalism as a means to development. The more rapidly such nationalistic tendencies developed, and the more successful they seemed to be, the more nervous the white mainstream grew. It is one thing to help a guy who's poor—it is quite another to have him take your aid and announce his independence as well. That is not exactly what most people had in mind.

All of this was conducted in the usual format of the big project, the grandiose idea. These projects would change the world forevermore, maybe by next Monday morning, or so the press releases implied. And when very little seemed to be happening, except negative things like tearing up shoddy housing for a new highway or housing project, which would not be ready until 1978, disillusion set in quickly. Indeed, some of the rising expectations of the black poor undoubtedly helped lead to quite unexpected and undesirable outcomes, such as riots. This led to disillusion in the mainstream, as observers noted that after all this work, all you get is more trouble, so why bother? Now most of the big programs are in financial trouble, as a reluctant government is not too sure that it wants to continue financing the monster it seems to have created.

What was not taken into account at all, except in a peripheral sense, was the cultural problem inherent in all of this. There is a black subculture, and many thoughtful persons perceived this in racial terms. That is, the blacks had a subculture because they were denied access to the main culture. True, no doubt, so the thing to do was to allow access. And those blacks with mainstream skills took full advantage of this new access. Few poverty planners worry much about black engineers, dentists, administrators, or any others who possess both skills and cultural attributes of the mainstream. When the doors opened, such people, along with the younger men and women who could acquire such skills, did fine. But somehow the really unskilled, hard-core poor stay about as poor as they were before. The money flows in, and someone gets it, but not the poor. And all those big expensive projects, those great dreams for the future, somehow they never quite come off. It's all very familiar—those who have watched AID programs in Pakistan, India, or Ghana have seen it all before. What went wrong?

A visit to any poverty program office suggests some of the problems. The place is typically rather chaotic, particularly if it is a relatively new organization. Offices are disorganized, people wander around looking for documents, and the harassed director is beseiged by tricky problems of where to put the typing pool for the new division, who gets which office, how to get the phones connected right, and similar important matters. After all, no one can go to work until these organizational and spacial problems are all worked out.

Since these programs are typically financed and supported by the federal government, the clear order of priorities quickly becomes evident. First, one must meet the necessary bureaucratic criteria of reporting, auditing, and other administrative matters. If some federal auditor or evaluator isn't in the office now, he will be within a month, so reports have to be prepared and updated, accounts must comply with complex federal guidelines, and so on. Since the staff is relatively new (none of these organizations has been around more than five years), this exercise takes much time and talent. The really capable staff people have to do this.

Second, all funding is short term, rarely for over two years, so the next most important thing to do is to prepare requests for future funding. This also involves very high-level talent, and as budget-submission time approaches, all the good people get drawn into this activity. And then there are the internal personnel problems. The new black typist is upset because she gets less than a white typist with the same experience; inevitably the top people will be drawn into the discussion. Some of the black administrators are not as experienced as some of the whites, but they have more power and pay—more problems to resolve. Any cross-cultural group of over ten people will spend a lot of time communicating with each other on all sorts of problems. And the latest reorganization, so carefully structured, violates section 213 (A) (4) of the enabling federal legislation, so the administrators have to go back to the drawing board to get it right.

Meanwhile, a delegation of welfare mothers is in the office complaining about their housing being condemned—they came to the wrong organization, but someone has to go out and face them, explaining what they should do. And in some cases, someone has to go down and bail out one of the more eager field workers, who also is involved in some sort of racket—or so the police say. He happens to be one of the more capable young people, so off someone goes. And the lease on office space is up for renewal, and the landlord wants 20 percent more, which is above budget, so there goes another long and tedious conference. The lawyers from Model Cities want to discuss some very complex land-condemnation problems with the organization head—another day shot. And before too long, the various administrators and technicians in the organization are worrying about their pay and relative status, casting envious eyes at some other antipoverty group which managed to get plugged in at some higher federal pay-scale level. Moreover, money and status mean power, and the various administrators are already beginning to maneuver to see who gets on top when the present boss resigns (which is always widely rumored).

The actual working personnel also know that everything is being done wrong. The money is being put into the wrong programs, the major effort is in manpower training when it should be in prisoner rehabilitation (or kids, or slum clearance, or whatever). Since employees tend to be very intense about what they believe should be done, it usually does not take too long before factions form and infighting starts. Resignations follow the loss of a point—new administrators have to be broken in all the time. Since these programs and organizations have a potentially short life, few old-timers who know government well want to stay with them or resign their present jobs to take positions with the agency. And business types almost never do—they are far too busy trying to keep their own complex organizations going.

So we observe a tremendous bustle and hustle of activities, involving very dedicated people. But nothing much has happened to the poor. Virtually none of the organization's personnel are poverty people—the blacks and ex-poor involved are likely to be secretaries, typists, or reasonably well-educated administrators, not hard-core types. Oh, the janitors and a few others may get a job, but nothing much else happens. The poor are still poor, still getting hustled by the numbers men, the slumlords, and all the others who live off the poor. There is no room in the organization for semiliterate, unskilled, half-sick people. There is no room for restless high school dropouts or welfare mothers with kids at home to watch. There is plenty of room, however, for the good and not-so-good middle-class types who typically inhabit the bowels of large and complex organizations, and there is also room for the very dedicated social-reformer types, also highly educated, who see in the program a chance to get their ideas implemented.

Note the mistaken premises built into these programs. The federal government is incapable of responding to crisis without a massive, large-scale organization being created to handle the job. Anyone who has bothered to read a law, taken a look at accounting guidelines, or tried to figure out how to comply with innumerable federal administrative constraints, will know why. The premise here is that big organizations are inherently efficient because they are inherently efficient. Indeed, anything else is not even considered.

A second premise is that there is an infinite supply of highly talented administrators to run new programs. Laws never worry about who does what—they just set up the system. Somewhere out there will be a group of dedicated, efficient people who are capable of easily and quickly locking into a new, complex organization. This hasn't been true since the New Deal days, though we still act as if it were true.

Another premise is that what is wrong with the blacks is lack of opportunity. If money and programs get into the ghetto, then what will emerge is a carbon copy of similar activities in the mainstream, with diligent men and women easily being absorbed into productive tasks. They will do this, of course, by behaving like WASPs, by being solid workers in the complex organization. This in turn implies that everyone thinks like mainstream types—that they have the same notions of time, diligence, ability to obey complex instructions, ability to read instruction manuals, ability to get along easily and well with their fellow workers, and ability to discipline themselves into a larger group smoothly working for the welfare of all. We create our aid programs in the image of ourselves, assuming that everyone out there who is poor will have the discipline and abilities that we have, the day something starts happening. And we also assume that this is the desirable way to go. Why else would we ask poor blacks to be like us, to behave as we do, to accept unquestioningly the values and mores we have? The ideal nonpoor black is a fellow who works hard, minds his business, earns good money, owns and keeps up his house, sends his kids to school to learn to be the kind of people who will survive easily and efficiently in big organizations, a fellow who is kind, honorable, thrifty—in short, a nice guy like us. The tacit assumption here is that locked in every adult ghetto-breast is this kind of nice guy, who will emerge full-blown as soon as we open the opportunity door. Somehow, it never happens this way.

Those blacks who do have these characteristics are doing fine. They are plumbers, accountants, secretaries, steel-mill workers, administrators, and all the other good middle-class occupations which get people out of poverty. Perhaps one-third of all black adults are already like this, and each year (no thanks to the big programs) more come out of college and high school to do the same. Perhaps another third are moving closer to this elusive black WASP goal, since it does pay off, and blacks are far from stupid. Most of them want the good life as much as anyone else. But somehow, the hard-core stays hard, and all the programs put together don't get at it. Why not? Because we have assumed cultural change without making any effort to figure out what kinds of change we are talking about. When it doesn't happen, and nothing works, we are puzzled.

One reason nothing works is that there really is a generation gap between anyone over forty-five and those younger. If you're over forty-five, you were young during the 1930s, when the Great Depression was in flower. At that time, there really was (for practical purposes) an infinite supply of highly trained, highly motivated manpower unemployed and eager to go to work to do anything. An ad in any metropolitan paper would turn up a hundred, or even five hundred, engineers, mechanics, secretaries, administrators, or whatever, willing to do anything for $25 per week. Many a senior administrator can ruefully remember when he was young and unemployed. Most people easily forget that someone like former President Johnson was teaching school in some Texas/Mexican community in the early 1930s, because there was nothing else to do. But Mr. Johnson never forgot.

As a result, older people tend to think that the administrative and technical talent problem is trivial—and just examine the ages of key Congressmen and Senators these days to see why this point is so critical. Why worry about manpower? There are mobs of eager citizens, unemployed, to do any job! True in 1935—but far from true in any year since 1940. We could also note that the slack in the 1930s' system was incredibly large. When we had to, we almost doubled real income in the United States in *three* years (1940–43)! If we could do this again, . . . but we cannot.

The Marshall Plan also fouled us up for a generation. These days we hear calls for a new Marshall Plan for the ghettos, for payments to allow the blacks to do their thing. We have tried the Marshall Plan abroad too, in poor countries, and it doesn't work there either. The reason is that the Marshall Plan was designed to provide money, goods, and capital to a group of Europeans who had seen their assets destroyed by World War II. They had skilled labor, a mainstream culture, plenty of good managers and technicians, but no equipment. When we provided the equipment, Western Europe took off economically, to the point where now it probably will reach or exceed our own high income levels.

If it worked there, why not in the ghetto? So push in the cash and wait to see what happens. The probable answer, nothing much, is a disappointment, just as big aid to foreign, poor nations has been a disappointment. The reason is that the battalions of skilled labor, the unemployed administrators, executives, and technicians are just not there. Neither are the work habits and personal characteristics of the typical, uptight Calvinist who rebuilt Europe, or, for that matter, created the modern United States. Money pours in; big organizations are created, and those who can run the organizations work hard, but the core problem is untouched.

If this approach doesn't work, what would? After all, lots of people have stopped being poor historically, and many are still climbing out of poverty. But some lag. If large numbers of blacks were poor *only* because of lack of access to opportunities, and had the skills and attitudes to do work in the mainstream, then the Marshall Plan approach would work fine. Indeed, wherever we find this situation in the black community, we find success.

Examination of America's past may suggest what could be done. In the old days, things were a lot smaller, and firms and other organizations did not cater to anyone's needs. If you fell sick and were poor, you died. If your boss was nasty, you quit and stayed poor or sighed and endured him. If you didn't figure out for yourself how to adjust to work in the dark satanic mills, there were always plenty of other immigrants fresh off the boat to take your place. No one gave a damn if you starved. In short, the price of not behaving was high. Rewards were small, but quick. The almost forgotten practice of piecework wages made workers faster—they had to be to get enough to eat. The only clerical type most early workers saw was the paymaster—no one tried to cull out the unfit before the job began. Hire fifty, cull out ten good ones and to hell with the rest was standard personnel practice. It was crude and cruel, but it worked.

Nowadays, we have shifted from the "all people are inherently nasty" philosophy, to "all people are really nice at heart." The poor are poor because they are ill treated, not because they need a kick now and then to behave. Their culture is valuable and well worth saving—we don't do what we used to with European immigrants, in effect tell them to forget their culture, or else. We long ago got rid of quick reward systems, like piecework, because the system was inherently subject to abuse. Nice people like you and me (and by inference, all those poor out there) deserve better than this. Our grandfathers got their teeth kicked in, worked hard, got paid very little—and somehow, in the process, got into the middle class.

They had their behavior changed radically if necessary, by threat and force. And now we pleasant middle-class types, freed from this sort of discipline and threat, can contemplate doing better by our modern poor. So off to Marshall Plans, big-ticket organizations with nice guys like you and me running them, and all the rest. To do otherwise is inhuman and evil.

But we do have prisons, and they are full of poor. We punish quickly, if we can catch those doing wrong, but we reward over long, long timespans. To a young black stealing hubcaps, we in effect say, "Keep on this way for a day, and the punishment will come. But if you are good for five to eight years, get a good education, and learn to behave like me, then you will get a nice payoff." For poor people, who typically have a very short time horizon, this is a bad bargain.

The modern liberal mainstream, which after all is thinking up these programs to lift blacks out of poverty, is not well suited to what is actually going on in the ghetto. Much of modern thinking in business and economics is not applied to many kinds of social problems. The main problem here is that the very basis of thinking in these fields is antithetical to liberal beliefs. The history of liberal thinking suggests clear reasons why this is so.

Three Premises

Economists and business scholars have long used as operational assumptions three premises. The first and third come from economics, while the second is from business-management theory, as derived from systems theory. These are:

1. The premise of maximization. Economists have long assumed that men and firms tend to maximize profits. More recent work suggests that the initial simple-minded maximization assumption is too simple for practical use, and that most persons tend to maximize some sort of complex bundle of things, including money income, status, perquisites, and so on. Whatever the mix, they do tend to maximize. Firms typically do not maximize short-term profits any longer (although many smaller, hard-pressed firms do), but rather, a complex mix of sales, profits (short- and long-term), executive perquisites, and what not. It is surprising, even after all due note has been taken of the complexity of human behavior, how workable this maximization assumption is. It underlies virtually all modern work in economics, which today is virtually the only operational social science, and much of modern business-school work is also based on this premise. While firms and individuals may protest that for them this is a poor assumption, most of the time most people will tend to move in the direction which will give them the highest income. Of course, one can except monks

who take vows of poverty, ministers, some highly socially oriented liberals, and so on, but if 99 percent of the people are moving toward profit or money-income maximization, it is still a good working rule to begin any discussion.

Even casual reading of many publications suggests that at this point modern micro-economics and American beliefs part company. Few citizens outside of business care to work with any sort of theory which holds that people will tend to be greedy, and there is a very long set of premises (going back to Jesus and the New Testament) which suggests that the liberals have plenty of company. This repugnance in a modern scene is suggested by what one might call the evil-man theory of liberal business history. Thus, cigarette companies are evil organizations run by diabolically clever fiends who would happily poison a generation; auto firms are run by monsters whose delight it is to build unsafe cars for people to kill themselves in; pharmaceutical firms both sell unsafe drugs and overprice the ones they do sell; and milk companies callously raise prices to deprive poor children of their needed nutrition. The image (only slightly overstated) is one of a bloated plutocrat arriving at his office on Monday morning, rubbing his hands gleefully as he contemplates just who he is going to torture, maim, or starve this week, all for the delights of a few more percentage points on his rate-of-profit return.

For the thoughtful American professional, contemplating the new job offer he has just received for a thousand a year more than he is getting now, this is a simplistic and delightful picture of gloom, depravity, and despair. Of course, if the working conditions are right and the schools okay, he may take the job. But his case is different. He is a little man, underpaid and overworked, taking a good opportunity to advance. Those bloated corporations out there are something else again.

This point is quite deliberately overstressed, because failure to accept the maximization principle leads to really serious problems in America. Among other things, it leads us to ignore much of modern economics and virtually all of modern management theory (both of which are built on this basic principle). But realistic theorizing provides much that can be quite operational for development causes.

2. The premise of goal qualification. If you want to accomplish something, it is nice to know when you have. This leads to the notion that few goals are particularly operational until they have been quantified. Everyone wants better race relations, but how do you know when you have them? We all wish to abolish or minimize slums, but how can you tell, after a lot of work, when you are achieving this goal? A real problem here, because many kinds of ethical problems cannot be readily quantified, yet until they are, it is extremely difficult to decide whether or not any progress is being made in solving them.

According to systems theory, the following process is necessary, if the system is to work at all:

a) Quantify your goal. This can be so many new toilets in a slum, so many dollars of profit, so many members, or whatever, but it has to be something that can be checked after the fact.

b) Get the program going.

c) Check back (e.g., get feedback) on what did happen, and see if what happened deviates from what was planned. If you expected to build five hundred new bathrooms, and only forty were constructed, something is wrong with the program, and the administrator should do something.

d) If deviations from the norm or goal occur, decide what has to be done to get back on course.

Try to figure out, using the above system, what to do if the goal is to make people better citizens, or some other rather nebulous objective which often seems to be at the heart of many government programs. One can quickly be swamped with evidence pro and con, and no one really knows if the program is working well, simply because there is no way to decide whether or not the goal has been achieved.

Many Americans dislike quantifications of this sort, since they implicitly appear to put numbers or boxscores on problems which truly defy quantification. If we are interested in happier, more ethically motivated people, it seems almost obscene to place numbers on these values. Yet unless some sort of quantification is attempted, a program wallows around, because no one knows whether or not the goal is being achieved. Engineers and businessmen use this sort of theory daily, and they get excellent results, because they do know what is happening, how it compares with norms, and whether or not corrective action is necessary. Liberal programs flounder because no one knows these things.

3. Resources are always limited. There are never enough resources to go around. Land is scarce (including minerals and climate); labor is available only in finite amounts; and money is always in inadequate supply. Increasingly, the scarcest resource of all is highly skilled managerial and technical labor, including such men as clergy, medical doctors, technicians of all types, and most particularly administrative and management talent.

This scarcity leads immediately to the concept of priorities and trade-offs. If skilled men are scarce, not everything one wants to do can be done immediately. So, what do you want to do first, second, third? Thus a typical medical problem may be to decide whether it is more important to do more cancer research by investing funds in special hospitals for this purpose, or to attack the level of infant mortality. One can do both, of course, but rather quickly the highly talented doctors and medical administrators will be used up. Where should the big push be made? Perhaps $10 million dollars invested in cancer research will save 5,000 lives; the same money put into infant mortality will save 50,000 babies. Take your choice—because there is never enough to go around.

Most Americans dislike this sort of decision. Their usual answer is to do both—but resources really *are* limited, and eventually the choice has to be made. Since the metaphysics of decision-making are such as to paralyze the intellect, the choice is not deliberately made. Which does not mean that the choice is not made, but only that it is made by others. The hospital administrator makes it, or the research-oriented doctor who may end up in the wrong place. The liberal, from the very nature of his philosophy, ends up completely out of the decision-making process. One of the hardest kinds of decisions to make in complex social situations is the one involving human-life trade-offs. Nevertheless, one has to make them. If not, they get made by default, given the fact that we never have enough resources to go around.

Some Applications

Since many Americans dislike all three of these premises, they tend to ignore their application to problems which interest them. As a result, the typical government program is a mass of contradictions, confusion, and wasted effort. Scarce resources tend to be squandered in all directions, and the impact of programs is far less than it should be. Consider here several types of programs now in progress (which are not very successful) to see why this is so.

1. Slum clearance. A common approach to this problem is to try to force people to do things they don't really want to do—that is, to work uphill against their own profit-maximization posture. Thus it is often true that slumlords are forced to make improvements to their properties. Armies of building inspectors find defects, the owner is hauled into court, and orders are given to force him to comply. The typical owner is either too poor or too interested in money income to welcome this sort of order, and he fights it all the way. As fast (or faster) as improvements are made, other properties deteriorate.

A second point is that few programs even bother to define what a slum is. Slums are complicated things, involving underdeveloped people, deteriorating housing, poor civic services, rats, and so on. We all know one when we see one, but it is difficult to quantify what we mean. Hence if improvements are made, it is difficult to decide if the slum is less a slum as a result. In this case, the premise of goal quantification is violated.

A third point is that few workers in slum renovation have any clear concept of priorities. What is more important: to get rid of rats; to improve housing; to get better education; to reduce the garbage problem; or what? Note that this point is closely tied to the question of resource availability. If we can get rid of the rats in six months for $100,000, and if it will take eight years and $200 million to improve schools significantly, then it is probably useful to concentrate on the rats first. Better school planning can start now, but other kinds of things can be done more quickly and cheaply.

With all three basic precepts being violated, it is not too surprising (to a management specialist) that slum clearance programs usually work very badly. By the time one slum gets improved a bit, others have expanded faster. The programs work uphill, in that they try to reform all mankind while curing social ills too. This is a noble objective, but it doesn't work out well in practice.

Now, what might be done to get more action and improvement at less cost?

a) Do things which make people want to do them, because they are money ahead in so doing. Instead of hiring armies of (relatively inept) civil servants to plan new programs, pay people to do the job themselves.

b) Decide on quantifiable short-term goals, and try to achieve them. Perhaps we will never decide what a slum is, but we can say something about the percentage of houses unpainted or otherwise in disrepair, the level of crime rates, the number of rats per capita, or the tons of garbage now in alleys in the slum. These can be quite hard figures to obtain, and the problem is to start thinking about how to improve the count.

c) Get a priority list. Realistically, this should be based on relative ease, in terms of the resources used up to accomplish them. If we can do something easily and cheaply, it may be worthwhile to do this first, rather than try to accomplish something grandiose all at once.

Consideration of these principles leads to this sort of suggestion:

The reverse English property tax: Try reversing the usual property tax. Now, if a man bothers to improve his house, he pays a penalty for it in the form of higher property taxes. If a slum situation exists, one sure sign of it is deteriorating housing. So if any owner wants to maintain his property well, cut his taxes. This approach might also meet the test of relatively little resources involved, since every city already has a tax-collecting unit in operation, and this sort of scheme could be attached to it. If an owner puts in a new bathroom or paints his house, he calls the inspector. The inspector verifies that the job is done, signs a chit, and the owner sends this in with his next tax bill to get a standard tax reduction.

2. Getting rid of rats. The usual proposal is to try to hire pest-control specialists (who are in very short supply) to figure out what to do. No one else in the slum cares much, since those in them have no chance to make any money out of the program. But in the west we have paid bounty hunters for wildcats for years—why not pay slum dwellers a bounty for rats? Set some price—say 25 to 50 cents each, delivered at a local incinerator, and pay off in cash as the rats are brought in. With this sort of money incentive for the very poor people living in slums, it might well be true that some of the rat population would disappear in a very short time, at much less cost than any formal program. One also suspects that presently totally apathetic slum dwellers would suddenly develop very ingenious ways of catching rats if they had a chance to profit from the procedure.

3. Getting rid of accumulated garbage. One reads of six-foot-deep garbage in alleys all over slums, increasing steadily

year by year. Sanitation departments apparently cannot keep up with the load.

Try paying anyone who wants to so many dollars per ton for any garbage he finds anywhere in some delineated slum. Never mind worrying about how he gets it in his truck and gets it to the dump—if there is money in it, he will find a way. In the process, he will employ a lot of supposedly unemployable people, thus raising income where it is most needed. One could spot (say, by helicopter or ground inspection) where the stuff was coming from and whether or not a dent was being made in the accumulated pile.

4. Getting in and out of the slum. Public transportation in many slums is very poor. Since many people do not own cars, they may well be unemployed simply because they cannot get to work.

Try letting anyone in the slum with a car carry other people anywhere for whatever price he can get. This sort of jitney operation is illegal in virtually every American city,* despite the fact that few public-transit companies make much money in slums. Let the car owners figure out where to go and what to charge—they may exploit a few little old ladies, but there is a real chance here that the added mobility of slum dwellers would more than make up for any exploitation which exists.

All of these simple schemes bother most liberals. For one thing, they appeal to man's avaricious nature, which is wrong. For another, they focus on such mundane things as garbage, the number of rats, passenger miles, and other quantifiable things. To liberals the important things are not these items, but human beings! And finally, other kinds of things, such as better education and health, are much more important. In short, they are not really acceptable in any liberal's scheme of thinking. And since most persons who worry about schemes for slum renovation are liberals, these ideas never even get suggested, let alone tried. What is suggested

* In Bloomington, Indiana, jitneys were made legal in 1971.

and tried are massive, billion-dollar schemes involving wholesale destruction of slum areas for new housing (which quickly goes back to slum), large, impressive projects involving many scarce experts (who somehow never are as competent as we would like), grandiose organizations which, after a few years, seem more involved in their own bureaucratic morass than the purpose for which they were initially set up.

Conclusion

Unless the basic premises of good organization are observed, it is quite likely that much of the thrust for a better America is likely to be frustrated. Problems are massive—and, so it seems, are the proposed solutions. However, many concerned people constantly ignore the first principle of good systems analysis, namely, that the simplest system is the best system. Since most simple systems which might work are based on three precepts which many find repugnant, there is a paradox here. Not too much is likely to get done on many kinds of social problems, because those who do all the thinking and proposing of projects don't set up their premises correctly. But the kinds of thinking which most liberals do leads to overly complex, wasteful systems of correction, which never quite get to the problems as they should. Until this paradox is resolved, many goals deeply cherished by many Americans may well be elusive.

In the end, we are faced with the familiar key problem: How do we change behavior fast? The usual attempts of working intensively with potentially nice people to get them to change their minds don't work fast enough—nor do we have enough highly talented, dedicated people to get the job done this way. So the ghetto stays relatively underdeveloped, while the big programs, which by now have developed lives of their own (few organizations ever commit suicide, no matter how poorly they are doing), go right on. They are fun, but they can't accomplish the task.

Anyone naïve enough to suggest the sorts of programs mentioned here will quickly find out what the true goals of reformist, wealth-creating bureaucracies are. The naïve part is assuming that they have anything to do with education or poverty. Education is for educators, not for kids; development programs are for developers and entrepreneurs, not for the poor. If we could stop poverty by doing simple things, then what would the organizations do? And what would the planners have to plan? Of course no one asked the poor what they think, because they are out of the game.

CHAPTER **VII**

· ·

Hypernationalism, War, and Other Humanistic Goals

The development image for poorer countries is now about as stereotyped as a minuet. Examination of United States documents or other public evidence of what is going on inevitably shows the same thing—clear-eyed young technicians labor in spotless labs; doctors give shots to wide-eyed kids; clean and efficient new factories are manned by intense workers; and presidents or premiers at the government palace smile from behind the latest in office desks. All is efficiency, copies of the best of Western medicine, technology, machinery, and decor. Strangely the image is true, at least some place in the poor country. This is what modernization is supposed to mean and be.

The goals are also clear cut. Income per capita is to rise; perhaps available income will be redistributed a bit in favor of the poor; the health, welfare, and education of the people is to improve; and each individual's personal fulfillment is to grow. None of this is particularly surprising to a Westerner from any affluent country, since all of these ideas were borrowed quite directly from the West. And our own ghetto people and other poor often present similar images, since they are attractive to most people. Who doesn't want better health, a bit more income, and a brighter future, particularly if one is now exploited and poor?

These images are so hallowed and accepted in development circles that nothing else is really discussed very much. It is taken for granted that poor countries will be trying to achieve as much as they can along these lines. The task of development agencies and aid missions is to get there from here as quickly as possible.

Meanwhile, out in the real world, things are a bit different. Western images of the nobility of poverty are fun, but really poor countries have desperate problems which cannot so easily be glossed over. Here are some of them.

Basically, most poor countries are in real danger of coming unstuck and lapsing into total chaos at almost any time. They *are* poor—which means that they do not have basic resources even to give those shots, build those factories, or do anything else but, with luck, give basic food and clothing to their inhabitants. And of course the population explosion has to be handled because there are more bodies to worry about every year.

It is common to find that most people in a poor country are in subsistence or plantation agriculture, and even this sector is coming apart. The countries cannot avoid considerable Western impact here, so tractors, rationalized agriculture, and fertilizers have already changed much of agriculture, typically in the direction of using fewer people. And increasing population on a fixed land base has also shaken this sector. So masses of really poor people drift off to the cities, trying to find some low-level subsistence work. The cities in the poor world are growing faster than those anywhere in the West. Ten or twenty years ago, they were provincial centers of 40,000 or so people; now they badly house literally millions of drifting, displaced poor.

Few poor countries can handle the problems inherent in modern government very well. Huge, ponderous bureaucracies do exist, and they make feeble efforts to handle problems of public health, education, welfare, and transportation. But given educational levels and social attitudes, most

of them would make the most venal American city-govern-
ment administration look like a model of efficiency and compassion. Everything is in crisis, including such fundamentals
as providing decent water supplies and sewage systems to the
exploding populations. It is quite common to find unemployment rates of over 30 percent. If there is a modern, efficient factory around some place, it may employ a few
hundred people, out of the tens of thousands of illiterate
and unskilled masses wanting work.

Still the people come in from the boondocks, since being
unemployed in a modern poor country city is better than
starving out there in subsistence agriculture. A few have
transistor radios, and maybe even an occasional TV set, if
the system exists, so the people see and hear about the wonders of the modern world. Politicians everywhere are used to
puffing up their achievements, and each modern school, each
new technological wonder, each new factory, is hailed as a
step toward the future. The implication is always that the
world is changing rapidly and for the better. But the poor
ex-peasant, out of the system, can only wonder why he and
his children somehow never get in on the game. And as his
expectations rise, and his awareness of the new potential
rises, the masses do become explosive. Things should be happening, and the poor man sitting on his dirt floor in his
shack at the edge of the city wonders why it never happens
to him. Competing politicians, like politicians everywhere,
have to make wild promises which can't be kept, so the expectations grow faster than anyone can produce.

Americans know all about this, since a similar process is
happening in the American ghettos. The black citizen, unemployed and bitter, has a chance to watch the mainstream
world on his battered TV set, knowing cynically that such
good things, like cars, nice housing, and all the rest, only
happen to someone else. Our communications revolution,
which is worldwide, leads to instant awareness of what is
being done, and what, by implication, should be done immediately for everyone.

To date, efforts to get things changed, always using systems borrowed from the West, also lead to role confusion and role destruction. In traditional societies, there were a few well-defined roles, such as peasant, landowner, lord, merchant, and so on. Everyone knew who was who, and where everyone fitted. But where in traditional society does the clear-eyed young technician fit? There is no precedent. Clearly such a man is educated and distinguished, but what status does he have? Or what status does the mechanic, truck driver, entomologist, or whatever have? No one is sure what is most important. Modern development literature often discusses the role of the technocrats, those bright young men who are busily restructuring society, and their conflict with more traditional political types. In such situations, no one is sure who really has power, and subtle, yet very real, struggles for power go on constantly. Older types such as the traditional political leaders begin to realize that there is more to a modern power plant or factory than merely technical activities—control of such installations may well confer status and power on those who run them. And as the traditional leader senses his power ebbing, he may well be not too enthusiastic for still more change.

The United Nations and other external development groups are completely dominated by the technocrats, so their positive images of economic and social change carry the message of political power shifts as well. No agency ever presented the image of the political ward boss of the traditional type (or his counterpart, the village chief), dispensing wisdom in the usual, traditional way. Yet the chiefs and ward bosses may well resist the new power shifts, leading to extreme political instability in a poor country. Power is the name of the political game, and one unexpected result of modernization is to begin power shifts in all directions. The result inevitably is conflict, confusion, and often weak government direction. The society seems torn and twisted, first toward modernization, then back toward more traditional values. The impassive peasants sit in the middle, pawns in the power struggle, but critical as a power base for those who would run the country.

Related to this is the keen sense of impotence felt by so many new and old political leaders in poorer countries. No one much cares what they do, since the world mainstream is out there in the affluent countries. Those countries with wealth, technology, high education levels, and not incidentally lots of guns and troops are the ones watched by the world. Switzerland and Sweden are widely admired models for small countries to emulate—who ever heard or cared about Burmai, Rwanda, or the Ivory Coast? Japan, West Germany, even the United States are places to watch and emulate for somewhat larger countries—who worries about or emulates Pakistan or Burma? When the chips are down, the poor countries are irrelevant in the worst possible way—no one really takes them, or their leaders or policies, very seriously. They are objects of pity and concern, not admiration. And this simple fact drives leaders and elites nuts. We all want respect, admiration, emulation—and if we don't get it, something tends to change. This is why the technocrats manage to get along as well as they do; at least they have some ideas which might lead to greatness.

Educational patterns in the poor country don't help much either. The usual pattern is Western, often English or French. Here the bright young men go abroad to get educated in the world's best universities. They live in the affluent world, pick up its values and ideals, and are trained the way young people in these countries are trained, which is to say that they are ready to enter complex, modern organizations in such a country. When they return home, those organizations aren't there. The lab technicians so common in the West are as yet untrained, so the young scientist cannot do his work right; the middle managers and administrators in the government bureaucracy are either incompetent or nonexistent, so the new civil servant cannot do his job correctly; the technicians in the factory are as yet unable to perform in the Western manner, so the young engineer is underutilized, or worse, unemployed; and so on. As a result, a lot of quite well-educated young people have relatively little to do. A pattern sets in—the very best join the brain drain and leave;

the next best are underemployed in shuffling papers around useless or inept government offices; and the others sit around coffeehouses to plot revolutions and coups.

Most Western university education tacitly assumes that everything is in place, that is, that the rest of society has done its job in the Western way, and that the technicians, workers, and others are well trained. Rarely does any Western university, even in its courses in development economics, bother to explore the problems faced in big organizations where nothing is in place. Young students or ex-students thus tend to assume that the system is rotten, that a few changes this way or that way will get them into the proper roles to lead their country to bigger and better things. Traditional Marxism helps out by assuming away this structural problem. Managers and administrators, together with their large and well-trained staffs, will emerge by magic when the system changes. The result is extreme instability within the country. Everyone has a good idea of what to do, but somehow few are around to do it. Tasks taken for granted in the West, like getting a plumbing job done, fixing a truck, or having a letter written, somehow never get done. There are plenty of chiefs, but few Indians.

And finally, many poorer countries have weird frontiers laid out by European diplomats long ago on some large-scale map. Modern national borders cross tribal lines and mix up historically homogeneous groups. It is common even now to find that tribes and peasants literally don't know what country they are in—their own frames of reference are quite different from our modern notions of nation-states. But the modern thrust is Western, and the nation-state is a critical central Western idea. So leaders are faced with the problem of getting their various peoples, often torn with racial, tribal, and religious animosities, into some semblance of a modern, developed people.

Add all these things up and you get a more realistic picture of the poor world. It is highly unstable, frustrated, and full of very real problems which no modern ideology can resolve. Its leaders are constantly torn between older patterns and new technocratic ideas. And while the bright images of modernization so popular around the United States and other foreign groups are there somewhere, these images are thin minority images for the most part. In short, the modern country is a mess.

Leaders of such countries are smart enough, and they are anxious to hold on to power as long as they can, like any other political leader. Given their real problems, how do they react? The logical responses are clear enough. The first thing to do is to adopt the trappings of nationalism as rapidly as possible. Keen observers of the European scene in the poor world have long noted that lots of defects can be buried and forgotten, if only the people can develop a keen sense of country. "My country, right or wrong," is now considered a trite statement in the United States, but it is the essence of policy in many poor nations. Since most poor countries are of fairly recent origins, the trappings of nationalism, such as one's own currency and stamps, an army, passports, visas, flags, and all the rest are not only novel, but a real way to push the idea of the nation-state. And leaders push enthusiastically in this direction. While Europeans move in the opposite direction, toward unification and easing of national pressures, the poor world moves enthusiastically toward a 1900-style nationalism, complete with all the trappings. Europe has had quite enough of this sort of thing—two world wars convinced it that this is a dead end. But the new poor countries have yet to learn this lesson.

This nationalistic pressure leads to projects which do not help development. The United Nations seat is the ultimate status symbol; of course, it costs money; other prestige projects are the international airline (run often by foreigners with foreign equipment); the huge stadium in the capital for games and political demonstrations; the steel mill; a big modern new capital building; and all the rest. Scarce, often very scarce, capital is plugged into new Boeing 747s, which will lose 20 percent of their investment. The new government building is built instead of housing for the masses, and the steel mill turns out to be hopelessly uneconomic. But the trappings of nationalism are seen to be important, often more important than silly questions like how to earn more income. The Roman emperors had bread and circuses; the modern equivalent of the Roman common man can squat at the end of the runway of the new international jet airport and watch the 747s take off, bearing foreign dignitaries and a few local elitists to better places. Or he can walk by the new public buildings and reflect on his country's importance in the general scheme of things, or try to get one of the very scarce jobs at the new steel mill. He won't, of course, because most jobs are reserved for highly skilled foreign or local technicians, not illiterate peasants.

Development in primary and secondary education in these circumstances becomes easy to predict. It will follow the mainstream West, including all the cultural indoctrination built into the system. Instead of country schools in shacks, nothing but the best will do. Since funds and personnel are so short, most citizens won't get to school at all, but at least the schools that do exist will be models of the best in the West, complete with audio-visual tools, excellent classrooms, and a diligent administration. The books will reflect the greater glories of the nation-state, just the way American and European books did in the 1920s. And education will be very expensive and very inefficient. Perhaps half the pupils will not get as far as the fourth grade, and 1 percent or so will finish high school. But costs, just as in the West, will continue to escalate rapidly.

What is the reaction to suggestions about doing things differently or cheaper—but perhaps more efficiently? The same one found in the American ghetto. Nothing is too good for the modern national state—and what is good, of course, is the model from the most affluent part of the West. If California, Michigan, or New York has a beautiful system of audio-visual instruction (and the income to afford it), then that is the one we want. If Pan American and Lufthansa have the most modern jet aircraft (and the wealth and technical expertise behind them to make the jets pay), then these are the aircraft we want. If England has a complex and elaborate primary school system (and the trained teachers and administrators to make the system work), then this is the system we must have. The results? A new elitism. Instead of reaching everyone, the brave new systems in the poor country reach 5 or 10 percent of those who should be reached. Instead of simple schools teaching people everywhere to read, we find elaborate schools which don't even work well with the top 10 percent. Instead of DC-3s plowing around in bush airports serving the whole population, we find 747s which can land at only one major airport in the country. Instead of simple factories fabricating lots of cheap imported steel, we find a huge steel mill working at 20 percent of capacity because no one out there can use its output. And so on. It happens because form is much more important than substance in this situation, and anyone who worries about substance is quietly pushed aside. It's too bad. All that is at stake is the survival and well-being of a few billion people.

Lack of self-confidence is common in the poor countries. Since their whole experience has been humiliation at the hands of the West, they seem incapable of doing the job their way. Better to try to emulate their betters than to figure out how to do it themselves. And to admit this point is to be in disgrace—it's just not very politic. But not to admit it is so very, very costly! There is a pseudo-logic here which makes rationality very difficult. The West is rich. They are rich because they have the big buildings, the elaborate schools, the shiny new jet airplanes, and everything else. Therefore, to become rich and powerful, build the things they have that are visible. Right? Wrong. Imposing the trappings of a modern state (in very inadequate amounts) on a poor culture just screws things up, since the population cannot handle them the way the Western countries do. But no one agrees, so the game goes on.

The second quite logical thing local leaders do in a poor

country is to build up a strong military force. Poor countries know all about this—after all, for centuries many of them were dominated by Western countries with exactly such forces. The guy with the guns wins every time. And when independence day finally comes, the obvious way to stay independent is to get as many modern guns as you can. Moreover, Western imagery is full of dreams of military glory, tight discipline, beautifully organized military systems, and dying for one's country. It's the only way. Moreover, enemies are everywhere. As the nation-state evolves, other neighboring nations are also evolving, and they are dangerous. Pakistan eyes India suspiciously; the Arabs know all about the Israeli danger; Iran wonders about Iraq; while Kuwait ponders potential invasion. And internally there are enemies too. The Kurds fight Iraqi central authority; Biafrans rebel against the Nigerian central government. The only way to handle such situations is with guns, troops, tanks, and planes, and few are around to question the wisdom of building up as rapidly and efficiently as possible all the military force one can. If it costs money and skilled manpower, well, that is the price of vigilance and liberty. If it also keeps you poor, that's life. And they learned it all from us.

When the generals begin to build up their nice new armies, they quickly discover that modern weapons systems are expensive. For the six or seven million dollars (always in hard currencies, of course) needed to buy even one jet fighter, a country could build a good factory. Moreover, such weapons always require lots of maintenance, done by superbly trained personnel with long years of experience, equipped with very expensive tools. If such people are around, though in very short supply, of course they work with the military, not in the civilian sector. And in really poor countries, there are not enough of them to cover the minimal military requirements. Even in affluent countries, it is common to find that about a third of available military aircraft are not ready to fly on any given day. In poor countries, it happens all too frequently that *none* are ready to fly. But the planes look good anyhow, sitting there on the airstrip, all shiny and menacing.

Military men also quickly find out that if one wants a modern trained army, illiterate peasants won't do for soldiers. They have to get better personnel. Even something simple like a burp gun requires sophisticated maintenance to keep it going, and illiterates are not likely to be very trainable along these lines. And the battalions of electronics technicians, armorers, artillerymen, truck drivers, mechanics, ordinance men, and clerks needed to keep a modern army going seem to drain off most of the country's talent. But it's all very necessary.

Talk to an Egyptian about this. He understands it very well. After all, his country has been clobbered twice since 1956 by the Israelis, and if any shooting starts again, it will be three times. This is not because the Egyptians are not brave—it is because this poor country just does not have the enormous number of trained military technicians necessary to keep the army going in a major campaign. The obvious goal for any Egyptian is to work diligently to develop enough trained people to get the military job done next time around. If as a result most Egyptians stay poor, that's too bad. First things come first, you know.

Talk to any Pakistani or Indian; they will also know what the military danger is. After all, the enemy is strong and crafty, and more defense spending will be required, more skilled men needed, to protect the homeland. It all sounds like Europe in 1914, and it's all very real to the participants.

Talk to any military strongman running a poor country. He knows all about this too. After all, he gained power because he had the guns, while others did not. He knows that if he keeps adding to his guns, his troops, and his material, he will stay in power a long time. And besides, when the troops march and the bands play, note the swelling pride of the populace. Here we are, a country to be respected! Prestige, power, and glory all lie in this direction. And the military dictator, sitting in the big government palace, knows for sure that he is right.

So we find reality in far too many countries—hypernationalistic sentiments, pushed diligently by those in power, along with the guns and trappings of a military force. These are the things that count—and if anything civilian matters, it is what is visible, the jet aircraft, the big factories, and the trappings of the modern state. In the bush, maybe a few kids get their shots, and maybe a few small factories do their thing, but most people are out of this game altogether. The investments are just going in the wrong direction.

As a culture-busting force, hypernationalism and militarism do have very useful purposes. It is difficult to see the idea of literacy for all in cases where its only use is to run small shops or craft-type factories. But if literacy is needed for the fatherland's troops, then by God or by Allah, we'll get everyone literate! If increases in income impress the peasants abroad and further the idea of the fatherland in the West, then we can sell such useful ideas that may lead to this activity. If roads are needed for the new tanks (and incidentally for the farm trucks), then the roads will be built.

Realistically, it seems improbable that anybody's army in a poor country is going to do anybody any good. We Americans, still locked into cold-war thinking patterns, sometimes appear to believe that 100,000 such troops will protect us or somebody from the communist menace. But we might start thinking, in our military-aid programs, how to take advantage of these poor country pressures to do somebody some good. A few models are around—once in a while a big army in a poor country actually goes out and builds roads or tries to teach peasants how to read. A bit of gentle pressure applied when military aid is given might prove useful here. After all, it is for the greater glory of the fatherland! Maybe this will sell, even if the more mundane and simplistic view of development won't. Unfortunately American military people have not done much along these lines. If they did, perhaps some of our lost prestige might come back. Hypernationalism also has its positive virtues. We can see what Afros and other symbols of black pride have done to our own minorities; perhaps the same kinds of positive feelings can be found abroad. It may be better to be proud of what you are than ashamed—as long as you don't go shooting your neighbor as a result.

In the development mainstream, the pressures of hypernationalism and war are ignored. They belong to generals and politicians, not to those technocrats dealing with the real problems of investment, health, education, and technology. But to ignore them omits much of what is really going on, and it omits some of the biggest pressures for change around. The affluent West managed to go a long way with similar motivations—few leaders in the United States or Germany worried much about economic growth, but we worried a lot about getting enough guns. We also know what we did wrong with such pressures long ago—perhaps now we can gently prod others to use these pressures as positive rather than totally negative forces. Poor cultures everywhere are being broken up, like it or not. Their leaders, seeing things come unstuck, respond in expected ways, with guns and appeals to patriotism. We did the same; no one really knows how to mobilize complete populations any other way. But few have really sat down to figure out how to use the pressures of militarism and hypernationalism for positive ends. It's about time they did.

. . . .

CHAPTER VIII

Marxism, Capitalism, and Other Religions

As the total organization of human societies has always intrigued scholars and thinkers, utopia construction has been a growth industry since Plato. How can we reconstruct our present inadequate system to give us what we want? Any philosopher can look around any country and find enough wrong to keep him busy for a decade or more. All is sin, degeneration, despair, poverty, and man's inhumanity to man. It's always been that way, largely because all societies have always been very poor. If life is nasty, brutish, and short, it is very likely that the society will be nasty and brutish too.

For the past hundred years or so, the reformist high ground has been occupied by Marxists of varying sorts, ranging from wild-eyed revolutionary types to moderate reformers favoring a modicum of public ownership. Following the tenets of Marx, they argue that the proper reconstruction of society will occur only if the dictatorship of the proletariat is established. Once this is done, utopian results will follow. There is by now a massive literature on the subject, although the problem is hardly academic. Governments have fallen, revolutionary bloodbaths have occurred, and countries like China and Vietnam have fought more or less continuous revolutions for twenty years on this issue. Who owns what is the key. The Marxists believe that if the means of production are in state hands, all will be well.

If the general goals of a country are of the sort we have already discussed, such as raising inadequate incomes, redistributing wealth, creating a better human-welfare system, and so on, it would appear that everyone has been arguing the wrong issues for a hundred years. The problem is the change in the ownership of assets really does not lead to rapid solutions of pressing economic and social problems. In short, Marxism, or for that matter traditional capitalism, just doesn't get the job done. In considering changes of this political sort, all the relevant variables are omitted. Strangely this fact does not bother revolutionaries, reactionaries, or politicians a bit. They keep right on fighting for their type of reform, and when they win, and when nothing much seems to change very fast, the new system chugs right on. Anyone in power, from right or left, can rationalize his mistakes.

Why doesn't the violent debate and struggle which has gone on for so many years get at the real issues? Nowadays the capitalists are on the defensive. The world ethical mainstream in both rich and poor countries is Judeo-Christian, and anyone who seriously suggests that the way to get things straight is to maximize profits and allow unearned income to accrue to various favored individuals in the form of rent and interest is very far out of the game. Such maximization principles smack of exploitation, dark satanic mills, and vulgar greed. The historic models of a purely capitalistic society are older than Marx, dating back to Adam Smith, and we now live in a different ethical world. People should be nice to each other; cooperate rather than fight; be decently human at all times. The fact that few people have ever behaved this way, and that almost no poor people do, is omitted in ethical discourse. When the millennium arrives, we may all be nice guys. But getting there from here seems very difficult.

So the Marxists preach their gospel and more often than not

win. If we need big firms, better to have the state own them even in nominally capitalist societies. If we want a society where income is distributed fairly, the dictatorship of the proletariat can do the job better than decadent feudal or capitalist regimes. If rapid change and growth is needed, then the revolutionary people's party can do what is necessary. Right-wingers mumble about individual initiative, working harder, and taking over with military dictatorships to keep the peasants in line—and often they do. But from time to time the Marxist theology wins out, and one more country is added to the communist list. In most poor countries, if communism doesn't win, some sort of socialism does. The public utilities and other big firms are more often than not state-owned and run by the people for the people. Such gentle socialism is widely considered to be more humane than the more brutal and unethical capitalist-type activities.

All of this would be exciting and interesting if Marxism worked better than capitalism, but it rarely does. The publicly owned electric power plant is neither notably more or less efficient than the private one; the state-owned railroad does not produce the ton-miles any better than a private one does. In communist countries, one looks in vain for extraordinary achievements, such as rates of economic growth far above the capitalist West. If anything, the affluent communist countries (the Soviet Union and Eastern Europe) are falling behind while poor communist states (North Korea, Red China, Albania) are doing no better and sometimes worse than poor noncommunist countries. Communism may have virtues, but getting societies' economies changed for the better does not seem to be one of them. On the other hand, before card-carrying capitalists gloat too much, it is worth remembering that lots of capitalist poor countries don't do all that well either. Places like Ethiopia, Ecuador, Sierra Leone, Rwanda, and Uganda are as poor and miserable as Albania, Mongolia, and North Korea.

The problem is that the general political structure of the society is not the whole story—although revolutionaries seem to think that it is. Key variables aren't even in the system. And that is why those who feel that capitalism, socialism, cooperative movement, or communism will save the world or their country are theologians, not economists.

Missing Variables

There is a screenplay in new communist countries which tends to be repeated over and again, like a broken record. The revolution has come, and the people are in power. The leader has nationalized this and that, restructured education, tossed out the decadent capitalists or caused them to flee. Foreign governments are concerned, particularly the United States, since so many valuable properties have been expropriated. The country is free of its past, free of the contamination of capitalism, free for the first time in its long history. And the people know it. The excitement of being important can be felt everywhere. The leader mounts the platform, perhaps on May Day, the day of days in the theology, or perhaps on the anniversary of the Revolution. And he begins to speak to the adoring masses.

What is he saying? Those used to old-time Presbyterian sermons will find it very familiar. Since the revolution, the workers have been very lax. Industrial discipline is failing. Workers must, if the revolution is to be a success, work harder, obey their superiors, make sacrifices. Absenteeism is far too high, and black-market activities are a disgrace. Workers are consuming too much—there are shortages of everything, and still more sacrifice is demanded. Loyal party cadres and new managers are not being diligent enough. We must save more materials, save more fats, save more money, save more everything, if the revolution is to succeed. Shape up, save, work, respect—it's all been said before, by a thousand times a thousand uptight Calvinists of the old school. And Castro said it; Tito said it; Stalin said it; Kaldor said it; and now Allende is saying it in Chile, right on schedule—or maybe even a year or two earlier than such things normally get said in the revolutionary state. The problem is that there is nothing in Marx which, when the society is changed by revolution, makes any worker, bureaucrat, technician, or manager any better or worse than he was the day before the revolution. If he was a sloppy worker, prone to absenteeism, he is likely to be this way the next day. A few dedicated revolutionaries gaining power may change and be more diligent, but the masses do not.

If a man was ill educated and bad at his job before, he will be ill educated and bad at it after the revolution. Moreover, revolutions have a bad habit of forcing out the decadent capitalist managers who just may know how to get something done. Those intolerable rules and pressures imposed by them on their slothful workers at least got some work out—now someone has to figure out new rules. From a worker's worm's-eye view of the world, the day after the revolution is the same as the day before. There is a new boss, but he sits in the same chair and does the same things as the earlier one did. And he may well be more politically than managerially adept, so things easily corrected in the old days now get out of hand. And the boss yells just as much, and he puts just as much pressure on as before.

If the workers are smart, they can play the game and get big wage increases together with some slacking of the earlier intolerable work discipline. Even radical revolutionary leaders need political support; and after all they are supposed to be pro-labor. But the factories and mills are the same, and the work patterns are the same, and one's personal problems with his wife and kids are the same. Nothing leads to productivity increases, and a bit more money for an underpaid worker only goes a little way. Within a year, new problems always arise. The spare parts so easily obtained before from the United States or Europe seem very hard to get, and more are needed as new managers and slack workers don't seem to know how to keep things going quite as well. Those capitalist countries seem unwilling to lend or give money to the revolutionary government, and Soviet parts don't fit.

Moreover, it is not too clear what is being produced. Before, the country was loosely locked into the West's way of doing things; now new marketing patterns have to be evolved, and few revolutionaries are good at such things. Plants run out of raw materials, as new planners fumble in efforts to learn; higher-paid workers with better housing (perhaps taken from some capitalist now gone) seem to enjoy life more and take work easier. After all, aren't they the chief beneficiaries of the new order? The newly nationalized industries have difficulty getting into historic markets; the American firms which used to own them are quite adept at tying up shipments to third-world countries with court orders, or undercutting the national firm on price or quality. Somehow foreign currency becomes very difficult to obtain, while needs for it grow inexorably. After all, the state needs more guns, since enemies are everywhere, and local industry cannot produce them. It needs more food, more clothing, more pharmaceuticals, more of everything to support the historic standard of living, which was pretty low to begin with. Remember that population keeps right on growing.

Since fair shares are now the rule, the technicians and professionals find their incomes reduced. In the old regime, they were creaming the society, since they were the productive ones, or at least the ones who knew how to earn income. And as the pressure mounts on them, they react accordingly. Some work less, since there is nothing much to buy anyhow, and everyone else seems to be taking it easy. Some leave, becoming new American or European immigrants (who seem to do very well as soon as they learn English). And some just sit and glower. It's hard to get a skilled architect to do his job properly, if he doesn't give a damn—creativity cannot be ordered by any police state. It's harder to get a dentist to do his job right, and considerably more painful to his clients. And, after a year or so, the leader mounts the podium and gives his uptight Calvinist speech—usually several of them. It figures.

The missing link is the whole behavioral and educational mix of the population, which simply is not in the Marxian vision. Essentially, the theology suggests that revolution will change directly and immediately the nature of man. It just isn't so. Every society, Marxist or otherwise, wants goods and services, and these are produced by productive organizations. And the way they get produced has more to do with technical and managerial skills, quality of equipment, and ability of firms to adjust to the complexities of the outside world than with the politics of the government. The capitalistic price system, however imperfect, tells what to do and when to do it—what planners are supposed to do in the Marxist state. Unfortunately, there is no law that says that good planners come out of the woodwork when the revolution comes.

Marx proposed his grand scheme when the common production unit was a small, family-owned firm. The modern concept of large-scale capitalism, complete with professional management divorced from stockholders, was virtually unknown, even in advanced England. Hence Marx didn't talk about it. Class war was supposed to lead to the destruction of the capitalist system, and those despised owner-managers would be evicted. Moreover, at that time, technology was relatively simple—a reasonably well-educated man could, in a few months, easily acquire whatever competence he needed in almost any field. Hence there was no reason to suspect that there would be any problem in the easy transition from exploitative capitalism to beneficent socialism. Until 1917, there was no communist state, and Marxist scholars could only theorize about how they would run the productive system. The idea of getting things done through complex organizations was an unreal concept.

This is the second key missing variable. A manager, in Marxist terms, was an owner who wandered around in a white collar and did very little observable work. If he vanished, not much would happen, except that the system would be more equitable. Since Marxist thinking has generally dealt with inequities rather than with expansion, the concepts of productive efficiency and economic growth have been largely ignored. About the only theoretical discussion of these points in Marxist literature up to the 1950s dealt with accounting problems inherent in fixing public responsibility. If available income were redistributed, all would be well.

As late as 1917, Lenin could say: "It is perfectly possible . . . immediately, within twenty-four hours after the overthrow of the capitalists and the bureaucrats, to replace them in the control of production and distribution, in the business of control of labor and products by the armed workers, by the whole people in arms." But by the early 1920s, Lenin was praising the work of Frederick Taylor on scientific management, and urging adoption of his principles. Having power focuses the mind wonderfully on economic-growth problems, particularly if your country appears to be coming apart because nothing can be produced. Every group of local Marxists have to learn this lesson the hard way because as Marxist doctrine hardened around the world, the view that management was unnecessary became a part of the dogma. Lenin's earlier views were adopted, not his later ones. The whole management question became a minor footnote of a problem, to be solved once the party took power. This position persists to this day. The idea that an administrator or manager just may be useful, and get something important done, escapes the radicals.

The early Marxian position on managers and firms seemed well suited to poorer countries. After all, here were still found the rapacious small firms, managed by their owners, apparently exploiting the peasants unmercifully. Management consisted of buying low and selling high—which is not exactly a problem worthy of note to a serious revolutionary. To the true revolutionary, the problems of who buys nuts and bolts, fills out the payroll, analyzes new markets, or works out export documentation are dreary things indeed. But if they don't get done right, nothing much happens. In short, management *is* important. And as various new socialist and communist countries have restructured their systems, they discover, to their total dismay, that total restructuring does not make the production system better, but worse. The dreary managerial and technical tasks still have to be done, and they can be done only by highly trained professionals, if they are to be done right. In the poorer countries of the world, intellectual lags are often as important as income and technological lags. The elites of poor countries have rarely seen a really modern, productive large corporation in action —in those countries, historic exploitative patterns still persist. Today the cruelest patterns of worker exploitation exist in such capitalist places as Ethiopia and such communist countries as North Korea. The common thread is low incomes, not political system. Running through this pattern is the inability, particularly before coming to power, of leaders to see that, in the end, what is needed is the proper and efficient management of the productive system, not theological reorganization of the country. They keep right on trying in the old ways, with the same old mediocre results.

Another missing link in the communist theology is the inability to understand what profits really are. In traditional Marxism, profits are to be eliminated, since they are all an income share which is immoral. As a distributive share, the ethic says profits should go. It might be noted that even in modern America, profits are somewhat disreputable. If we want to do something useful, we set up a nonprofit corporation—by implication, a profit-seeking one is somehow not too nice. We all live, one way or another, in the shadow of Marx.

But profits are something else, too. They tell managers what to do. If a firm finds itself in a very profitable field, it is being told by the system to expand, to make new investments, to hire new workers. If it is losing money and goes broke, whatever it is doing is not what is wanted. Few Americans (or anyone else) worry much about such trivia as the fact that their local supermarkets always seem to have milk, or that gasoline seems available at any station, or that the key part for your 1967 Buick somehow is around (well, most of the time, anyhow) when you want it. Failures of supply almost never occur. The reason is that it happens to be profitable to many merchants, wholesalers, and manufacturers to get these things to the right place at the right time. Here the profit system is telling people what to do. And if errors occur, we all see the big inventory and fire sales, where someone's mistakes are being liquidated. If real shortages occur, prices go up, and once again it becomes profitable to supply the item.

In capitalist, market-oriented economies, such things are taken for granted, even in poorer countries. The economy is oriented to providing whatever people seem to want and be able to pay for. There is nothing ethical about all this—rich widows may buy caviar for their poodles while beggars starve, or old people may spend more than their share because society makes sure they get good pensions. Income distribution is one problem, resolved by taxes, ethics, and abilities, while pricing is quite another. Note that the usual attacks on profits and the price system are actually attacks on income distribution or absolute poverty, not on whether or not there is a quart of milk in the corner grocery, or whether a mechanic can obtain easily the part he needs. These trivia can easily be ignored.

So come the revolution, and the price and profit system goes out the window, to be replaced by planners at the center. Their task is straightforward—all they have to do is plan for the next five years every possible demand for every possible good in the total economy at every moment in time —and then plan for every possible factory input to produce all these things for every moment in time. And they have to do this with no realistic price system and no feedback or information which the profit system gives.

A mechanic in Taiwan needs a certain bolt to fix a truck. He goes to the local parts shop, and there is none there. The shopowner, anxious to make a buck, calls his wholesaler. He doesn't have one either, but he wants money too, so he checks around among his friends. The special bolt turns up in a dusty corner of the local Ford agency. For a price only six times what the bolt is worth, the mechanic gets it, fixes the truck, charges the truck owner twelve times what it's worth, and gets the truck back in operation. The bolt cost 2 cents to make and deliver to Taiwan; the truck owner paid 24 cents for it. Since even in Taiwan his truck earns $100 a day, he's happy and productive.

In North Korea, a mechanic finds he doesn't have the same bolt. He checks with the state parts house, and they don't have one either. Since there is no particular incentive for the parts manager to find one, he writes up a requisition and waits. The mechanic, a state employee, doesn't have any incentive to get the bolt either, so he turns to other tasks. Meanwhile, back at the planning center, information finally begins to trickle in that certain key bolts are out of stock and that lots of trucks are down for repairs. It seems that in the last Five-Year Plan, a minor planning official miscalculated usage rates for this item. Moreover, the plant manager was being rewarded for output of complete vehicles, so his interest in spare parts was very, very small. Even the allocated quota was not met. So, the plan has to be changed, which isn't that simple. The bolts use steel, and the total production is already allocated to other uses. Some other plans have to be changed. Steel uses coal—and this sector needs some jiggling to get a bit more steel. But it seems that the coal is hauled in trucks to the steel mill, and they are largely out of service because for some reason parts can't be obtained to keep them running.

This sort of misadventure is very common in every communist country—their newspapers talk about such problems every day. Simple problems which no one in the capitalist world even worries about somehow become horrendous in Marxist states. The reason is that such countries have tossed the baby out with the bath water. In getting their income distributive shares right, they threw away their major managerial feedback loops. As a result, no one knows what to do, and even the most perceptive and intelligent planners, by the millions, cannot plot a simple economy in advance without some idea of what's happening out there.

It is no accident that Castro went back to sugar. He started ambitious industrialization plans for Cuba, and he assumed away all three of the key missing variables noted here. But they could not be assumed away. His managers and technicians were no better after the revolution than before; indeed, given the flight of half a million Cubans to other countries, they undoubtedly were worse. He assumed that management was a trivial problem—but in trying to produce new and unfamiliar items, this was discovered not to be true. And he got rid of the price system, which meant that even good managers didn't know quite what to do. After five years of fiasco, back to the sugar fields, where at least problems are straightforward and simple, and where someone knows what the score is.

No one on the other side of the ideological fence who has worked with capitalistic poor countries imagines that there are any utopias there either. Problems of monopoly, incompetent and uneducated workers, technicians, and managers abound. Price systems work very badly, since one key to a good price system is very widespread knowledge about what is going on in markets. Illiterate peasants or shopkeepers without good communications (like telephones) are not likely to take full advantage of any price system. But at least it works in a gross way, and things get done. In Taiwan, the trucks run, though not as well as they should. But in North Korea they run much less often or not at all. In economic development, everything is relative.

Communist and capitalist theologies also get all mixed up in class structure and power problems. Poor countries are poor in part because their elites tend to sit on their butts and avoid change—hence it is easy to draw the conclusion that changing the elite will lead to dynamic development. So, reform is certain. But there is no free lunch. Shifting from one group of power-holders to another won't get at many problems, nor, as suggested above, will it avoid the usual grubby details of managing, pricing, and production.

All of this thrashing around in the political arena often obscures the suppposed name of the game, which is to get incomes up and people in better shape than they now are. Too often, the name of the game is power per se—not change and development. And the poorer and more disorganized a country seems to be, the more likely it is that some revolutionary doctrine of the right or left will appeal to both elites and peasants. There must be some simple magic that will solve our problems! The Marxists offer one brand; the military dictatorships of the right offer another; the American capitalist still another.

But explorations of the different brands of magic in practice suggest that there is much more to the problem than the magic suggests. Development isn't easy—it involves lots of hard work, imagination, good management, slow technical progress, cooperation among various parties, capital investment, and so on. This sort of work can't be done with incantations. It's too bad that so many people think that it can be done this way. If they were more realistic, then a lot of energy could be channeled into productive use. But then, humans have always put more stock in their gods than in mere mortals, and Marx is no exception.

. . . .

CHAPTER IX

Open and Closed Economies: The People's Choice

A long time ago, there used to be a customs station on the Saudi Arabian-Neutral Zone border, as far away from the world as it is possible to be. Out in that empty desert, fifty or more miles from anything, a small brown building sat on the top of a knoll, a bit off the sand track a few travelers used to go back and forth between two improbable cultures. The first time I drove there with Samir, my driver, I was a stranger. Few foreigners of any sort had ever passed that way, and after the usual courteous greetings, the official asked us to stay for tea. One of his subordinates inspected our Dodge pickup closely, not because he was looking for contraband, but because he had never seen this model before. We spent some time showing him the new V-8, the special new-type sand tires, and the water carrier our shop boys had rigged up. He approved of it all.

Night fell as we sipped the overly sweet tea, chatting with the two senior officials in broken English and even more broken Arabic. We talked about this and that, about the world, about what was happening out where people were. Someone turned on the battery radio, and we listened to an Arabic orator, far away. One official was old, and he recalled

times when only caravans came this way, not really so long
ago. Now, with you Americans here, well, things are different. We learn something new all the time. He hadn't seen a
truck or a car until he was twenty; this radio was the first he
had ever owned. The world, by the grace of Allah, was
changing fast, and he rather liked it. After all, more and
more people were coming down this track—they had as
many as four or five trucks a day now—and there was even
talk of a new paved road between the countries.

Someone brought in a part from the broken-down Land-
rover I had seen in the yard when we drove up, and Samir
showed the worker what might be wrong. I corrected Samir,
and we argued good-naturedly about it for a while. The
worker brought in some tools, and we tinkered with the car-
buretor for an hour, under the hissing Coleman lantern.
The older official carefully explained a new government de-
cree about border crossings, and we maybe got his carbu-
retor right. After another hour we took our leave, with four
lonely men watching us drive down the track.

I guess we all have our desert islands, the places where we
can get away from it all, and when my mind turns that way,
I think back to that outpost, so far from the world as to be
all the way out. Four lonely people sitting and tinkering
with carburetors, pondering their religion, talking with the
handful of strangers, listening to their radio, away from it all
in a total way. Yet, we got there, and with the pickups, the
radios, the jeeps, and the Coleman lanterns, strangers in-
trude even on the most remote parts of the world. There is
really no place to hide and no man is really alone anyplace.

Strangers are dangerous, as any small American backwater
town knows. They have a bad habit of introducing new and
sinful ideas, and they rarely show the respect due local institutions, leaders, or people. Why should they? After all,
they've seen other petty tyrants and ideas from someplace
else, and to them all the locally important activities are
nothing more than quaint customs enjoyed by the local
peasantry—who are definitionally a bunch of dullards who

don't understand the world's problems. But strangers are fun too. They bring in gimmicks and gadgets, along with strange ideas and new life-styles. They bring in money and new technologies, and it's fun to see how a stranger, particularly a rich stranger, behaves. He may be nuts, but inevitably, some of his kooky ideas are borrowed, usually by the more radical young people. Any American who has speculatively eyed the new family down the block, noting their cars, their hairstyles, and the way they talk, knows this. And it's particularly interesting if the strangers have money. Of course, we all know that cash doesn't count, but if a stranger has it by the bale, then we can't resist taking a closer look.

New poor countries have the same reactions. Strangers are culture-busters, particularly if they seem to have something the locals don't, like healthy, happy kids, lots of money, and an apparently easy ability to make still more. Everyone likes a nice home, a good car, plenty of health services, and an easygoing way of life which the strangers seem to bring. Well, almost anybody. The local conservatives, those in power and with whatever local wealth is around, will mumble about upsetting traditional values. Local revolutionaries, conscious of the about-to-be-realized local destiny, will be upset, particularly if the strangers appear to be introducing ideas and values alien to proper revolutionary concepts. The elitists, in short, will be upset, since they sense quite clearly that it is their turf which will be threatened by the stranger. If you run the park, don't let a competitor in.

We live in a world of nation-states, and each state has a choice about strangers. They can let them in and welcome them, trying to learn what is going on, or they can keep them out, build a high fence, and do their own thing unbothered by others. In this case, the local elites have to remember that war remains an instrument of national policy, and on occasion the strangers may force their way in. Unless your guns are as good as your neighbors', the isolation strategy may not work too well. Many a new poor country knows all about this point, since not too long ago British, French,

Belgian, or American troops took the place with relatively
little effort. Colonies didn't exactly volunteer to become
colonies—they were forced. So, do leaders open up the country or close it off? The choice is not only a social but an economic one, since whatever is done will have major implications for wealth creation. And whatever is done will have a
lot to do with culture-busting too.

The Closed-System Choice

Quite a few countries take the closed route. Red China, Albania, North Korea (good communist states all) have opted
for a quite closed position. A few others also go a similar
route, though not quite as tight. India, Pakistan, and Burma
are examples, along with fabled Nepal. The reason for communist countries staying closed is obvious and theological.
The devils out there are likely to contaminate the culture—
therefore, keep them out, allowing in only a few trusted
(more or less) friends. Ideological contamination is sure to
follow if the wicked are allowed entry. And the leaders are
right—the West is tricky and attractive, so it must be excluded. A good way to measure this factor for any country is
to see how tough it is to get out—if one needs exist visas,
permissions, and all the rest to leave his own country, it can
be concluded that the establishment feels strongly that *they*
out there are evil.

Countries such as India and Burma follow a semiclosed
pattern. Here the problem is to do one's thing in relative
isolation from the world. Moreover, such ex-colonial countries have had quite enough of arrogant foreigners, and they
would like to do it their way. Hence block off imports with
exchange controls, make investments difficult through licens-
ing and profits-remission restrictions, and all the rest.
Strangers can get in, but not as easily as they might like,
leaving the local system on its own to solve its problems as
perceived at home.

While relatively few countries outside the communist group want to be left alone and try to implement policies to make this loneliness happen, it is typical to find in every country, including the United States, groups of people who would enjoy being isolated. American liberals and radicals tend to be quite provincial, as one example. Give a good liberal the choice of righting a domestic or a foreign wrong, and he will go domestic every time. If underpaid Mexicans are sweated in American fields (but come by the thousands, because to them this is a good deal), then send them home to lower-paid jobs, and give Americans a chance. What happens to the Mexicans is their problem. If American firms go abroad to invest in Taiwan to take advantage of cheap labor (but the Taiwanese flock to the factories, because to them these are high-pay jobs), then force the American firms back home where they belong. And if great social-engineering schemes are to be realized, they always seem to involve only Americans, not the rest of the world. In a sense, this is fortunate, since if American liberals and radicals, concerned as they are with human misery and suffering, had to worry about 500 million Indians or 800 million Chinese, most of whom live in poverty that would make the American ghetto seem like Beverly Hills, they would really have some problems.

Since the idea of isolation to solve problems always has seemed attractive, countries shut off the outside as best they can. They are then stuck with the problem of doing everything (or almost everything) themselves. If they are poor, they typically are not very good at such taken-for-granted things as production of goods—so the first problem is to figure out how to produce. So much is needed, so little is available. It seems logical to do this first. And always remember that the guns have to be around—neighbors are suspicious and jealous.

This approach inevitably leads to a production orientation of the world. First you produce things, then you worry about everything else. If you can't get production, nothing much else matters. Of course, your closed society begins to come unstuck here, since you have to contact the outside to get your technology. Import a few trucks, to figure out how to get them made at home. Import a few machines, so they can be copied. The Soviets used to do this (and so did the United States, a long, long time ago), so precedents are clear. But somehow, the physical thing doesn't embody everything. Anyone can take a truck apart and see what's in it, but the truck itself doesn't tell you much about the personnel policy of the firm that produced it (actually it does, but only a very sophisticated observer could spot this). The truck does not tell you much about marketing or after-sales service which gets the thing used and sold. It doesn't tell you much about the organization of the components manufacturing plants which made the thousands of bits and pieces that go into the finished product. The truck itself tells nothing much about the management of the firm that made it. And other evidence is hard to find, like how the axles were heat treated, and what kinds of steel went into the springs. If a country has battalions of capable engineers and metallurgists, it can find such things out, but few poor countries have such talent.

Production-oriented people tend to forget that there is a lot more to the problem than production, but they will call in the foreign engineers. At least these people are sanitary, more or less. And the country may even get its plants built. Once again, this is not the whole story. Perhaps the trucks are not really what the country needs most; perhaps it is much more difficult than anyone imagined to get all those 20,000 parts produced so the finished product will come out right. No one remembers that over 2,000 American auto- and truck-makers went broke trying just this—everyone knows all about Ford, Chrysler, and General Motors. It looks easy—but it isn't. The Russians have been at this auto-truck business for over fifty years, and even though they have talented engineers and workers, somehow the things never quite come out well enough to sell in a freely competitive market. Poor countries, with but a fraction of the Soviet human talent, find it very difficult to beat the affluent Western countries at their own game, even in items much simpler than motor vehicles.

Simple things do get done. The closed country manages to get along somehow, and even to expand outputs a bit each year. Often such countries do have some internal cohesion, a sense of doing great new things, a sense that enemies are everywhere, so the people must be alert. Certainly the leaders of such countries do everything they can to foster such illusions. Since in many closed countries such vital data as any output, birth and death rates, and certainly national income, are top state secrets, it is a bit difficult to deduce exactly what is going on. But generally, after stripping away the glowing reports about tractor production and images of stalwart workers doing great things, what emerges is a pattern of modest growth. If such a country can manage 2 or 3 percent per capita real increase in income, it is doing well, and that includes the communist countries.

Smaller countries which choose this closed-economy strategy normally have more trouble than big ones. The reason is simple—if you do everything yourself, you have to have all the well-trained people, all the organizations, and all the capital equipment to do everything. A really big poor country, like India or Red China, has at least some chance of finding good engineers, metallurgists, statisticians, managers, personnel specialists, accountants, and all the rest. A small country like Nepal, North Korea, or Albania has no chance at all. All of these countries have a fairly high incidence of illiteracy, very low incomes, and poorly developed organizations. The culture stays pure—but nothing much happens.

Perhaps the worst aspect of such a situation is the gradual drift to irrelevance. If you never let anyone in or out, and if your internal system doesn't seem very exciting to anyone, who cares? No one knows or cares who is premier of Albania or North Korea, because this information is irrelevant. No one listens at the United Nations (if you belong) to your

statements, since they don't matter. You *know* that you have
the word, and that your cause is just and true—but somehow, no one else gives a damn. This can be very frustrating
to any elite establishment anywhere.

Bigger countries are noticed, because they are big. But
they are noticed for all the wrong reasons. No one wants to
try the Chinese or Indian system—they are worried, however, that the internal convulsions of such a large system
might affect them negatively. So they are watched. But keen
observers end up sympathizing, not admiring, unless the big
closed system can show that it has something someone else
needs. And so far, not much has been needed.

We now see in the American black-power movement some
of the same yearnings for aloneness and isolation so common
abroad. It is tough to live in someone else's world, the world
of the *man*, where he dominates everything. It is tough to
try to get something done when *they* seem to block off every
move. Indians in 1946, Albanians in 1945, and lots of Africans in the 1950s and 1960s would be sympathetic, because
they went through the same process. Someone else was controlling their destinies, so they wanted to be alone and
proudly independent. And it always appears easy to do the
simple productive things which have to be done to run your
own show. After all, factories are nothing more than buildings with some equipment; most highly skilled managerial jobs
are merely sinecures held by exploiters, and once independent, we can go our own way in peace, dignity, freedom,
power, and wealth. And if American blacks really want it
this way, they might even get it. The hooker is, if you isolate
yourself, you have to do it all on your own. The ex-colonial
power may give you freedom, but don't expect much in the
way of help after Independence Day. And if you can't do it
well by yourself, you have to face the consequences. Experience to date suggests that this isolationist way has a low
probability of significant success.

Dependent and Open Countries

Lots of small, poor countries have seen the unpleasant possibilities of doing it all themselves, and they haven't liked what they saw. The idea of being a peaceful, independent, pastoral nation with per-capita incomes staying below $100 per year forever (or at least for a few centuries) is not all that appealing. So what else is there?

Well, there is always the raw-materials export route, and this road is very well trod. Leaders know all about such improbable places as Kuwait, Saudi Arabia, and Libya, where oil exports from huge pools have led to really big money. In 1958, Libya was considered a write-off country—no resources, 90 percent illiteracy, no way to get into the human mainstream. Now the country has a per-capita income approaching $2,000, and it is going up all the time. Within fifteen years, Libya has moved from a world charity case to one of the more affluent countries in the world.

How did it happen? Easy—Westerners found oil in the distant, sterile desert. With the country getting half or more of the profits, and with Western Europe next door badly needing more energy, petroleum exports exploded. Libya exports oil and imports everything else—and it has the highest growth rate of any country in the world, unless some equally improbable country like Abu Dhabi, which has followed an identical pattern, has managed to edge them out. And with wealth came relevance. Not only does the oil supply directly interest the West (and East), but all those hard currencies buy guns, jets, and new public buildings. Leaders are very important men, both at home and abroad. Perhaps the country would just as soon the evil foreigners went away—certainly a place like Saudi Arabia is not very anxious to adopt Western ways in a hurry. But all that oil money breaks down even the most stubborn isolationists.

Oil is usually the magic commodity, although iron ore (Liberia) and copper (the Congo) can be lucrative also. The idea is to get Western foreigners to exploit the mineral wealth that can be sold in the West, earn a share of the profits, and use them to build up the country with imported stuff. It's a great strategy if you're interested in money, and if you're lucky enough to have a big supply of some key raw material on hand.

Such places are lively enough, and their incomes are going up very fast. A visit to any one of them would show tremendous signs of life. Japanese motor bikes fight with Mercedes and Cadillacs for inevitably inadequate street space. Local merchant millionaires are at the big new airport, waiting for jets to take them to Europe or the United States. The local army, too small, to be sure, seems well equipped with the latest weaponry from the West, all paid for with those delightful hard currencies. Leaders flit from country to country, working out oil-cartel deals with similar states, or plotting revenge on ancient or recent enemies. At the United Nations, representatives are listened to with considerable respect by other poor-country leaders (nothing succeeds like success and money). And back home, new schools, mosques, and public buildings, all air-conditioned and in the latest neo-functional modern styles, sprout everywhere. Whatever else is happening, such places are swinging.

Like everyone else, these countries have problems. Those foreigners are in the country, exploiting something scarce, holding all the good jobs, linking up your shaky economy to Western affluent countries in mysterious ways. Local radicals want reform now, like taking over the production of the key raw materials. Conservatives get restless, since those foreigners typically have the wrong religion and an expressed or implied contempt for local religious values and customs. And the country gets only half, or maybe 60 percent, of the profits. If only it could get 100 percent.

Because such places are so totally locked into Western consumption patterns, total expropriation is not yet seen as the only way to go. Iran tried it in 1951, when it expropriated

its petroleum properties—and all it got for its trouble
was sharply lowered income as Western countries shifted
suppliers. After a few years, a new arrangement was worked
out with the West to get back to the old game. Perhaps expropriation will be more common in the future, since the
pressures to do your thing as you wish are strong and growing. But if many countries take over the oilfields, copper
mines, and iron deposits, it is not too likely that the countries involved will do much different from now. The exports
will flow, if at all possible, and the imports will continue to
come in. No country in this group could do much of anything along modern industrial lines itself, and their leaders
know it. Whatever happens to asset ownership within, the
open pattern and linkages to the West will continue. Countries that as yet haven't got into this game typically are most
anxious to do so. If a poor agriculturally oriented country
could only entice a big Western firm to come and get the oil,
copper, or whatever, then they too could get in on the high-
income game. Unfortunately, not every country sits on a
major oilfield or copper deposit, so this strategy is not open
to all.

A few other countries with good agricultural possibilities,
such as Thailand and the Ivory Coast, have used a similar
strategy in agriculture. The Thais can grow rice cheaply and
well—why not sell it to others and import whatever is
needed? And if the country can get its agricultural outputs
up faster than the inevitable increase in population, this will
work too. Models exist—Canada, New Zealand, and Australia got rich this way, so others might too. But the agricultural idea is against the modern mainstream. Development
means factories, steel, urbanization, not a bunch of peasants
doing their traditional thing in a more efficient way. Yet a
few countries that have moved in this direction have done
well.

Economists call this comparative advantage. That is,
everyone is good at something, so do that and buy from others the things you're not so good at. Even if others can grow

rice better in absolute terms than you can, if this is your best advantage, do it anyhow. Your income will be lower than theirs, but it will be higher than if you tried to do things you are not too good at. Of course, this sort of theorizing is ignored by politicians everywhere—but if a country really gets off track on this point, as the closed economies tend to do, then they are poorer than they should be. Prestige, power, and the ability to have one's own culture may be worth more than money, but such things may really mean that someone else gets rich. And in spite of everything, we admire and respect the rich.

Open Economies

Plenty of poor countries have very little to offer the rest of the world. They really don't have much good agricultural land; their resources are small or nil; and the skills of the population are low. They can stay isolated, and very, very poor, or they can try something else. Like what?

Well, one thing they might have is a large supply of cheap and relatively disciplined labor. In such countries it is common to find peasants working for 15 or 20 cents a day. A factory job at 30 or 40 cents an hour would look like a good deal to many. The difficulty is that there is no capital, nor is there any managerial or technical skill in the society. Such things are the product of long decades of industrial experience, which such a country hasn't got.

Such defects can be easily remedied. If the economy is open to all, if local money is freely convertible to foreign monies at whatever price is relevant, then maybe something will happen. If foreigners can come and go, and if foreign firms can easily repatriate profits, then perhaps they will come and do something. After all, those Americans, Japanese, and Europeans are always looking for a chance to make money, even abroad.

And come they do. In places like Taiwan, South Korea,

Hong Kong, and Singapore, or even along the United States-Mexican border, the foreigners come. They set up the kinds of labor-intensive factories which are so hard to operate properly at home, given high wage rates. Television-tuner assemblies, other electronic gismos, toys, and all the other light industries are fair bets here. The foreign firm provides management, the technology, capital, and the organization; the host country provides the labor. And the country begins to take off, exporting all these light industrial products and importing everything else. You as an American can see this down at the local variety store in your nearest shopping center. Just look at the marks of origin of textiles, toys, cheap transistor radios, and all the rest. You're at the receiving end of a long and complex supply chain which started perhaps a decade ago when a premier picked the development strategy of open-ending his country's economy. It took a while for American firms to figure out how to take advantage of the idea, but now the movement is in full bloom. Instead of paying fifty bucks for an American-made radio the way you did in 1940, you pay ten to get a better one carefully assembled in Taiwan.

Meanwhile, in Taiwan, things are pretty lively too. Income per capita is going up at 10 percent per year or better, as the twenty-cent-a-day peasants are rapidly getting locked into forty-cent-an-hour jobs. The streets, like those in the oil-rich states, are clogged with too many cars, motorbikes, and bicycles, and the new local jet airport is filled with businessmen of many nations coming and going. The cities are crowded, lively, and exciting.

Of course, there is never a free lunch. Local radicals, like local radicals everywhere (except in the closed economies, where they are either in power or in jail) are agitating for expropriation and a return of the nation to itself and its traditional values. All sorts of social inequities are observable —the rich seem to be getting richer, and the poor get richer more slowly. Social overheads, like schools and hospitals, never seem to be adequate to house the population (in earlier days, the population was scattered around on marginal farms, so of course they did not demand such services, even when they were available). Everything is in flux, and lots of things are wrong. But somehow, most people seem to be a bit better off this year than last.

Indeed, such places vaguely resemble the American ghettos—lively, sometimes crude, full of all sorts of social problems, overcrowded, bubbling with radicals, reformers, itinerant ministers and missionaries, and short of every possible social amenity, such as schools, hospitals, roads, sewers, and policemen. Why not? After all, the American ghetto is also an open economy, and its citizens also came in from the farm not too long ago.

But there is a difference. While the Taiwanese find the job market booming (though there never seem to be enough jobs to go around), the ghetto occupants find jobs very tough to find. In the old days, when the ghetto was Irish or Italian or Jewish, there were plenty of jobs (though never quite enough), and the number was booming. But after 1945, America decided on a freer trade policy, and American firms discovered the big outside world at about the same time. And since as early as 1922, American policy has been to exclude the poor, particularly the nonwhite poor, through immigration restrictions. So gradually the modern pattern emerged. Instead of sweating our own poor in whatever ghetto is around in this generation, we have exported the jobs to those countries which accept the sweat. Remember, they really don't have many options, and one man's exploitation is another's good fortune. Then we import the products of the cheap labor to be sold at even lower prices than poor sweated Americans ever could have made possible.

You can see the effects in any American ghetto. Drive around and note how many small shops and factories are closed; how many lofts are for rent. Those small shops and factories used to produce the toys, clothing, and cheap electronics we consumed. Now there is nothing left in the ghetto but bad housing, and those who work have to leave the ghetto to find a job, if they can.

Of course, we want it both ways. We want the three-dollar-an-hour jobs *and* the cheap goods. But even our most ingenious industrialists cannot provide both. We can have the cheap labor and the cheap goods—or we can have two-dollar-an-hour jobs and expensive goods. As usual, if we go this way, the foreigners get screwed, which becomes their problem. The present pressures for higher protection through import duties and quotas on such items as textiles reflect our interest in having it both ways, or at least trying to. And here again the interrelationships in this spaceship earth creep up on us. Because some Asian potentate decided to have an open economy, some Chicago Negroes get into trouble. Actually it has always been like this. Even the countries that choose to hide and close off the frontiers have no real place to hide.

So far, the open economies are doing fine. And there always is the Japanese model to ponder. They opened up fifty years ago, trying to provide the world whatever it wanted. After some decades of experience with simple things like textiles, they graduated to more complex things like cars and machinery. And they continue to grow faster than anyone else. The danger is that as the world goes, so goes your economy—if you are taking a total marketing approach to the rest of the world, and if their markets decline, you're in trouble. In short, you have given up some sovereignty in a very fundamental way. The other danger is, if you open up, your culture is contaminated very fast. The alluring products of someone else, like motor bikes and small cars, to say nothing of radios and TV sets, can wreck anybody's petty local traditions and customs.

Reformers in the affluent countries, interested in tighter controls on people, don't attack TV and auto ownership for fun—they know that such things give people strange ideas, like being able to do what they want. With a bit of luck, a

reformer who knows that his view of the world is correct
can totally control TV (simply by not letting outsiders in)
and get rid of cars (if people ride trains and buses, you can
make sure they go where they are supposed to go). In the
end, with luck he may wind up with a Soviet model, where
such foreign things are excluded, and life is correct, sedate,
and extremely dull—to say nothing of being where the action decidedly is not. Without luck, he may end up with the
Albanian model, where life is equally sedate, correct, and
dull, but poor as hell, and where no one gives a damn what
you do. The basic trouble with closed economies is the same
as their basic virtue—you can run an uncontaminated culture which will never get busted up by outsiders. But you
also pay the price, namely, that you never quite know what
the others are doing, which means you just might fall farther and farther behind.

So far, the open economies are most people's choice, although it is fun to watch the so-called revolutionaries (and
their curious arch-conservative allies) push hard to close up
the system. It is clear why they want it this way. If you let
the foreign devils in, they will bust you up, in ways far more
fundamental than selling you a truck or a TV set, and these
reformers know it. They are welcome to their petty,
cramped worlds. Most humans want something better.

. . . .

CHAPTER X

The Ghetto Abroad

You see them when you're riding in from the airport in almost any poor country. Before you get to the city, you pass a string of shacks, sometimes put together with old oil drums, sometimes made of bits and pieces of wood, sometimes just tents. An incredible number of children seem to be everywhere, and even the casual observer can note that there is little or no electric power, no plumbing, no water. Ragged inhabitants may stare at you as your taxi plows through the area, horn blowing, scattering everyone. Then you reach the built-up part of the city, and the buildings become very substantial, often built in the latest neo-functional high-rise patterns. More are being built everywhere—poor countries are always having a building boom of sorts, and the impression is one of dynamic activity, striking architecture, and long-range planning. The streets are a bit narrow, and cars and taxis and trucks fight for space, but downtown, or its nearby inner city, does not seem all that different from what you're used to at home.

It is a bit different, when you think about it, because those new high-rise buildings are being put up exactly where the American ghetto now is, in the inner city. The luxury

apartments for the upper middle classes are within walking
distance of downtown. Look once again—there is little or no
parking space in them, either, because in poor countries,
even the upper middle classes are not likely to have automobiles. So they want to be close to the center, close to downtown. Those without money or hope are stuck out where the
American suburbs are, at the edge of the city, in the shacks
and tents. The city in a poor country is inside out to an
American one, and to what European and Japanese cities are
fast becoming. Autos do make a difference.

Cities also are growing explosively in the third world. Urbanization is the new development, and cities no one in the
West ever heard of in central India or some such place now
have a million or more inhabitants, and they are growing at
10, 15, or even 20 percent per year. Those luxury apartments and high rises can accommodate only a fraction of
these new people, even if most of them could afford the rent,
so the bulk of the growth is out in the fringe, where the
shacks are. Some cities have several rings—the outermost
one is tents and other portable housing; the next one consists of semifixed shacks, old auto packing crates, and other
partially portable buildings; the next one is now pretty well
established, with quite well-constructed houses built out of
cement blocks, oil cans, some good lumber. Maybe even electric power and water reach some houses; and finally, the real
construction begins, within a mile or so of downtown.

Aside from a few Peace Corps workers and religious vol-
unteers, few Americans spend much time in the shacks, so
they go largely unnoticed in the West. Few elitists in the
country have ever spent much time in them either, and the
leaders tend to be ashamed of them, so there is little local
comment either, unless some of them are being knocked
down for a new housing project, or unless a crime wave or
epidemic is seen as emanating from such housing. But the
shacks often are surprisingly ingenious, and in warm cli-
mates (remember, many poor countries are subtropical)
rather comfortable. They lack the usual amenities taken for

granted even in bad urban slums in the West—running water, indoor plumbing, electric power, and sewers—but they accommodate enormous numbers of new city dwellers who have moved in from the bush to gain whatever they can from city life.

Everyone is new to the city in such places. These migrants typically are from the agricultural sector, and they normally have little to sell but their own unskilled labor. Yet still they come, in a worldwide movement which seemingly has little to do with the country's politics, religion, or location. Why?

The population explosion has a lot to do with it. Remember that some countries are now far enough along in their own population growth to have doubled (or in a few cases, almost tripled) population in the past forty years. With relatively fixed agricultural-land supplies, the excess peasants literally have no place to go. There is no need for them in the countryside, and jobs are very low paying and often nearly impossible to obtain. So they come to the city, where the new development plans and activities at least suggest some modicum of hope for employment. Of course, this sort of person has no money or skills, so he ends up in the last ring of temporary housing on the outskirts. With luck, he may have a cousin who has a job, and who can support him for a while until he can find a job. Often he never does, given the huge supply of unskilled labor and the few jobs available. He may pick up an occasional day's work unloading a truck, working at the port, or stacking crates in a factory yard, but most of the time he will be unemployed. His kids, with luck, may get to a poor school to learn a bit, but they also will be hustlers—tourists see them in swarms, as shoeshine boys, gum peddlers, and junior pimps, all over the city. And the children will continue to be born and they will live—the man may have five, eight, or ten children. As I said, death control is cheap, and once in a while the health van will come along and give cholera shots or smallpox shots to everyone in the area. Who wants an epidemic right next door? The planners will be quite good about such things.

They also will be good about making sure that the one water tap which may serve fifty or even two hundred shacks runs pure water—not a difficult job. Ten years from now, there will be twice as many adults scrounging for perhaps 10 percent more jobs even though the unemployment rate is already over 10 percent. In some places right now it runs over 30 percent. Try to figure out what kind of home life the eighth child of an unemployed illiterate might have in a disorganized shack city, and you may understand why so many people are worried about the future of the poor countries.

The agricultural revolution has also hit the less-developed countries. Modern, productive agriculture is all machines and fertilizers and good planning, not unskilled bodies laboring in the fields. A tractor can replace twenty men; a combine can eliminate the need for several thousand at harvest time. The smart landowner uses capital, not labor, because he can get better results this way. Remember, too, that many poor countries encourage the use of capital and discourage labor through their pricing policies and social-welfare legislation. Thus the foreign-currency exchange rate may be artificially low, and only favored buyers have access to foreign equipment. But who is more favored than a good farmer who is producing a lot of badly needed food? So he gets his import permit, and he buys a nice new American or Japanese tractor at an artificially low price. Meanwhile, the recent social legislation has just set a new minimum wage for agricultural workers, which is above the price desperate people are willing to work for. What is more logical than to use more tractors and fewer people, under these circumstances? And still more peasants are forced into involuntary unemployment and off the land. In Pakistan, a tractor costs less in terms of bushels of wheat than in the United States. If you want to overurbanize your country in the fastest possible way, this is a great way to do it.

The new green revolution, which is the term given to the introduction of new varieties of wheat and rice which have yields two to five times the old varieties, also is hurting.

These new miracle strains are making massive increases in food production possible, and for the first time in twenty years, it appears as if countries with exploding populations can feed their peoples for some time to come. But the new varieties involve careful planning, better fertilizer use, and in most cases more mechanization. In short, they favor the agri-businessmen, not the peasant farmer. Those who quickly seize the new opportunities make more money, buy more land, and push still more people off the land.

Some countries, seeing this problem, try land reform. But, given doubling populations every twenty to thirty years, this option has limited value. If the plots are small enough to accommodate even the farmers in this generation, they will be too small for optimum uses of the fertilizers and equipment. And wait twenty years—the population will have doubled, and the problem will be right where it was—with the surplus people going to the city. If you try to make reasonable-sized plots, then the surplus people are here now—and again, back to square one. A real problem in land reform is that the new tenants may not be very sophisticated and able to take care of their new lands. So, the country starts the usual pattern of agricultural credit extension, rural education, and training in new techniques. The results are the same as noted above. The sharp farmers get very good and very rich—the poor have static production and lots of kids. And sooner or later, the kids go to the city.

Another factor which pushes people into cities is that now they can get there. Most countries, even poor ones, now have some trucks and cars, along with a number of roads, some good, some average, and many terrible. But trucks can go lots of places where only a simple dirt track exists. And peasants can ride atop the loads. In the old days, a fifty-mile trip might have taken five days; now, a peasant can go see for himself, in a day, and even come back to talk about it in his village. If the driver is a cousin, the trip is free—or even if the driver is merely a distant relative of almost anyone in the neighborhood.

Trucks also can bring in the basic necessities from a wide area to feed and clothe the new city dwellers. Little is needed: a bit of grain (usually rice or wheat), a few bolts of cotton cloth from the textile mill (and behind that, the bales of cotton from the farms), and the other odds and ends needed to keep someone alive, such as drugs, fruits, and the like. This could be done only with difficulty in the railroad era, since railroads in poor countries were few, and vast areas were not served. It costs over 20 cents a ton-mile to move anything by animal-powered vehicles, even if labor costs are very low, and it costs over 50 cents per ton-mile by pack animal or porter. Even beat-up trucks can do the job for 5 cents a ton-mile, which expands the supply system for any rapidly growing city. And the range and flexibility of trucks mean that previously untapped agricultural areas now are in the system.

Note the interlocking here. The good farmer buys or rents some previously unusable land, or land used in subsistence agriculture, far from historical transport modes, such as rivers or railroads. He gets a good crop, using trucked-in fertilizers and machinery. Then he sells at a good price, because someone (maybe the government) is willing to pay a good price for the grains he produces. As the trucks roll into the exploding city, you can see some of the displaced agricultural workers sitting atop the load, coming in from the boondocks to seek their fortunes.

And finally, the exploding cities reflect the expectations revolution. Even poor peasants have access to transistor radios, and along with the entertainment and educational attempts, any government will be inclined to brag a bit about the tremendous new development activities. So, why not go where the new growth is, in the cities? Why not try to get to the new factories, the new power plants, the new port developments, where the government speaker is talking in glowing terms about what opportunities exist? If you're going to be poor and unemployed, you might as well be poor and unemployed where the action is, which is the city. Americans, singing praises about the delights of bucolic rural life, have long since forgotten the incredible monotony of the village, without phones, radios, TV, movies, or anything. People sit —and that is all there is to do, except copulate. You go to bed with the sun, since no one has lights, sometimes not even candles or kerosene lanterns. And no one reads, because no one can. If someone can, he can't afford even a newspaper, let alone a book. So somebody brings in a transistor radio, and everyone listens. And a second cousin, Hamed, who left ten years ago, is now a truck driver who gets around, and once in a while comes back to the village with wild tales about the outside world. The peasant notes with interest Hamed's new bicycle, his good clothes (old army fatigues—used clothing is a big business in the poor countries; but an old fatigue jacket can be a very impressive shirt to a man who has none—everything is relative). Perhaps if he went to the city . . .

So the expectations revolution begins to work. And there are *some* opportunities: an uncle now has a job as a porter; another village worker actually got a job as a laborer in the new factory project; somebody's wife's aunt is a maid with a wealthy family. Even if the unemployment rate is 20 percent, this means that 80 percent are working one way or another, so perhaps there is a chance. And agricultural labor seems to be less needed every year. So why not? In the city one hears tales of movies, TV, and other entertainment. Men with few options tend to try to find new ones, and they do. In this generation, all the opportunity is in the city.

In the city, the modern men of the poor country look, act, and work much like modern men everywhere. Their offices and factories look about the same; their behavior and work habits are some place in the same ballpark; everywhere you see the same serious, hard-working people you might find in Milwaukee or Oakland. But they are the tiny minority. They are the ones who live in the apartments; who take the bus to work every morning; who worry about how well their kids are doing in school; and who tend to have small families. But out at the edge of the city, the new urban poor swarm, trying to adjust to a way of life which they or their ancestors never knew. And somehow, it is very difficult to lock them in. They are illiterate; they lack skills; they often are partially sick and lack stamina. Slowly they do get accustomed to modern ways, but it is a very slow process. And they quickly lose whatever ties they may have had to their traditional way of life. The culture they left behind—the one of simple peasant life in some village—is gone forever. Their culture has been destroyed, to be replaced by some bastard version of modern Western life no one knows much about yet.

This is why, when we see efforts to preserve the old ways, complete with smiling peasants in their traditional costumes, the whole deal seems very phony. It is rather like Disneyland—a nostalgic, prettied-up picture, less the inevitable diseases, bugs, and boredom, of a way of life which is gone forever. The model man in a poor country today is a fellow living in a shack at the edge of the city, wearing some old work clothes or a tattered Boy Scout shirt from the affluent West, watching a public TV set, or listening to someone's transistor radio. He is a man buried in the hustle and bustle of God knows how many crowded people, learning as he goes a very new way of life which is neither very Western nor very traditional as yet. And the model child is not a smiling schoolboy in a stiff new uniform, but a ragged hustler on the edge of the city, selling candies, shoeshines, or girls. Remember that after twenty years of 3 percent population growth, over half the people will be under fifteen years of age —no country can provide enough schools for this many kids. So a child learns the hard way, much the way our own ghetto children learn, on the streets. And he decidedly will not grow up to be a traditional kind of man.

Planners and thinkers in poor countries can see all this happening on the edge of their cities, but they can do very little about it. It costs perhaps $5,000 to $10,000 of capital to provide one job in Western mainstream-type economic activities. When you have 1, 2, or 20 million people in this situation, no one has that kind of money, to say nothing of the skilled administrative, managerial, and technical labor needed to provide the jobs. The big capital projects, such as machine-tool factories, power plants, and petrochemical complexes, where perhaps $50,000 to $100,000 in capital is needed to provide just one job (and that for a highly skilled man), does absolutely nothing for the urban poor. And the municipal government is in worse shape. It needs billions of dollars to provide housing, schooling, sewers, water, police and fire protection, and parks for the exploding population, and of course the money and skilled men are not there. So only the bare minimum gets done, and sometimes even this doesn't get done. The American urban crisis looks like a paradise on earth compared to the problems of a city like Calcutta.

In this area, Americans may be more harmful than helpful in their advice. When an American expert sees this situation, he is appalled, and he suggests remedies based on his American experience. So some really nice public housing is built—and the 10,000 units which cost $5,000 apiece, and take two years to build, are put up. While this is being done, maybe 50,000 new migrants have entered the city, and things are worse than before. A better way to do the job, if anyone wanted to help a maximum number of people, would be to make available lots more old oil cans and cheap lumber, so those in tents could get into more permanent houses.

Or one beautiful school is built, which costs a half million and accommodates perhaps 500 pupils in the American manner. While it is being built and staffed perhaps 15,000 kids reach primary school age. The absolute number of illiterates in the world today is going up, even as the absolute number of those becoming literate also rises. What works well in the United States may well be very dysfunctional abroad because Americans, used to total solutions, are likely to suggest similar solutions in poor countries. The usual result in urban problems is that a handful of lucky people live in the American manner, while the masses get nothing. Indeed, since the scarce capital and manpower are going into big, total-solution systems, they may well be worse off than before.

But no one, in this world of good ethics and the belief in the dignity of man, is likely to suggest that the way to get something done is to put out some cheap two-by-fours and old oil cans (which cost a pittance) so that the scroungers can improve their humble homes. No one is likely to suggest that the way to run schools is out in the streets, with teachers and pupils using whatever facilities, including the oil-can shacks, they can find. No one is going to suggest that the scarce capital be put into things which could yield very cheap jobs for illiterates. No, the way to travel is the Western way, with model housing (that few ever get to live in), big factories (where few can ever work), huge new power plants (whose electric power few will ever enjoy), very capital-intensive sewer systems (which stop short of the distant shacks), and complex planning offices (which never have the resources to apply their plans for the masses). These things count—they are big, impressive, and they are what the rich countries do, so they must be right.

Meanwhile, out in some shack, the illiterate ex-peasant sits, waiting for work that rarely comes. His kids are out hustling, when they should be in school. His wife is again pregnant, and the roof leaks. Sitting on his dirt floor, listening to his neighbor's transistor radio sing praises of the new order, he can perhaps count his blessings. At least here, in the city, there is a chance—out on the farm, there was no chance at all. Maybe it didn't work out as he planned, but at least he is alive and eating. And maybe, with just a bit of luck, one of his sons may latch onto one of the scarce jobs, and be able to support the family. It's a tough world, but it could be worse.

. . . .

CHAPTER XI

The Farm Problem, World Scale

Every oil-producing country has at least one export point. It rarely looks like much—just a few tin sheds on shore, and way out in the bay, maybe four miles or more, a buoy and some almost invisible tankers, waiting to be loaded. The huge ships, running up to 400,000 tons, over 1,000 feet long, carry the oil to Europe, Japan, and other big consumers. In Arabia, over 2 million barrels per day go out, and standing on shore, seeing ships as long as two city blocks looking like models, it's hard to remember that you're looking at almost $2 million a day for the government, 365 days a year. No one in the country ever sees the oil, but it accounts for virtually all the income the country earns from abroad. The import docks are some place else where dry-cargo freighters unload everything under the sun, from wheat to trucks to generators to canned goods. These docks look like those in some old movie, with cranes, lighters, longshoremen, bustling small locomotives, and all the rest. And they look a lot more like money and income. But those tin sheds and a few pipes leading out to the tankers pay for it all.

The less-developed countries export raw materials and foodstuffs, and import just about everything else. It's a lot

like Kansas in 1910—and, like Kansas in 1910, leaders of
poor countries spend a lot of time worrying about how to
get farm prices up, and they complain bitterly that the in-
dustrialized part of the world is always giving them the business. Their dream is to get a sort of international price-fixing deal going similar to the one in the United States. If this
could be done, farmers would be better off, at the expense of
someone else. But unlike Kansas vs. the rest of the United
States, this argument is between the poor countries and the
rich ones. And as a result, there are some differences.

Poor nations tend to be single-crop economies. They export one or at most two key items, usually low-grade materials, and buy machinery, motor vehicles, and all the rest of
the industrial products from wealthy countries. The one
crop depends on where the country is and what its luck is—
subtropical countries tend to export coffee, tea, sugar, bananas, or copra; countries lucky enough to have big mineral
deposits export iron ore, copper, tin, or petroleum; and a
few others go for wheat, rice, or other grains. The really
lucky countries are those exporting oil—indeed, many of
these are not poor financially, although their populations
look about like any other less-developed country. Kuwait,
Abu Dhabi, and Libya are actually quite affluent countries
in the world scale, with incomes over $2,000 per capita per
year and growing. Saudi Arabia, Iran, Nigeria, Venezuela,
and Indonesia also rely heavily on oil for foreign-exchange
earnings, which runs into the hundreds of millions of dollars
per year for all of them.

Oil is particularly nice, because it is extracted, refined,
and sold by giant multinational British, French, and American firms. The countries get a rentier's share for their troubles, along with some employment. While there are problems aplenty in the oil business, and while the countries are
decidedly not happy with their lot, not having hard cash is
usually not one of their problems. Petroleum consumption
rates have been growing at over 8 percent per year since
World War II, and countries in this game have been able to

enjoy both rising oil prices and even more rapidly rising profits shares.

Other segments of mineral and subtropical agriculture also have attracted much foreign investment, usually from Europe and the United States. The reason is simple—minerals are where you find them, so the firms go to get them where they can. And if you want tea, sugar, coffee, rubber, or bananas, you have to go to the right climate. The term "banana republic" stems from the ancient practice of buying a country in the subtropics to get such items. There is a long and tortured history of expropriation, political agitation, and troubles over such investments, but even now lots of foreign investment is still out there, although modern images of colonialism are formed on what happened long ago on the British tea plantations and the United Fruit Company's banana plantations.

Now, if a country sells one or two things, the prices for them will be of critical interest to everyone. If the price falls, and production stays constant, incomes will drop; if prices rise, everyone grows prosperous. Americans who have followed American agricultural history know all about farmers' reactions to price drops—our own history is full of riots, political activities, and hassles about the price of corn or wheat. Farmers were once urged to raise less corn and more hell, and our overseas friends from poorer regions have taken this admonition to heart.

What is alleged to have happened throughout most of the postwar period is that prices for agricultural products have fallen relative to prices paid for industrial goods. Remember the old agricultural price-parity arguments? In the new world, it's the deterioration in the terms of trade, which in a one-crop country means the same thing. The price of the export (a raw material) has dropped relative to the price of imports (the manufactured goods). If so, the poor countries are being forced to export more to pay for the same amount of imports. Worse, import prices tend to rise, since all major industrial nations have some price inflation, and most industrial prices are controlled by producers. The lower agricultural and raw materials prices go, and the higher industrial prices rise, the worse off the poor country is.

There is no doubt that in some cases the above allegation is true. Specific countries have had real troubles with sharply declining prices for their export, and the things they buy have risen sharply in price. But to cover the 120 countries that are poor might suggest that the breaks of the game are different for each country. Some poorer countries, as suggested above, have done very well with oil; others have had some product which did not go down so much in price; and still others expanded output enough to offset the price changes. Incidentally, if you want to lie with statistics on this point, be sure to pick as a base year the highest possible prices for your raw materials and agricultural products—this means that when declines occur, they will be sharp. A good base is 1951, since this was during the Korean War, when many raw-materials prices reached an all-time peak. A similar good year for American agriculture was 1914, so parity prices used to be computed with this year as a base. Incidentally, the synthetic revolution hasn't helped. Already it is possible to use synthetic rubber to the exclusion of natural (although we don't); various sugar substitutes make cane growers nervous; and quinine is sometimes replaced with synthetics. If prices go too high for too long, it is quite possible that we may see synthetic coffee, tea, and maybe even bananas. Wool and cotton growers have already felt tough competition from synthetic fibers.

Richer countries have some of the same problems right at home. The United States and Western Europe both produce wool; cotton is a major product in North America; wheat is grown in both rich and poor countries; and sugar is produced from northern beets as well as southern cane. Even in the more affluent countries discussions of what to do about prices in such industries inevitably get involved in various domestic political considerations.

Doing Something About It

As one who has lived in the United States or almost any
European country might suspect, suggestions for improving
the poor country's lot usually take the line of price supports
(this time, on a world scale), plus some sort of output restrictions. If you hold the price above the market clearing price,
there will be surpluses; hence someone will have to figure
out what to do about these. Since in dealing with poorer
countries and their markets we get involved with from ten
to fifty countries, each with strong ideas about what should
be done, it is not easy to reach agreement on the best policy,
though some agreements have been reached. The United
States, partially for domestic reasons, has long controlled
both price and output of sugar, in cane and beet form; it has
also agreed to restrict coffee imports (along with many European countries) and to pay higher prices for the coffee it
does import; and from time to time it has participated in
various international wheat agreements, though usually as an
exporter. In all cases, the idea is to give farmers a better
break—they get higher prices, and the consumer pays the
bill.

As you sip your next cup of 15- or 20-cent coffee, you
might reflect that the coffee is priced above the market because of our coffee agreement; the sugar is twice the world
price because of our sugar production and import policies,
both at home and abroad; and the cream is also way over-
priced because we try to protect domestic dairy farmers. You
are doing more for development than you thought—unless,
of course, you use some synthetic sweetener and synthetic
cream. Wait five or ten years—if the coffee price stays as
high as it is, you may be able to have synthetic coffee as well.
The gainers from such policies, if they work, are the poor
countries that can get the higher prices—the losers are the

consumers. This is typical all around the world—one major
American export has been its domestic farm policy.

It is true that such international price-and-output fixing
agreements have a bad habit of coming unstuck. Prices are
artificially high; countries not in the game are attracted to it,
and they may try to break into major markets by cutting
prices. Surpluses do accumulate and a poor country desperate for foreign exchange may well dump some of these at
lower prices to earn more hard currency. And of course, in
any game where a piece of paper is worth money con men
quickly climb on the gravy train (here, as one example, an
American coffee importer, who is allowed to import only
specific amounts at specific prices). If you are interested in
lucrative illegal activities, you might examine the import
control system for both sugar and coffee with great interest
—having the right piece of paper might give you a six-figure
income every year for the time and expense of obtaining the
right documents alone. Others do it—why not you?

So world history shows a long, sad story of international
agreements coming apart, of recriminations, or efforts to put
together the next agreement. The world coffee agreement
has worked better than most because it has included the consuming countries as a key control system. The United States,
under this agreement, polices imports and does not allow too
much coffee in. Note that if this country, which is by far the
largest importer, did not cooperate, and tried to buy from
the lowest-priced source among the forty producing countries, then the whole thing would collapse. By in effect accepting higher prices for its consumers, the United States
makes the agreement work.

Another thing that has been happening in a major way in
agriculture is sharp productivity increases. This has forced
people off the land all over the world, as I noted earlier; it
also has minimized some of the impact of lower prices. If
prices drop by 10 percent, and if you can produce 20 percent
more with the same labor and equipment, you're better off.
This has eased the price problem a bit, but it decidedly has

not eased the question of what to do with the released labor.

The countries involved in all of this may have very little in common—indeed, they may hate each other's guts. Both Pakistan and India produce jute—if either could get the other, their citizens would celebrate in the streets. Cuba, the Philippines, and the Dominican Republic are all cane-sugar producers; they have little in common except poverty and their export crop. And the coolness (to put it mildly) which various countries have for others does not lead to mutual assistance and cooperation in getting world price-fixing agreements; this particular problem is not likely to get any better.

This issue really led to economic-development thinking in the 1930s. Latin American countries, which were having grave economic difficulties at the time because of their one-crop economic position, began to consider alternatives to what they were doing. Such considerations led to ideas about industrialization, import substitution, and shifts away from the one-crop system. We've been arguing about such ideas ever since. Such thinking also led to similar ideas in the United States about the same time, and they are still with us. Almost any issue of *Business Week* or *Fortune* has ads about the industrial opportunities in the southern states; and notions of cheap and disciplined labor, along with power supplies and eager towns, abound. And if black Americans ever manage to set up their independent states, either in town or out in the country some place, you will see the same kinds of ads for the same reasons. The new states will probably be one-crop economies, and they will need to diversify. But instead of being able to call on the general taxpayer to do the job, they will be stuck with the problem themselves, and so, the ads will run—and probably they will work about as badly as they work elsewhere in the world, for the same reasons.

In considering options, poor countries have roughly the following possibilities to choose from:

First, they can go open or closed. As we discussed, for most smaller countries, some sort of openness is about the only choice they have, but big ones can go either way.

Second, the country can decide to live with one crop or to diversify. Diversification is usually chosen, simply because the one crop, be it oil, cotton, or bananas, does not use up all the available labor. If diversification is chosen, the options become those of inviting in foreigners (to take advantage of cheap labor, and possibly to orient output to export markets), or to produce for local consumption. This latter course involves import substitution—a country merely tries to produce the things it imports, beginning with the simple ones.

Import substitution usually works out badly, in part because the local manufacturer is in a position to give everyone trouble. He gets a high tariff and often import-quota protection to begin with—which is necessary to get him in the business. The usual result is that prices for the product are now higher than they were before, so consumers get taken. A nice example from long ago (1946) was the Australian manufacturer who managed to get tariffs on shock absorbers up to the point where one which used to cost $8 delivered could only be imported, duty paid, for $28. Then he manufactured them as a monopolist in the country and sold them to General Motors of Australia for $26. GM of course passed on the added cost to Australian buyers. It's a nice racket, which rarely gets much development done, but it's fun and dramatic, particularly in countries where there isn't much industrialization. Nevertheless import substitution begins to get people doing something besides being in the one export industry. Even if the products are expensive and the industrialization is badly done, it might be better than nothing.

The third major course a country can take is to try to develop light, labor-intensive industries using its major asset—cheap labor. Here the problem is to find new foreign markets for such things as textiles, toys, and similar products. The domestic market is quickly saturated, so exports are needed. And the major export markets are in the affluent countries. But the affluent countries have their own problems in these industries. Such things as textiles were the first major industries in most countries, including the United States, and they often, in high-wage countries, are most vulnerable to both foreign and domestic competition. They also tend to be rather far down on the productivity scale—an American worker in textiles generates from $4,200 to $5,000 of value added per year, depending on what part of the business he's in, whereas a computer or machine-tool worker produces from $12,000 to $17,000 of value added per year. This, incidentally, is why people in computers and machine tools are very well paid, while textile workers worry about minimum wages. They just don't produce enough. If imports come in from low-wage-cost countries, the guy who loses his job is not going to be a computer programmer, but rather, a textile worker—and he can vote too. The usual result is high protection for inefficient industries and great difficulty in poorer countries cracking markets in richer ones. Western Europe has exactly the same problem as the United States along these lines, so potential markets there are also severely restricted.

Poorer countries have pushed hard at the United Nations for lower tariffs and trade restrictions in such labor-intensive industries. Here is a real split—the wealthier countries, keenly aware of their domestic problems, are very reluctant to allow importation of such stuff; the poorer countries, in the majority and anxious to find new alternatives to their present one- or two-crop status, keep insisting on open trade. The results to date are not too encouraging for the poorer countries—in 1971, the United States imposed still tougher import-quota rules for textiles, and it is not alone among the affluent. The 10 percent import surcharge imposed in 1971 did not help either. If the wealthier countries finally agree to cooperate, this push to labor-intensive, light-industrial output for sale in the West will pay off—but so far, the poorer countries have run into major problems in getting markets.

The real money seems to be in the brain industries—high-technology things like computers, advanced machinery, and even education. But no poor country can realistically consider this option, considering the state of its human resources. So the realistic options involve worrying about how to use masses of cheap, unskilled labor. This is about all the poor countries have. And of course the options also involve getting poor labor to work better—which inevitably involves culture-busting on a major scale. So, back we go to the basic theme. There's no other way to increase your income.

The final possible option is to live with one's one-crop status. Oil states can do this, since their incomes are high, but even here they have problems in figuring out what to do with labor. Other countries have to do something. Once again, light industries and diversified local agricultural development (e.g., truck gardening) seem likely options. Other countries with crops or minerals sold in price-fluctuating markets have to take the risk that they can somehow win in a volatile game—and most, seeing how the game goes, try to work out other options.

When hard-working farmers in South Dakota, North Dakota, Kansas, and Nebraska couldn't make it they left—way off, to California or the East. Even price supports and other agricultural subsidies couldn't keep them down on the farm. The same thing is happening in poorer countries—the peasants are leaving the farm, moving on to better places. But there is no California to go to, where even a peon's income, or an unemployment check, would represent wealth beyond the wildest dreams of an affluent citizen of the third world. They go to a city, one of those inside-out places mentioned earlier, where a family can squat and maybe hope while planners and government leaders ponder their slender options to get something better going for their people. Unless the country is very lucky, there is little help available from abroad, and the help that comes always seems too little and too late. The country has to do it the hard way, on its own, and it has very thin margins to risk. If it is wrong, people could starve. Every option involves changing people around, often in the most brutal ways. Shoving an ignorant peasant off his farm into a textile mill may not be our idea of improvement, but, as usual, what else do you do? In the end, the people change, for better or worse, because no country can afford to do otherwise.

· ·

CHAPTER XII

Expropriation

Sometimes it seems that poor countries are every day grabbing American-owned assets in their countries. Actually, cases of expropriation, as compared to total American investment abroad, are rather rare, though each case makes headlines. The usual pattern is that a nationalistic or hypernationalistic government, under lots of pressure at home, finally bites the bullet and takes over some large American-owned concession, such as an oil field, a copper mine, or some banks. The American press headlines the situation; the State Department is concerned; and the local citizens jubilant. Finally, the American tiger has been tamed! Senators darkly hint that the Hickenlooper Amendment, which provides that no foreign assistance be given countries that nationalize without compensation, be invoked (it rarely is). The company concerned counts its losses and tries to determine what kinds of negotiations are possible to salvage something from the wreckage. Editorials in the United States suggest that communist thinking and power has advanced yet one more step. Expropriation is a real gut-issue conflict. The foreign firm, and certainly the United States, will lose, while the poor country will win, because it now has grabbed the key

assets in the country. Everything is black and white, and as
one might expect, the locals are satisfied. Their incomes will
rise, they will get the good jobs, and their country will be
wealthier and more influential in the world economic and
power league. There is no question that the West, or the
United States, has lost again.

Or has it? Clearly the American firm whose assets are gone
has lost—unless it can get the money back through the government insurance program against expropriation (if it has
had the wisdom to pay the premiums and take out a policy).
It clearly loses all future income which it might have gained,
which can be substantial when the asset grabbed is something like Standard of New Jersey's Peruvian oil operation,
or Anaconda's Chilean copper mines. But has the United
States lost much? Let's see.

All affluent Western countries, including especially Japan,
need a variety of raw materials and foodstuffs from the poor
countries. Indeed, the classic pattern of trade between the regions is a flow of raw materials from the poor, to pay for the
return flow of industrial goods and consumer items from the
West. Unlike the earlier images of neo-colonial exploitation,
there is less money there than in trade between the affluent
countries—if you want to sell someone something, it is better that he have a big income to be able to buy more. Hence
trade between European nations, the United States and Europe, and Japan and the United States, is many times larger
than trade between any affluent country and any poor one.

Raw materials and agricultural products are emotional
items. Land ownership in agriculture is a hot issue everywhere in the poor countries, and much land reform has already occurred. The idea of rich foreigners owning huge estates rankles many local citizens, so much expropriation has
occurred here, directed largely at ex-colonials, such as Great
Britain and France. Since there are not too many really big
estates left, this issue rarely makes headlines.

Minerals, particularly oil, are not only a rich source of foreign exchange, but the companies are often foreign. More-

over, these are depleting assets. When they are gone, there will be no more. These factors lead to quite emotional feelings about foreign companies, and fuel is added to the fire when local citizens observe that the well-paying good jobs are also held by foreigners. Hence, demands for expropriation are frequent (every day in most countries). Since the affluent West clearly needs the raw materials, and since they are clearly exploiters, and since local citizens can clearly do the job themselves, why not?

Factories rarely get involved in expropriation, perhaps because they are not so visible. Their contribution to skills and knowledge may also be persuasive. Anyone can pump oil out of the ground (or so it seems), but not everyone can manufacture things in mysterious factories. Moreover, factories are more often than not a piece of the whole. If you grab a Ford plant, you may find that all you have is an assembly facility with the ability to make a few of the thousands of parts you need to get a complete car or truck. The idea of having an empty factory with no jobs or output is not too appealing even to the most diehard radicals.

When Western-owned facilities are in place in poor countries, there is a tendency to try to get the highest possible price for the product. Governments of affluent countries, well aware of the contributions to foreign-exchange earnings, security, and so on, are likely to agree. There is a long history of cartels, price fixing, and efforts to restrict competition in such situations, and of course the Western consumer eventually pays the bill. The world still has a tin cartel, and the international oil companies are not exactly like the models of pure competition used by economists.

Some countries who are not in the business of producing oil, such as Japan, Brazil, and India, get upset by all this. The fact that they have to pay the high prices rankles, since their companies are not producing in other poor countries. Moreover, the poor countries themselves have formed their own producers' cartel (OPEC) to get prices up still higher. The United States, France, and Great Britain may object, but after all, if the higher prices are finally achieved, companies from these countries will share the gains. If Japan and India get screwed, well, that's life. And if American and English consumers pay somewhat higher prices, at least the companies can pass back the gains in the form of taxes, prestige, power, or whatever.

It is not too surprising that the United States will try to keep the proper regime in power in countries where large mineral assets are exploited by American firms. If the leaders want guns, technical assistance, or maybe foreign aid, our government is happy to oblige. After all, the commies may take over if such support is not forthcoming. And if the country is rich enough to do it on its own (Kuwait or Saudi Arabia), then military missions and salesmen will be encouraged. Another thing which American firms and their employees do for many a poor country is to catch flak. That is, something is always going wrong, and usually badly wrong, in a poor country. It is very handy to have on hand a big multinational American firm, which can conveniently be blamed for everything. One even suspects that some perceptive American firms hire professional flak-catchers for this purpose. These fellows are the type who can stay calm no matter what is being said to them, on any subject. They smile, nod, and subtly take the blame. After the storm blows over, and the papers and other media have had their fun, the company goes on producing and exporting, the radicals feel better, the government may get off an embarrassing hook, and everything works out in the end. This sort of flak-catching can divert local radicals and reformers from very real problems, such as raising local incomes, problems of maldistribution of income (the rich get too much by far), health issues, educational problems, and lots of things which merit close attention. If they are spending all their time fighting the detested Americans, the local elites can literally get away with murder—and sometimes do.

So, We Get Expropriated

Sometimes the radicals win. They may actually get elected, as in Chile; they may take over in a revolution, as in Cuba; or the local radical military may pull off a coup, as in Peru. In any case, the reformers are in power, and after a while, the American firms are grabbed. The grabbing may be total, as in Cuba, or highly selective as in Peru, Chile, and Bolivia. In any case, the poor country has a nationalized oil company, copper producer, or what not to operate. What happens?

Not much, as far as the Americans are concerned, particularly if the expropriations are selective. Selective expropriation is a good tactic, since most thoughtful Americans are afraid that too much pressure will lead to still more expropriation, or maybe a communist takeover. Maybe the latest arms deal is postponed, or perhaps a small piece of foreign aid is cut back, but not much else. Of course the communist nations are jubilant—American imperialism has been defeated once again! But the Soviets and the Red Chinese do not offer much tangible aid—they have learned the hard way that it doesn't do too much good, and it can cost a lot. Better to give moral support instead.

The poor country is left with some new problems to face. The American managers and technicians go home, but, contrary to popular American opinion, the locals can usually produce the oil or copper. There are short-run problems, since things have to be sorted out and new men have to become accustomed to their jobs, but output flows. To whom? Oil has to be refined; sugar must be sold in world markets; copper is merely one raw material among many for firms who further process it and create much higher values. Often, particularly in oil, the key to profit is in refining and marketing, not in production. In sugar, the country of course loses its preferential American market, where tight quotas

and very high prices prevail. In copper, the country has to
sell as best it can in a competitive world market.

If the expropriation is selective, the country also has real
problems in attracting new capital from abroad to invest in
other sectors. Which foreign companies want to invest in a
country where something has just been grabbed by the government? If foreign capital investment has been important
(as it was in Chile and Peru), then new guarantees and
bounties will have to be made to attract nervous foreigners
—and often they are not reassured. Hence foreign-exchange
supplies from this investment source go down, and the country has to find new sources to replace them, or suffer a drop
in living standards. Remember, a poor country has to import
innumerable critical manufactured goods from the West,
and they have to pay in hard currencies.

Meanwhile, countries like Japan and India, sensing a kill,
move in. They will be happy to buy the goods—perhaps at a
significant discount. The poor country may well face some
real legal problems in selling in Western Europe or the
United States, since anything shipped there will be legally
seized to pay for assets grabbed. For this reason such an offer
might prove very tempting. A deal is made—but somehow,
the price is lower, and the foreign-exchange earnings are less,
even if the profits which used to belong to the American
firms are included. India is a poor country too and has its
own problems. Why should it support another poor country
which may well be richer than India?

Another problem, never mentioned in the dialectic on this
subject, is that the American flak-catchers are gone. Instead
of blaming the evil Americans for everything, local citizens
are responsible now that the country owns the asset. If workers get too little, it is not imperialistic exploitation anymore,
but rather, local socialist exploitation. If there are legitimate
(or for that matter, illegitimate) grievances, then the government stands responsible. The whipping boy is gone, replaced by long and tangled infights between local factions in
the government and out of it. Poor countries have great

difficulties running large, complex organizations efficiently. Moreover, instead of a private, profit-seeking organization, they now have a public, socialistic one, whose goal system may be obscure. Instead of just making money, the firm is also supposed to provide jobs for the needy (including endless political hacks); it is supposed to give the country the benefits the hated Americans did not, such as more education, more housing, more medical care, more income, and more of everything. It is easier to yield to political pressures and put an extra thousand men on the payroll at good wages than to resist and use the money for general purposes; it is easier to build a new air-conditioned office building for the clerks than to use it for rural housing; and it is easier to spend cash for worker education than for plant and equipment. The end result is that costs go up, and often they go up a lot. The people who get the extra income try to spend it, but foreign exchange, you see, is tight—so some more price inflation may well occur.

About the time that all of this has happened, the somewhat concerned government, facing shortages of foreign exchange, lower prices on world markets, and lots of clever bargaining from Japan and others, decides to approach the Soviets to see what can be done. Unfortunately the Russians have got smart. They were mousetrapped into Cuba, which costs them $300 million a year. Sure, they will send some obsolescent jet airplanes and burp guns, and maybe even a few piddling factories that the country doesn't really want anyhow, but they will not provide the critical Western foreign exchange, the consumer goods needed to keep the peasants from getting restless, or anything else which might entrap them in the country's problems. In short, lots of talk, but not much action.

Meanwhile, the Americans and West Europeans are beginning to play another game too. They may well buy the raw materials, but now, since none of their firms is involved, they push for the best price and terms. And they can try to force the country by playing it off against another—and they

succeed. If optional supplies are available from more tracta-
ble poor countries which still permit American or European
firms to operate, why reward your enemies? And of course
the other capital flows for other purposes tend to decline
even more, as official government policy makes it clear that
such investments are not really the best thing to do.

A further problem the poor country discovers is that oilfields, mines, and often plantations are not very labor intensive. They require massive investments (which the country
grabbed), plus a little high-skill labor. The masses, underemployed, want those juicy jobs—and again the pressure
mounts. As one example, a work force of about 20,000 provides over a billion dollars of Saudi Arabian income (and
they still give 40 percent or so to their Western company).
Hiring lots more people in such a situation may relieve political pressures, but it won't raise output—to do that you
have to invest hundreds of millions more in drilling, pipelines, gas-injection facilities, and all the rest. Who provides
it? The Americans won't; the West Europeans are very dubious; and the Soviets can't. So the system stagnates. After
ten years or so, the country is in deep trouble, and is frantically casting about to solve lagging output, shortages of exchange, lack of new investment, and all the rest. Look at
Cuba: it's had enough time now to go through the whole
cycle. After almost fifteen years of revolution, incomes are no
more per capita than they were in 1958. Perhaps better distributed, but no more, and half a million Cubans have emi-
grated to make the situation as good as it is. And that $300
million per year subsidy from the Soviets is also ominous—
suppose they bailed out? Other countries are not likely to be
lucky enough to latch on to the Soviet aid program.

So the poor country stumbles on. Instead of reform and
sharp improvement in incomes, at best it can look forward
to moderate gains, which it would have received anyhow. Instead of jobs for all, it finds that the capital-intensive mines
and oilfields can only use the very scarce highly trained technicians and managers. Instead of vast new markets, it finds
them constricted, and buyers more willing to bargain hard

and regardless of consequences. Instead of receiving military aid and other support from the United States, it finds that it has to develop new sources of supply. Instead of more foreign exchange, it has less. On the other hand, the country does have more prestige, independence, and the feeling of running its own show. You can't eat it, or use it to impress your neighbors, but maybe it's worth it. All the problems the country had before—lack of education, the wrong attitudes toward work and achievement; the poor social overhead capital facilities; the one crop economy; the extreme dependence on imports from the rich countries—are still there, only now the country has to figure out how to outpsych the Soviets or Red Chinese, or do it themselves the hard way, on their own.

Few people can add in highly emotional situations. A poor worker, seeing the $100 million of profits flowing out of the country to the foreign firm, may well conclude that if his country could only get that cash, his life would be much, much better. But $100 million a year may well be only $10 or $20 per capita—and a man with an income of only $200 can spend that in a night. And after he has a drink, gets his transistor radio, and maybe a dress for his wife, he's right back where he was. Next year, when the $100 million mysteriously shrinks to $50 million, he may well be worse off than he was in the one golden year. Unless the country can figure out how to compound the $100 million, the one- or two-year shot won't do. Castro found this out the hard way, and lots of other poor countries have pondered his experience.

For the true revolutionary, all of this is irrelevant. Power and prestige is the name of the game. If the peasants stay poor, what the hell—it's more important to have form than substance. So the game goes on. And to give the devil his due, the revolutionaries may even equalize a bit the available education, health care, housing, and all the rest. People will still be dirt poor, but at least they can have the satisfaction of knowing that they are all in the same boat—the filthy rich are dead or departed. Maybe this is worth something.

CHAPTER **XIII**

. . . .

Private Business and Development

Visiting the headquarters of an American-based multinational corporation in a less-developed country is like moving into another world. One moment you're out on a hot street, swarming with flies, kids, beggars in rags, vendors, beat-up taxicabs, and dirt; the next you're in the quiet, clean, air-conditioned office building, with its calm atmosphere of workmanlike efficiency, attractive secretaries, and images of progress and wealth. It's almost impossible not to think about what's just outside the door. "If only the whole country ran like this," you ponder, "what a difference it could make!"

The biggest wealth generator in international affairs since World War II has been the large American multinational corporation. Over $80 billion have been invested in foreign countries by over 2,500 companies, and any firm which is active only in the United States these days is seen by sharp managers as retarded. The real action is out there, in foreign countries growing faster than the United States. Naturally, most of these investments are in Western Europe, a continent not exactly seen as poor by most observers. The bulk of the rest is in extractive investment wherever the materials are. Places no one knows about, such as Saudi Arabia, Kuwait, Liberia, Abu Dhabi, Qatar, and Libya are the fastest-growing countries in the world because of oil and iron ore, extracted by American (and sometimes English, Dutch, or French) firms out to make a fast buck. The usual rules of the extractive game in the postwar world are that the firm shares its profits with the host government. If the raw materials are really good, local incomes can take off spectacularly. But oil is where you find it, and lots of poor countries don't have much. It is rare for big firms to invest in manufacturing or marketing in a poor country—incomes are very low, so markets are small, and skilled personnel are very hard to find. Political instability and lots of foreign-exchange controls also discourage investment. Hypernationalistic sentiments don't help either—every month or so it seems that some poor country is taking over foreign investments. Actually, it's not all that bad, but why bother with a poor market when juicy opportunities beckon in Western Europe, Australia, or Canada?

All of this activity by private firms is for profit, and the companies are very good at making it. They have the skills, manpower, and talent to get the job done. They are so good, in fact, that they are not only the most productive organizations around, but also the most admired, hated, feared, and observed groups anywhere. Even Marxist countries pay a lot of attention to them, trying to find out what the magic is. Why is it that a private, for-profit group, aimed only at a limited range of production of goods and services, can make any publicly oriented, socially active organization look sick? What have they got that others do not have?

American criticism of private, profit-making firms is vociferous. If you're so smart, why not solve traffic congestion problems, poverty, racial discrimination, and all the rest of the social ills we have, rather than design a better electric toothbrush, or a new car that no one really wants? Why not save the world with the talent you have, instead of being antisocial? Ralph Nader is presently the most vigorous critic, but down through the years there have been many, many others. Yet, when the chips are down, most countries tolerate such firms, because no one can really present a good alternative. Yet the question persists. If we can be so demonstrably good in our private sectors, why not utilize all this talent to do something useful in a more general social sense?

Examination of very successful private men in public life does not bring much comfort. Too many brilliant and gifted managers eventually get to Washington—and too often they fall flat on their faces. Somehow, running a complex government bureaucracy is not quite the same thing as running a complex private bureaucracy, even though the people are about the same, the problems seem identical, and the man clearly has not changed. It is even possible that most government agencies have superior personnel to private firms, particularly in poor countries, where a civil-service career is highly prized and relatively well paid. But the performance is not there. How come?

American firms abroad, if anything, get far more static in the poorer countries than they get at home. Local critics focus on the enormous profits being sent home, and forget the equally enormous benefits accruing to local government. Writers spend much time noting that all the really good jobs belong to Americans, forgetting that any jobs which exist are there only because the firm is there. Firms are violently criticized for failing to believe in whatever local theologies happen to be important at the moment, from Marxism to Islam. If one baby lacks milk, somehow the foreign firm is responsible. All that wealth should be used for more social purposes than whatever it is being used for.

An unstated criticism often arises as well. This is the absolute inferiority of the local culture compared to the American. The Americans cannot only afford the usual amenities of cars, good air-conditioned houses, the best health care and nutrition for the kids, and all the rest, but they have a bad habit of gently or not so gently reminding their hosts of this superiority all the time. Even being there is a reminder that somehow something is wrong. If your local gods are so good, why don't they provide as well as the American gods seem to? It's a tough life being poor, and few of us will ever admit that it just might be our fault. Better to blame the devil foreigners, to demand more, to suggest darkly that some international cartel is screwing us all in ways we cannot quite understand. But the image of enormous competence lingers. The firms are so good. No question about it. Now, why can't they get to work and fix up the world everywhere?

As a matter of fact, the private, profit-oriented firm can never do this job. Moreover, hiring away all their most talented people won't work either—the problem is deeper than just individual or collective competence. And the reasons why this point is true are the most overlooked and important of all.

The Efficient Private and the Inefficient Public

Private, profit-seeking organizations have very simple goal systems. Public agencies have very complicated, relatively undefined, multiple goal systems, where some goals are mutually inconsistent with others—and that is why they get paralyzed, while the private sector remains efficient. Most people, including me and possibly you, have much more fun with process than with overall goals—which is why it's so difficult to find people who can manage really complex large organizations.

Private organizations, like public ones, have one overriding goal, which is to survive. Many scholars and observers have noted that almost never does any organization of any sort voluntarily commit suicide. After the first few organizing years, the thing acquires a life of its own, and efforts to dismantle it will be fought to the death. Too many people have their economic, social, and political interests too intimately bound into the organization to have it disappear without a fight. But private organizations have to survive by making money. If they don't, they do disappear. Hence the profit motive becomes goal number one. If you don't make at least some money through time, you're dead.

As I have suggested, profit is an interesting concept, because most people see it in its insignificant aspect, which is as an income share. The important thing it does is tell a manager what to do. He does whatever yields profits through time. To do otherwise is suicide. Moreover, profits give managers orders of priorities. If the new petrochemical plant in New Jersey yields 8 percent, while the marketing-system investment in Japan yields 12, it is clear which comes first. And because firms are constantly investing in the high-pay-off things, they tend to be highly productive. Profits also lead to managerial discipline. One of the hardest things for a young manager to learn is that every possible profitable project is not done—simply because some are more profitable than others. After you cream the good ones, then on to the not so good ones, but not before. The results typically (for well-managed firms) are familiar—high profits, incredible technical competence, and sometimes apparently antisocial activities.

Consider the poor public manager, equally intelligent, but faced with multiple goal systems which are always ill defined. One goal is to keep costs down; another is to keep workers well paid and satisfied, along with having all the social amenities, such as health and dental care. The organization's goals are inconsistent—if you lower costs, you minimize wages. Which do you want? The usual answer—some of each—doesn't solve the problem. In poor countries, it is common to find that major goals of state-owned firms are to maximize employment and make some money. But if a quarter of the country's work force is unemployed, so that getting them all working would lead to staggering losses, which one do you want? Any competent public administrator learns very fast that he never takes a position on such an issue, if he expects to remain in his job. There are too many political enemies on any side. So he stays in the middle—which is to say that the issue never quite gets resolved.

One curious aspect of this particular problem is that profit-seeking firms are typically much better to work for as an employee than a public one. The private firm pays as little as it can—but its managers know full well that talented and productive people are scarce, so as little as it can is often quite high. Its managers know that if good men need social benefits, it is wise to supply them. But in the blundering public system, with its battalions of incompetents, it is more difficult for the good people to get what they want. So they find other options.

It is common in public organizations everywhere to find all sorts of weird things going on in the name of progress, decency, and humanity. Pushed far enough, there is no output at all, because everyone is so busy trying to achieve goals which have nothing to do with output. Process is everything, because in process one can find fulfillment, happiness, and the good life. But in the end, someone pays the bill. So if public organizations somehow cannot get the job done, then let's get our private sector to do the job—and we're back to square one.

Large private firms have caused one major problem for the whole world—they do their various jobs so effortlessly (or so it seems) that most countries and individuals who worry about how to get jobs done think that it is easy to set up a big organization, usually in the public sector, to do the job. But there are in the whole world perhaps only a thousand or so big (e.g., over 10,000 persons) organizations which are *efficient*. The goal-system business is one reason why. It is easy to think at the planning stage that a big organization can do things—but normally, public organizations cannot set up meaningful goal systems which make any sense, so they are doomed before they start. Many Americans wonder why billions of dollars and tens of thousands of very competent people cannot somehow resolve poverty problems. The fault lies here. The organizations simply cannot decide what is important, and hence everything is. Lacking a meaningful goal system and order of priorities, they wallow in problems without much being done. It's the same in poor countries.

There are some other reasons why large private organizations cannot work too well in poor countries. They are as follows:

Such organizations are highly selective of their personnel. No one has to work for them; the company doesn't normally have to hire anyone it doesn't want. If someone doesn't fit into the system for any reason, he is out. In modern democratic, egalitarian thinking, this is all wrong—it is better to get everyone in. It is no accident that many poor countries have laws and other pressures designed not only to force foreign firms to hire local citizens, but also to keep them employed no matter what they do. Insofar as such laws and pressures are successful, the firm finds it just that much more difficult to get its specific, narrow job done. Organizations which are nonselective, such as public-school systems, have all sorts of problems meeting objectives. The discipline of being able to require performance of participants disappears.

Now this point is fascistic, un-American, antiegalitarian, and all that, but if you want something done, e.g., creating an efficient producer of goods and services, then you must turn to the selective organization with precise goals. Not only will the organization know exactly what it is supposed to do, but it will be able to select exactly the right kinds of people to do it. Life is like this, however much we would like it to be otherwise.

Furthermore, really large organizations (of over 10,000 workers and managers) only work under rather specific conditions, most of which are not present in poorer countries. The need for clear-cut goals has been mentioned, but as important is the need to have the ability and the opportunity to select the best person for any job. If a culture has an extended family system, where family members are more important than outsiders, it is very likely that someone's cousin gets the next job rather than the most qualified person. This happens once in a while in any company, but if it happens always, then trouble is certain.

It is common in poor countries to find that there is little social insurance, poor or nonexistent old-age pensions, and little health care available. The cultural pattern has historically been tribal, so the modern pattern tends to be extended family. Every family member has primary responsibility to the rest of his family, not to the broader society. When such a person achieves power, his personnel choices for vacancies are very clear. Western countries, with somewhat different ideas about family responsibility and broader social programs of support for the less fortunate, tend to think in quite different terms.

The old phrase, "From shirtsleeves to shirtsleeves in three generations," reflects this family pattern in the West for the family-owned firm. There are a few big family-controlled firms still around, but most of them have drifted into obscurity or failure, as families, no matter how brilliant and capable, proved unable to generate talent for endless generations to man really big companies. And even where the family still is in power (e.g., at Ford), most of the managerial and technical talent is selected in the modern way. Poor countries have great difficulties on this point, even with publicly owned firms. It seems obscene and antisocial to many people *not* to hire the family, because that's what the game is all about!

Related to the above point is the need to hire and promote people on a competence basis. The best man, however defined, gets the job. Meritocracy is the criterion and the norm. In underdeveloped countries two problems come up here. One is that the best man may adhere to the wrong religion, caste, or social group—and poor countries, all protestation apart, are hotbeds of religious, racial, and tribal intolerance. The second is that it is so very difficult to define "best" for a big company, where new roles may be so unfamiliar that no one really knows what the guy should be doing. American firms with generations of experience often miss on this point; it is not surprising that new corporations in poor countries make plenty of mistakes, even when they try to do the right things. What should a production manager be and know? Only a handful of experts could even set criteria, let alone pick the right man for the next ten years, and so errors are common. Even American firms in poor, unfamiliar countries are misled here. They may not know enough about local conditions to get the right man pegged for the right slot, particularly if he is a local citizen, with all the biases, advantages, and obscurities such a fact may present. Too many errors about who is best, and the firm is in deep trouble.

It is helpful to any firm to have lots of hard-driving, high-achievement-oriented people around. If talented people try hard, it is easy to select and train a good crew. But the up-tight, Calvinist type who happily works his eighty-hour week is not all that common around the world, and American managers constantly complain that foreigners don't work as hard as they should. This has been a complaint about the poor for about as long as man has been around, since the poor normally do not get too excited about working hard for nothing. Moreover, it is very common to find that the poor are sick most of the time, and their normal vitality is hampered. Still, if the dominant cultural theme is leisure, reflection, and the finer things of life, and not getting some dreary production or marketing job done, the company will be in trouble.

There is much folklore on this point. The image of the driving executive, full of complexes and phobias, unable to enjoy life, is contrasted with the much superior person who knows how to live more leisurely and effectively. Few want to become the hard-driving man. But the point is simple—if the hard-driving types are not around, the firm and the society won't be as rich as it might be. There *is* a trade-off here. Of course, it also is useful to have large manpower pools of highly trained technical, managerial, and craft labor around from which to choose your work force. And the poor countries do not have this sort of personnel available. Hence the big organization must either import talent, as American firms do, or get by with something less than the best. Which is one reason why multinational firms look so good in action. A local company has to pick and choose in the local market. If some problem comes up, such as continuing poor quality of painted finishes on the product, the company may literally be unable to find anyone who can help out. So the product is poor and stays poor. The multinational firm, on the other hand, has a whole world of experts to choose from. Given the same problem, its local manager can call for help at headquarters. Within a few days, an expert from somewhere is on hand to resolve the problem. He may be American, German, English, or Brazilian, but wherever he is in the organization, he can be called upon. The usual results are lower costs, better products, and more wealth and income being generated.

Note how all of this ties together. If the expert was the son of the president who really wasn't an expert, but needed a job, problems would occur. If the firm was unable to self-select its own best men, the fellow probably could not do the job. If the poor country had sticky visa requirements for such men (an all-too-common occurrence), then he might not be able to get into the country to solve the problem. And the country would stay poor—which is what has happened for a long time.

This point also suggests another critical ability of really large, multinational organizations. To a very high degree they have developed communications and information linkages all over the world. Their financial, production, marketing, and research and development activities are organized on a global basis. The poor country's organization, being provincial, locked into a culture with poor human resources, and unaware of what is going on out in the world, finds it very difficult to compete. A seemingly minor development in Brazil may have tremendous implications for Pakistan—but the Pakistani firm may not hear about the development for twenty years. The multinational firm, operating in both places, has the innovation in place in Pakistan within a year. Such linkages are critical to rapid progress, yet it is very difficult for provincial organizations to handle the problem.

Efficient big organizations can also get rid of persons who don't fit. But firing people is always painful and often seems immoral; so far too often big organizations in poor countries don't. Because they don't, the firm loses one key disciplinary factor which does work, particularly with persons who have a great deal to learn. The concept of tenure for professors is now under attack in the United States—the same point applies to the state railroad or power company in a poor country. People just don't respond as well without pressure as they do when the heat is on.

A curious point here is that really good and successful big companies have *de facto* tenure for all but the real bums and crooks. The reason is simple—it pays to keep good people on the payroll, and there is a lot of work to be done. A man or woman may not be good enough to be president or general manager, but that does not mean that he is incompetent —there are plenty of places where a good person can be used. And the morale implications of wholesale firings for trivial reasons can wreck any company. Hence it is rarely done—the major exception being when a big firm gets into really deep financial trouble, and survival is threatened. Remember that the private firm, lacking unlimited public support, has to generate some profits or die. Public firms, lacking this discipline, not only don't fire, but often don't care if they make money. The all-too-common result is that they become an efficiency drag on the economy. And private firms normally reward people about the way they have to, to get and keep good people. If an outstanding man wants a special office or more money, he can get it—if he is really worth it. But such goings-on lead to pay inequities, which are undemocratic, so often we find that poor-country organizations have civil-service-type pay scales, with relative equity built into the system. This often means that the really good people are found elsewhere, doing their thing. Why work for half what you can get some other place? A few dedicated reformer types will do so, but the bulk of any given group will not.

And finally, private firms, particularly Western multinational ones, are growth oriented. They have to be, or they will stagnate, grow senile, and fall apart. Their managers are used to living with dynamic change—something new is coming up all the time—and managers are expected to get sales up 10 percent a year, start new product lines, cut costs, revise production facilities, open up new markets, spend money on research and development, improve the efficiency of financial planning, and all the rest. That is what the game is about, and that is why these organizations are multinational and expanding. Those people who like relative stability and the cycling of static systems can find plenty to do in quieter government offices, schools, and provincial firms.

Of course, economic growth is involved. If you don't change, your economy will stagnate. If your personnel don't shift attitudes and ideas all the time, the organization will begin to cycle. It is surprising how static most organizations in poor countries are, in these terms. The thing is set up, gets established—and fights for no more change. After all, change is unsettling, leads to personal-power base erosion, and possibly even inability of managers and administrators to hold on to their jobs. New ideas are dangerous, unless the individuals handling them can adjust very rapidly to their implications. Since many cannot, the idea of no change is attractive.

All sounds very familiar to most Americans—after all, we have been in this big-organization game for decades. But every point made above is revolutionary in any poor culture. The sophisticated citizen of any such country who really buys the above ideas is culturally isolated from his countrymen—in short, his own culture is destroyed for him, and he becomes a cross-cultural citizen. He has been brainwashed by the most revolutionary thing to come down the pike in a millennium—which is the American modern firm and its management. If you define revolution as a situation where there are large, discontinuous gaps in the evolution of human affairs, then the American manager is the revolutionary in today's world.

It's a quiet revolution, which makes it more dangerous. Personnel decisions are made quietly in big offices, not in the streets. If the best man, not your uncle, gets the job, few will know or care. If the local manager gets permission to expand his product line into new areas from the home office, no one will riot. If an unprofitable branch is cut back or closed down, few except those directly affected will care. If a quiet technician from England steps off the plane at the local airport and goes out to solve a minor but irritating technical problem, no local revolutionaries will even know about it. If a bungling idiot is released from his job by a sad manager, only the two of them and their families will get very excited. But put it all together, and it is the most revolutionary thing that has happened in a long time.

Until very recently in the West, and right up to now in the poor world, big organizations were static things, activities which changed little from year to year. We can find plenty of examples of them even now all over the world. Yet somehow those improbable, profit-oriented systems seem able to get things done! Somehow, our noble local organizations, full of good will, with nebulous yet socially desirable goals, have great difficulty in functioning at all, let alone correctly. Moreover, it all looks so easy, and the revolutionary part of it is well hidden in ideas and concepts and accounts, not in anything visible. So let's get our own organizations, with new head-office buildings full of reasonably competent people, to do the same thing. Let's copy the Western style. So it's done, but somehow the new organizations aren't quite what they should be. They are, in fact, only pale copies, in form but not in substance, of the efficient, dynamic foreign firms.

Examination of failures among the big, private firms in the West suggests the validity of these points. If you force a big organization into a model which it cannot live with, failure is probable. The Penn Central, to take one recent exam-

ple, is bounded, unlike many modern firms, by publicly pre-
scribed goals which have nothing to do with profits or
efficiency. The company was forced to keep men it didn't
want and probably couldn't use—the goal of employment
maximization was more important than profits. It was required to provide services such as running freight trains on
unprofitable branch lines and passenger trains which lost
money. The requirement was for service optimization at any
cost. And the result was inevitable. So it takes a few hundred
million dollars of public money to bail the system out.

One Penn Central can be lived with, but if every big organization needs perpetual bailing out, who pays the bills?
The productive part of the economy is taxed and its resources drained to provide support for the unproductive.
When there is not enough of the productive left, incomes
fall and growth ceases. This is a possible world—the English
in particular are very good at it—but it is not exactly a rich
world.

Now, on Saving the World

The foregoing may make clear why private firms cannot save
the world. If you want confusion, lack of development and
growth, inept and chaotic activities in your economy, it is
easy. You can do the following (as many poor countries
have):

First, set up lots of big, complex organizations with diffuse
and contradictory goals, such as: maximize employment;
maximize social welfare; maximize medical and health care
for the workers; give them good housing; and by the way,
make money. Any manager, no matter how gifted, will find
it impossible to function well with such directives, so rather
quickly the organization will become process oriented, focusing on its internal problems rather than on whatever it was
supposed to do.

Second, don't be too strict about not hiring cousins and all that. Many poor countries have some sort of civil-service law, but any capable manager can usually figure out ways to get his uncles, brothers, and cousins on the payroll. After a while, it doesn't really matter what the organization was supposed to do—it can't do it.

Third, get the organizations as big as possible, on the logical grounds that really big organizations like General Motors are the most efficient. Given the cousin problem, along with relatively unskilled personnel and diffuse and contradictory goals, the system will quickly become so bogged down that nothing much will happen.

And finally, make sure that no outsiders can compete. If your big organization is functioning about as expected, it will be rather inefficient, and many a small fly-by-night operation of one to two fellows who know the score can provide the services or goods for less money. This is a disaster, so make sure that they cannot.

The results of your efforts will be those seen in too many poor countries. Output will be very low, if there is any at all; the organization will be a drain on the economy, rather than an asset; and nothing much will be happening.

The above may also suggest why private, profit-oriented firms really cannot do much to resolve social problems. If you saddle such companies with diffuse social goals, they come apart. Their job, which they are very good at, is to maximize the production of needed goods and services. Now we have lots of pressures to convert big private firms into systems of social welfare. But unfortunately, such systems get bogged down on the goal question—that is, deciding, given always limited resources, what *is* important. If you can't decide, you are in trouble, because any activity can be justified on the grounds that someone benefits.

Big firms, particularly foreign ones, do a big service to poor countries, aside from merely generating income and wealth. The local citizens have a chance to see what is going on. That is, they can get an interesting education by watching managers and workers from abroad in action. After cen-

turies of seeing small, bungling organizations fumble to succeed, it can be useful to see how a really efficient firm gets
the job done. But far too often, the wrong conclusions are
drawn from this observation. It is more fun to contemplate
being in that air-conditioned office, with the attractive secretary, doing paperwork, than it is to think through what is
really going on—so the office is established, but the productive underlying system is not. It is more fun to contemplate
the absolute power over thousands of men than to figure out
why such power exists—so the power system is established,
but the productivity is not.

All of this leads to the suggestion that the real problem is
to avoid big thinking, big organizations, and big-time emulation in most poor countries most of the time. There are always a few things that have to be done on a grandiose scale,
such as a major electric-power generating scheme, or an inte-
grated steel mill. But given the inability of most poor countries to accept or quickly adopt the subtle social and cultural
implications of big firms, it is useful to consider options.
The small, family-owned unit is the viable one in most poor
countries, because this sort of thing meets the local cultural
and manpower situation better. If a country can do something small, it is better off. But few foreigners pay much attention to small Western firms, which typically stay home. A
shop that efficiently winds generator armatures in Indiana,
with a total work force of six, is never seen. The local office
of General Motors is. It is easy to conclude that everything
Western is GM, and thus the poor country should go that
way as fast as possible. Which just isn't so.

CHAPTER **XIV**

. . . .

Anyone Can Run Anything, Maybe

Anyone who has spent time around large organizations in various countries is aware that they operate very differently from place to place. Some are models of efficiency and productivity; others often seem not to function at all. Since productive firms get out the goods and services which in the end add up to national income, and since the affluent Western countries have the biggest incomes, it is no surprise to find that most efficient managements are Western, concentrated very highly in the thousand or so biggest American and the approximately five hundred biggest European and Japanese firms. If this sort of expertise and ability could be transferred to poor countries, then many economic problems would be solved.

Even in the affluent West, differences in firm (and presumably management) performance are high. It is common to find that an American firm operating in England can get 30 to 50 percent more output per man from its work force than an English management can. The very idea of a management gap grew up between the United States and Europe, as thoughtful Europeans, trying to figure out why the United States is somewhat wealthier than Europe, seized on the

201

quality of management as the key factor. If European management were as good as American, then Europeans might be a thousand dollars a year better off per capita than they now are.

Earlier, the idea of a technology gap was more popular. Again, Europeans observed that American firms had, or seemed to have, better technology than the Europeans, and moreover, the gap was growing. Hence the way to get ahead was to obtain more technology faster, so that European firms could catch up. This idea is still alive and kicking, but it has yielded to management-gap ideas as the key problem, since it gradually became clear that just having a lot of good technology rarely did any country or firm much good. The key is in how the technology is used—which is really a management notion. Any company who really wants to improve its technology can get help from lots of sources; there are plenty of research institutes, colleges, research centers, government laboratories, and other companies to borrow or buy from. The trouble is that so few companies take the trouble to do this, which suggests that the managers, not the technicians, are the real culprits.

Poorer countries are of course in much worse shape than Western Europe. They have many fewer big firms to get things done—indeed, in many countries, there are virtually no large local firms around to do much with either better management practices or new technology. But the idea persists that if only the country could borrow from the West, particularly the United States, then all would be well —or at least all would be somewhat better than the miserable state the country is in at present.

Management is a peculiar kind of thing. We usually know (or think we know) when management is good, but it is very difficult to define what is going on. If we are going to talk about a management gap, then presumably we can measure good and bad. That is, we could say that firm X ranks 96; firm Y, in some poor country, ranks 22. The gap is 74. The problem is that no one has ever measured management so precisely, and no one really can say for sure what is good or bad.

We mentioned earlier another emotional or behavioral fact about management which still persists. Managers are grubby, low-grade technicians; the real thinkers are economists, political scientists, sociologists, and planners. If vast new projects are to be started, the problems of getting capital, planning the new activities, and setting up the structure are important. What happens in the marketing or personnel section after the great works have been done are petty problems which can be left to low-level technicians. Modern and not-so-modern economics have always made an assumption about firms that has cost this world a lot, given that economists typically do economic planning and thinking. It is that firms are assumed to be competent. That is, their managers know all that they need to know to make good managerial decisions.

Because this assumption was made by great economic thinkers in the past, and because every modern economic thinker knows who was good, the same assumption is built into modern projects in the poor countries. It may be reasonable to assume that General Motors or IBM has a group of managers that know what to do, given a problem such as building a new plant, but it is a wild-eyed assumption to make in a country where no one has ever managed anything large, and where middle managers may well be semiliterate cousins of some important politician. When funds vanish or are wasted; when supposedly competent technicians cannot handle simple problems in production-line balancing; when product piles up and cannot be sold because no one knows how to market it; when checks bounce because financial planners cannot add or forecast correctly; when half the machinery and all the trucks in the place are down for maintenance at once, because parts men forgot to order key items —then people begin to think about management problems and talk about management gaps.

It is no accident that my business classes now are perhaps

10 to 20 percent foreign, with many diligent students coming from countries few Americans have ever heard of; it is no accident that copies of American business schools pop up like weeds all over the world; it is no accident that foreign journals are filled with discussions of how to get better managers. Nothing works right any place, and after having tried the magic of technology in the 1940s and 1950s, and found it wanting, the new magic is business management.

What Is Management?

If you walk into a store, and the clerks are surly and uninformed, this is one kind of bad management. If you see a brand-new plant, built in the wrong place at the wrong time, now unused—it is another kind of bad management. If you read that the X company just went into bankruptcy, it is still another. If a government commission chastises a public utility for having costs twice as high as a neighboring utility, it is still another. Anyone who reads the *Wall Street Journal* can find dozens of examples of bad management every day, as can anyone who needs to get his car fixed, buys some groceries, or tries to find a doctor. Even very affluent societies, with plenty of good mechanics, excellent sales clerks, and the best medicine in the world, cannot seem to get its managerial house in order. Poor countries, lacking these basic resources, do much, much worse. What's going on?

Rather curiously, although the science and practice of management has been studied for over one hundred years, there is no single definition of what management is that is generally accepted. Some scholars see it as getting things done through people; others see it as the science of making good decisions; still others feel that it is the science of getting people to work together in harmony to achieve agreed-on goals. Computer people see it as the linking up of thousands of variables in complex interacting systems to get things done. Various specialists see it as the science (or sometimes art) of marketing, production, logistics, or accounting.

Like the blind men examining the elephant, what management is depends on what your perceptions of reality and importance are.

Management is all of these things and more, and if anything doesn't get done reasonably well, then the company gets into deep trouble. Incidentally, a lot of time and energy has been spent arguing about whether firms should be publicly or privately owned, but all of these management problems are common to all productive enterprises, regardless of ownership. Just making a company public does not solve much. It merely makes problems worse, since public firms have a lot more political problems to resolve than private ones.

But we can say something about what managers do, and all of it spells trouble for poor countries and their peoples. Managers generally plan to take some inputs, like labor, machine hours, and raw materials. and process these things into outputs, like medical services, autos, furniture, and everything else. To do this, they plan what to do—that is, get objectives, organize the system to get the job done as easily and efficiently as possible, and monitor the process constantly to correct whatever deviations occur. In any complex system, such deviations will be very common.

So managers plan, organize, structure, and get feedback on results. If they are reasonably good at these things, then something useful might occur. All of this constantly takes place in a situation of scarcity—firms lack money, well-trained men, the right kinds of components and raw materials, and so on. Hence they have to be highly disciplined men, well aware of the fact that a key scarcity can break them any time. They have to take risks too—who knows if the new product will pay off in the market, or whether the new research program will work out? Who knows if the production people can really handle the new high tolerances demanded in the new engines? And they take rational risks. If the odds are good, then they may move. But if the odds look bad, then they hold off.

This process also requires immense knowledge about the

managers' business. How are toothbrushes marketed in Rio? What kinds of consumer-goods financing are needed or available in Paris? What are the common types of fire insurance available in Tanzania, if any? What is the market for blister copper in London? What kinds of ships are needed to get through the Panama Canal? Young top managers are rather rare, since it takes time, and a lot of hard work in the bowels of any company, to find out enough to be able to make judgments about what is going on.

Managers are also very abstract thinkers, particularly in large organizations. The president of General Motors will probably never even see half the plants he is managing, since he won't live long enough to get to the thousands of facilities scattered around the world. Instead, he has to deal with reports, numbers, and other abstractions. A list of figures, or a cost report, or some data about output form the basis for decisions affecting thousands of men, and maybe even entire countries. No man can know all of reality, and managers, concerned as they are with all sorts of problems, know less about it than most of us. But good managers can perform well with those numbers, that intangible and abstract information which leads them to decide what to do.

If a man can visualize and predict the thrust of the future; can evaluate feedback on what is going on; can visualize the correct structures and organizations needed to get the job done; and can somehow get thousands of other people to work well for the company—in the end, the firm is well managed and efficient. Maybe there are ten thousand such people around in the world today, and very few of them are in the poor countries unless their American firm sent them there.

It all seems so easy. Find a bright guy, give him a good education, and set him up as manager. Only much later, when the organization is coming unstuck, do people start talking about management gaps and problems of catching up with America or Europe. It is also surprising to discover how incoherent so many really good managers are about what they do. When they are asked, they mumble incantations about working hard, having good subordinates, and all the rest, but few can really say what they are doing right. It's a tough job, and damn few people can do it very well more than half the time.

Transferring Management

So now we want to transfer such management to other countries and cultures. Although the bright young men are in American business schools, it is clear that something is very wrong at home, since output is stagnant and the West is pulling away. What do we do? After all, this is a human activity, and the fellows out there in the poor countries are pretty smart. Surely we can easily transfer a few things to them and get things going right! Here we run into some real problems, which so far have proved very difficult to overcome.

The first is that if something is to be transferred, there has to be a receiver out there. And the first difficulty is that there may be very few persons able to receive such information. Semiliterates speaking and reading a language other than English may not prove very good at obtaining and using complex accounting, financial, or marketing concepts. Even translating all the material takes more people than lots of countries have.

Second, there are more books, manuals, studies, and monographs around covering business materials than any fifty countries could use in a hundred years. Exactly what should be transferred? Since no one is quite sure what is missing in the poor country, or what is important to have, the usual answer is that such transfers are random. Anything that strikes the fancy of some young man abroad might get sent home, but no one, including the Americans, is in a position to evaluate what is good or bad. The usual result is that a jumble

of useful and not-so-useful information is sent along—
with not very good results.

Third, even though the material is sent abroad, it does
not follow that anyone will use it. In any country it is common to find more unused than used materials around about
managerial and business functions. This is true in the
United States as well, incidentally. Good accounting practices, how to set up budgets, planning manuals, and all the
rest may be there, but managers don't pay much attention.

It is also true that what is dramatic and seemingly dynamic gets a lot of attention, but the solid, sedate, and even
dull aspects are ignored. Few persons, except professional accountants, will spend much time on a manual which carefully explains how to order your books into better shape,
but everyone will be excited about IBM's new computer, or
machine tools which seem very dramatic. Anyone who has
seen the ludicrous efforts of a company trying to use a big
computer without first even having some basic accounting
information, or a set of purchasing manuals on hand, or perhaps even good salesman's route books set up, can only smile
sadly and wait for disaster.

Fourth, information normally costs a lot of money, and
there always are questions about who is going to pay for it.
Who hires the translators, the professors, the instructors, the
computer programmers, the other experts who are going to
make the management transfers? The usual answer—"Someone else"—normally does not get the job done. And if
governments try to set up transfer agents at the taxpayers'
cost, the problems of what to transfer, and to whom, tend to
bog down the whole process.

Finally, the question of who has useful information keeps
coming up. The business schools are supposed to have some,
and they usually do (though few practicing managers pay
much attention). But others also have very useful information. Many well-managed companies know a lot which is useful, but they may be unwilling to let others have it for free,
or even for money. Libraries have plenty, but again someone

has to figure out what to take. Trade associations often have much useful information, but once again, the users or borrowers have to figure out what to take and what to leave alone. And since there is so much more around than anyone can use, someone has to make choices about where to use his very scarce transfer resources, which basically are well-educated, smart people who can perform this job. Since poor countries have huge shortages of exactly such people, the tendency is to hand the problem over to Americans or Europeans, with the plea to "give us what we need!"

The Receivers

Meanwhile, in the poor country, management is a mess. Nothing is getting done very well. Actually, the small family-owned firms seem to be more active and aggressive than the few big government-sponsored ones, while the foreign-owned firms, if any, are doing better than anyone—but of course *their* managers are foreigners. Local leaders and thinkers watch the foreigners and wish that they could do as well.

But too many people do not have the education, talent, or inclination to do the managerial job. Moreover, the very nature of management—namely the discipline, the ability to plan far into the future, the ability to abstract from data about reality—all of this is exactly what the poor country doesn't have. Those who acquire the ability tend to get cross-cultural very fast—that is, their own cultural fix has to be fractured before they can do it. We find these people everywhere, particularly working for foreign firms, teaching after having come back from the United States, and working here and there in the modern sector. But they number in the hundreds, where tens of thousands are needed. And since no one is anxious to tell anyone that their behavior is wrong, the necessary attributes of good managers are ignored. The same old culturally oriented fellows try to run their organizations in the same old way. And if some bright young man is around with good ideas, he is very likely to be ignored, since he represents a real power threat to the old guard. And nothing much happens.

It is also true that good receivers are change-oriented people. Why not? Their business is to find out new things and apply them to strange organizations. But once again, traditional cultures are not very strong on change—indeed, this is why they are traditional. If something is working badly, but working, why change? The manager has his power, his prestige, and his salary. Change could just break up this set. So nothing much happens. This no-change attitude is very noticeable in family-firm situations, where the little company is doing reasonably well. Why break up a good thing, even if the payoff might be very large?

What this typically adds up to is that firms in poor countries are not very good receivers of information, managerial or otherwise. They are not typically change-oriented, or at least their managers are not. The smaller firms often cannot use high-powered information, and even if they could, they may not be too interested, particularly if they are doing reasonably well. And the ones doing well are exactly the ones that we would like to get at, since these are the ones which could move ahead the fastest. The failures won't do anyone much good.

An often overlooked point is that management information is developed for the kinds of environments it is needed in. If an American scholar starts figuring out new uses for computers, he rarely worries about the possibility that there will be an absolute shortage of the kinds of specialists needed to make this management material work. If a production specialist works out new assembly-line-balancing techniques, he does not worry about such trivia as the availability of electric power or whether or not the transportation system is adequate to handle new burdens placed on it. In the United States, planners and innovators can take such things for granted.

But in the poor countries, there will be absolute shortages

of skilled labor, electric power, transportation, and all the rest. A good idea which will work beautifully in America will often cave in within days in some poor country. Since no one bothers to point out all the assumptions about the whole economy every time the production specialist notes a minor change, this point is easily overlooked. It is also true that few citizens of any poor country are willing to admit that their undereducated citizens cannot handle whatever a major country can. So this point is ignored.

The management gap is indeed a bit peculiar. Serious writers point out that such gaps exist, and in some intuitive way, most of us agree with them. But then one drifts quickly to a discussion of how to transfer some undefined thing in an undefined way to an undefined situation in some other country. It is not too surprising that not very much gets transferred, and that if anything, management gaps are bigger now than they were in the past. We don't know enough yet about the problem to nail down what we really want to do —except to note that there is a problem and something should be done.

As a matter of interest, virtually all of this discussion would apply to the American ghetto. There just aren't enough skilled managers or receivers to get the numerous jobs done, in either the public or private sector. Efforts to transfer managerial skills in from the WASP mainstream run into the same kinds of problems poor countries experience. Note also the reactions. One federal government reaction is to pretend the problem does not exist (as when they start pumping money into a Black Entrepreneurship Program. Note the reasoning—no big firms, because there is no capital. Hence, more capital leads to more big firms. It's the Marshall Plan all over again.). Another reaction is to demand the top spots even though the people who get them may not do the job. This is a common demand coming from blacks —and from lots of well-educated people in many poor countries as well. It's one major pressure for nationalization and expropriation.

If it really were true that all you need is capital, and that there are many competent people around who could manage well, but who have been cut off because of being black or being in the wrong poor country, then we would expect that such programs would work extremely well. After new ventures were set up, very quickly they would begin to produce big and efficiently, and, lo and behold, we would no longer have poverty problems. Too bad it isn't this easy.

Another reason for accepting the money/discrimination excuse is because one can always find evidence that such things are true. Ghetto-based firms (along with many in poor countries) *do* need capital; and there *are* some individuals who could manage very well but who have been cut out in some discriminatory way. So such approaches do work— but not as well as we would like. And if a country, or a federal program, operates as if these two premises of discrimination and lack of capital were absolutely true and the total solution to the problem—well, prepare for more and continuing poverty for a long, long time. It will be a long while under these operational conditions before everyone now poor gets out of poverty. Maybe two hundred years.

Unrealistic Transfers

Everyone is impatient in this business—it sometimes sounds as though the solution should be to give every poor country a Ford Motor Company or Xerox Corp. by next Monday morning. When such transfers do not occur, some conclude that evil men are deliberately blocking the transfer of wealth to the poor country. After all, those Xerox fellows just sit around and think—what's so hard about that? But such transfers of large, complex, and efficient organizations take years, decades, or even half centuries—they do not occur because someone thinks that it is a good idea. Such organizations mesh well with their American environment— the facilities, education, training, and cultural attitudes toward change are there already. So, the big complex organization works pretty well.

Everyone knows about Xerox, but no one knows or cares about the small operations in the United States. There is nothing very glamorous about that armature-winding operation in Indianapolis, employing six fellows, or a little ad agency with an owner and his secretary getting something done. Who cares? What is important is the drama and excitement of the big companies, powerful, affluent, efficient —and capable of changing the world. People tend to forget that when the United States was poor, semiliterate, and did not have the environment for large firms, lots of management transfer was going on. Little operations like Henry Ford's first auto company (with a $25,000 capitalization) kept popping up trying new ideas. Most of them went broke, usually rather fast, but the survivors are now the big ones. These firms didn't start big—they began small, often with no more than an idea and a prayer to get them going. If their managers and owners learned fast, they survived. And learning fast meant that they had to figure out quickly what to use of what they knew or could learn. Management transfer takes place very well under such conditions. But nowadays we are impatient. Countries want to short-circuit the process, to build big and fast from scratch right away. The petty things are ignored. And somehow the management and technological transfers seem very slow and painful, if they take place at all.

An option would be to try to replicate both American and European experience—to say nothing of Japanese. Try to give the little guys something to chew on. Try to give them a chance to stretch and grow. The usual observation that most of them don't give a damn is quite correct, but it misses the point that you only need a few Henry Fords or Alfred Sloans to get things going. And most countries just might have a few such characters hidden away. But if the major thrust is to get the big-ticket organization put together from day one, the odds are high that such characters will never get off the ground.

Such big organizations just don't mesh well with the educational and behavioral characteristics of the populations of

poor countries. Hence they don't work very well. But the little enterprises, the kinds of things that no one pays much attention to, do mesh well. If family-owned, small firms are the
rule, and if such firms are accepted and used, then innova-
tions suitable for such firms will be picked up and used
rather quickly. Every poor country has already done this,
more by accident than design. You can wander around cities
and see the little craft operations, the small retail shops, the
mechanics who make auto parts, and all the rest. These
small operators have managed, on their own, to pick up all
sorts of good and bad ideas from the West. And more often
than not, this sector is expanding faster than the really big
things which are supposed to change the country. But they
aren't too interesting or dramatic, so they are ignored. It's
too bad, because if you're interested in changing cultures
and countries, it would seem logical to begin with things
that might have the maximum leverage on the most people.
Instead, we see the efforts directed at changing a very small
number of people in a small way. But then there is nothing
necessarily very logical about the whole development process.

· ·

Corruption:
The Festering Sore

It does not take much wandering around any poor country before a visitor runs into some sort of corruption, bribery, or other illegal activity on the part of government officials. Sometimes such corruption is petty, as when one has to tip a customs guard to get his bag back, or pay a porter to get ahead in a line at the airport. Other times such activities can really get big, as when a contractor's bagman takes a million dollars or more to a cabinet minister to make sure the latest dam contract is awarded correctly. Many countries seem riddled from top to bottom with corrupt practices, and both local citizens and visitors comment indignantly about the evils under the sun, which seems to grow larger each day.

Some argue that such practices merely indicate the low morals of the natives, forgetting that at similar states of development, presently affluent Western countries, including the United States, were not exactly pure either. Indeed, even today one occasionally runs into corruption in the police or among city officials which makes what is going on in poor countries look very tame indeed. But petty corruption is fading from the affluent West, while it flourishes in poor countries. Accepting it and noting that it is inevitable bothers many earnestly moral people.

215

Another common attitude is to exhort citizens to be honest, and to carry on campaigns directed at such practices. But
these never work for more than a short time. It may be possible to make citizens morally indignant for a while, and perhaps even a few bribe-takers are arrested, but shortly the
situation drifts back into traditional patterns. There are too
many persons in the game, and too few moralists.

Rarely is corruption analyzed to see what is really going
on. We all have strong ethical postures about it, but no one
really has any handle on the problem to see what could be
done if anyone were serious about reducing the incidence of
corrupt practices. Actually, corruption is built into the
framework of most countries so tightly that a major reorganization would be necessary to get rid of even a small part of
it. And, as usual, the affluent West is to blame for much of
it, however indirectly, as we shall see. Corruption is important. It is a dry rot that eats away at whatever economic and
social gains a poor country can make, and it erodes confidence and morals. Getting rid of even a little corruption
could lead to some interesting gains.

The Economics of Corruption

Most poor countries have borrowed rather heavily from the
West in regard to their administrative structures. Often,
such borrowing comes more or less accidentally, as when an
ex-colonial country sets up or continues a government department patterned after the corresponding English, French,
or even American department. When the country achieves
independence, these agencies keep right on going, run by influential local citizens. Whether such a structure really meets
the needs of the country is rarely questioned. It is enough
that the pattern resembles the affluent country's. Hence we
find similar agencies around the world to handle the routines of government, such as obtaining driver's licenses; getting permits to sell pharmaceuticals, taxi service, milk,

bread, or whatever; obtaining passport forms; getting building permits; having construction sites inspected; receiving
public-utility connections for water, gas, or electricity; and
all the rest. Thousands of such routine affairs are handled by
local bureaucracies everywhere, and if we trace back in the
affluent country's history far enough, we normally find that
these rules and permits were set up initially to protect the
body politic. No one wants to ride in an unsafe taxi, driven
by a maniac; no one wants to live in an apartment with unsafe wiring; few would wish that known criminals obtain
passports and leave the country; and so on. Hence simple
controls have been instituted, and the state is responsible for
health, welfare, and equity.

It is also common to find that some notion of fair shares
for all becomes important. Hence entry into the local secondary school or university is controlled by systematic
screening of all applicants, and the selection of the most
qualified. If only a few taxi companies are to operate, all applicants are given equal opportunity, in theory, to present
their case. If all deserve medical care, than all should have a
chance to apply at the local government health center, and
the most critical are admitted. In these cases, the bureaucracy is responsible for determining who is most deserving,
and once again it is common to find thousands of examples
of such controls and screens.

It is one thing to decide that simple permits or entry controls are to be established, and quite another to make the re-
sulting system work right. The common thread is that something is made scarce. A piece of paper (e.g., a type of license
or application form) is now scarce. Someone wants it and has
to approach the bureaucracy to get it. At this point, the possibilities for corruption begin. The petty official in charge of
the piece of paper can charge for it, since the applicant
needs it. Perhaps the charge is only a few cents, but the official is ill paid, and besides, he needs the money. So corruption begins.

Where the piece of paper becomes more valuable, the potential corruption price also rises. Many poor countries have very tough import-control and exchange-control systems, where anyone wanting to buy something abroad has to get permits to import, plus often permits to obtain scarce foreign exchange. If my factory is about to close for lack of a key piece of machinery, and the cost to me will be thousands of dollars, then the corruption price goes up sharply. The official in charge can obtain a bit less than the cost of closure to obtain the key foreign exchange. Where the taxi entry control leads to very high profits, then the official can also extract a much higher bribe, since the applicant in effect shares the excess profits with him. Where issuance of a building permit allows a contractor to build a large and profitable luxury apartment house, the permit issuer can cash in.

All the scarcity adds up to juicy possibilities for corruption. Officials up and down the line can take advantage of their particular scarcities and share the gains with applicants. The same possibilities exist in the affluent West, but note the difference. Instead of inspectors being paid perhaps $30 or $40 a month, we pay perhaps $400 to $1,000. Wealthy men can afford to be somewhat more honest than poor ones. Moreover, Western organizations are better structured and often much better audited. Affluent countries have more auditors and more financial control specialists to keep track of things. They also have more lively newspapers and a more educated citizenry to scream if some graft is attempted. But even in the West, we read constantly of efforts by building inspectors to extort; of police who accept payoffs; and of city officials who accept bribes for key contracts. Where the organizations are badly structured; where auditors are few and far between, to say nothing of being less competent; and where officials are underpaid, we will find plenty of corruption. Not surprisingly, much American corruption occurs in city and state government, where managerial and administrative efficiency is typically much less than in the federal government or private firms. Being able to take full advantage of corruption possibilities usually implies a sloppy, ill-structured, badly managed system to work in—which, alas, describes all too well many American local-government administrative systems. The key is to make something scarce that might not be. Where something is scarce, but rationed according to fair-share principles, then the rationer can extract his fee and the corruption potential goes up.

The corruption index goes way up when something really important, such as a multimillion-dollar construction contract, is being tendered. Here the payoff can be in the millions, and normally only a few key top men are in on the game. The petty officials may get theirs by allowing access— I have seen the bagman make a payoff to the secretary who makes appointments for the minister (note the scarcity problem again—this secretary controlled the scarce time of the key man). Those fabled numbered Swiss bank accounts don't come from nowhere—lots of them are the property of key men in lots of poor countries.

If you also toss in the occasional government payoff for services rendered by the CIA or the Russian secret police, along with occasional payoffs from other organizations in many countries, the picture is complete. Being a key man cóntrolling a scarce thing in a poor country can be a lucrative activity. It may be nothing more than a routine printed government form, worth a penny or two, or it may be your country's vote in a key United Nations debate, or it may be the award of a major contract, but the principle is the same —something scarce is controlled, and someone is willing to pay for it.

Corruption and Ethics

Curiously, much corruption potential comes out of our ethical desires to be fair, just, and honest. We make things scarce because having them too common creates problems. If there were too many taxis, or too many building permits given to incompetents, then the public would suffer. If only those who could pay could send their children to the few good schools, the qualified but less affluent kids would be excluded. All we need is a good rationing system which will make our societies more sane and pure.

We also make some curious assumptions about administration, and the poor countries follow right along:

1. All public administration is perfect, well organized, and honest.

2. All administrators are just, compassionate, and honest.

We would never trust a private organization with such problems as far as we could throw it, yet when the same men go to work for the government, all changes. A man becomes a wonderful, public-oriented fellow, capable of Socratic decisions about who gets which scarce things.

As our earlier discussion of complex big organizations suggested, it is ill-advised indeed to take for granted the efficiency of any big organization, particularly where ill-trained personnel have to operate them, and where decisions which would tax Solomon are necessary. But we do, and hence so do the poor countries. Then many seem surprised that major corruption problems arise.

In the real world away from the theorists, the fair-shares system ends up in the worst of all possible worlds. The notion rarely works, since those willing to do a bit of bribing come off with the scarce items. The noble, smart young man about to enter college, but unfortunately without funds, does not enter; the semiliterate son of the wealthy man does, because he was willing to pay off the examiners. The contractor who was honest and tried to get a permit to build low-cost housing does not get one; the sharpshooter who is building a luxury high rise for civil servants who presumably can afford the rents gets the permit. The poor but honest man who wants to run a taxi fails, to be replaced by a cousin of the minister, who knew how to get his license. All the "wrong" people end up ahead.

Moreover, the system provides ample corruption possibilities. The bright young man who might have had an honorable career ends up in a high-bribery-potential spot at low pay. Sooner or later, he needs some more money, as we all do. And he weakens, to become part of the corruption system. The schoolmaster who would like to spend his time teaching smart young people finds it easy, sooner or later, to accept a small gift so that the not-too-bright son of a key man gets in. The system rewards those who cheat, and punishes those who try to be honest—which is not what the political and administrative theorists had in mind when the thing was first put together.

So the young become cynical; priests and wise men despair; honest bureaucrats agonize about the problem; and growth planners wonder if anything is possible. Somehow the system seems hopelessly bogged down in a morass of dishonest activities, where all the smart people are too busy looking for an angle to worry much about economic development or any such silly thing.

All of these problems are compounded in many poor countries because of the strong family orientation of most people, as compared to the more organizational orientation in many affluent countries. In a poor country without effective unemployment insurance, old-age pensions, or generally available medical care, it is common to find that everyone's focus is on the family. It is more important to protect the extended family than to show loyalty to the organization one works for. Tribal and agrarian customs tend to reinforce this attitude. Yet the big organizations busily creating scarcities are taken from the West, where organization loyalty is more important. An American customs official might hesitate to take advantage of his position, since he has accepted certain responsibilities and obligations by taking the job. A citizen of a poor country, responsible mainly to his family, sees the problem quite differently. His major responsibility is to his extended family, and his mother is sick. So why not take advantage? He may not even consider he has much of a moral choice here. When a country borrows ideas from other cultures, it is wise to question the premises on which the ideas are based. They may not be what is useful in the new environment.

Reform Problems

Like the weather, everyone talks about getting rid of corruption, but rarely does anything happen—except that it spreads. The reason it spreads is that as the economic-development process proceeds, new organizations are set up, new licenses are needed, new contracts must be let, and the potential for corruption keeps growing. So does actual corruption. Moralists preach against corruption, and urge honesty, though it seems every man has his price, and often the price is low. If temptation is always present, then sooner or later someone will weaken. Organization experts take a look at the problem and urge more and better audits, along with still better control systems, and improved personnel to keep track of things. These suggestions might work in more affluent countries, where the supply of well-trained accountants, computer-control men, and similar personnel is large. Normally they do not succeed in poor countries, where key men are always hard to find. So governments publish white papers, and many worry about the problem, but nothing happens. The basic reason is that the key constraints are wrong. Unless they are changed, countries will be struggling with corruption for a long time.

Reform efforts often come to grief because there are too many people with a vested interest in corruption. The persons taking cash view honesty as a pay reduction, and we all fight that. The hustlers, five percenters, and other con men who can fix something for you for a small fee also resist. Not everyone likes to pay bribes, particularly affluent Americans, and they often hire a specialist to handle the problem for them. It is common in some poor countries to find that a large percentage of the really talented people in the country earn good livings by getting things through customs, obtaining licenses for busy rich foreigners, getting permits for local citizens who don't quite know who to approach, and performing similar services. If the game became honest, lots of sharp people would be unemployed. And way at the top, the key people might suffer. After all, even cabinet ministers in poor countries are not all that well paid, and what would happen to them if there were no chances to get ahead in this world by controlling key bids and such? Like everything else that has been around for a while, vested interests tend to block reform.

Suppose a country really became interested in getting rid of at least some corruption? There are lots of easy ways to do it:

First, it is useful to keep in mind that there are no 100 percent control systems anywhere. It is common all over the world to find moralists demanding the total end to something, on the grounds that it is immoral. This is ethically fine, but impractical in the real world, as our experiences with such things as prostitution control suggest. Hence any anticorruption system should be cheap and *reasonably* effective. It will never get all of the cheaters. Accepting this reality can make all sorts of things possible. It is common to find that the costs of getting the last 1 percent are as high as the costs of getting the first 99 percent—so to hell with that last bunch. Businessmen, worried about profit and loss, normally think this way, but moralists and government officials rarely do. If you really want 100 percent control systems, you're in the wrong world. It will never happen.

Second, it is useful to analyze the government system to determine what is now artificially scarce. Even casual inspections of long-lived bureaucracies turn up endless items. In one country, it turned out that passport applications were made scarce by putting them in charge of one key postal official in each town. Most of these officials quickly learned that they could be sold for a small profit. Reformers then printed a few million applications and placed them on the counters of every post office, and the artificial scarcity, as well as the petty corruption, disappeared overnight.*

At this point, we run into our ethics about what is proper. We may restrict milk dealers because we want clean milk, and the restriction system is supposed to protect the public, as competent, wise inspectors screen applicants and reject those who don't understand milk sanitation problems. Unfortunately, the usual result of the system is not that clean milk handlers get into business, but rather that those willing to pay off enough get into business. Clean milk has little or nothing to do with the problem. Yet the feeling persists that this is all wrong. In theory, we *should* have clean milk!

Here is the non-100-percent system in action. What do you want—theoretically clean milk but practically a system where the rich get richer, or an open system which would give anyone who wants in a chance to compete, but with potentially unclean milk to boot? In either case we are quite likely to end up with unclean milk—the problem is to decide whether or not we want unclean milk provided at fairly high prices by a few operators, or unclean milk provided by anyone who thinks he can do the job. If we choose the operator route, we also end up with a very large corruption potential.

If things are really scarce, like street space, university places, or hospital beds, then one way to beat corruption is to sell off the scarce spots to the highest bidder in a public auction. Of course, in this case the ones who can pay get the slots, while the poor don't, so the system is unethical. But since in practice the rich get them anyhow, by bribing the gatekeeper, the result is the same as before without bribery, except now the government gets the revenue, not the cheaters. This course of action can drive ethically oriented

---

* After a short time, the reformers found out that the filled-out forms required the signature of another key government official in the town. Of course, he began to charge for his free signature. Eternal vigilance is the price of no corruption!

people up the wall, both in poor countries and in very affluent ones. At Indiana University, where I teach, there is a
lively black market in registration cards each semester for
certain courses, where the professor is great and the class size
limited by room size. Note the absolute scarcity. What happens is that students and petty administrators who handle
the registration cards get them to friends and operators even
before registration. The poor but honest student who is
dense enough to think that he can obtain a card for a key
class at registration is misguided, since they are all gone before the registration opens. Several of us professors suggested
that this petty corruption could easily be eliminated by selling the cards to the highest bidders. Anyone who really
wanted in would have to bid above the usual credit-hour
price for such a card. The reaction was amusing: we were re-
garded as unethical creeps who had come out from under a
rock—our suggestion was *unfair!* So we still have the same
system, and the operators still get the cards in advance, and
the petty corruption still goes on. But the system is *fair*.
Many thoughtful observers wonder why the young people
here and in other countries are so cynical about big organizations, the world in general, and corruption in particular.
After all, aren't the big organizations fair, just, and ethical?

Whenever something is scarce, and more people want it
than can have it, you end up with a rationing system. The
usual mainstream approach is to set up the rationing system
for public goods through the government bureaucracy, and
to use a price system for nonpublic things like bread and automobiles. But the nonpublic system works pretty well
(though unfairly), because those who pay get. The public
system works badly, because while in theory those who need
get, in practice, those who pay (or operate and hustle) get.
Since we feel that this is ethically desirable, we are stuck
with corruption, which we don't think is desirable. But unless we recognize that it's going to be this way, no matter
what our ethics, we will be stuck.

Another useful possibility to minimize corruption would

be for impartial groups of distinguished citizens to examine
all proposed new government systems (and maybe older existing ones too), with the view to determining the corruption potential of the system. That is, they could inspect the
points where some scarcity arises, note the probable value of
the scarcity, and show about what will occur, in terms of
prices and bribes. Lots of people know a lot about this—it is
one place where distinguished and wealthy five percenters
and hustlers could perform a real public service, after they
have made their pile. Rather curiously, this point is never
made, although in most proposed projects, it is very easy to
see exactly what will happen, from top to bottom. But we
are so used to assuming that all public bureaucracies will
perform perfectly and honestly that no one ever raises the
question. It seems a bit sticky and dishonest even to suggest
that perhaps some official just might do something wrong.
But he will, and if a new system has lots of corruption potential, it just might be possible to restructure it so that the potential is minimized.

The key points are easy to spot. Wherever something becomes scarce, it will be corrupted. Hence, minimize scarcity.
Where absolute scarcity is inevitable, sell the item to the
highest bidder. That's all there is to it. Nothing will work
perfectly, but far too many poor countries have discovered to
their dismay that they are spending more time playing
games with bureaucracies than they are getting honest work
done. Corruption is dysfunctional, and it does slow down ac-
complishment of the real job of economic development.

Here again is an example of culture-busting, although not
in exactly the positive way we would like to think. The
West has done a beautiful job of selling its big organizations,
its huge public bureaucracies, to a lot of poor countries. Because these organizations were orignally set up for different
places and different times, one thing they did was to raise
the corruption level of lots of countries, and poor people
everywhere jumped on this particular bandwagon. It's hard
to be corrupt in a peasant village where everyone knows

everyone else, and where wealth is so small as to preclude much wheeling and dealing. But it's very easy as a petty official in an imported organization, where artificial scarcities abound, and where eager clients are willing to pay off various amounts to get things done. Poor people need money, so many learned very fast how to take care of themselves.

Old line Marxists, who may feel that this problem is only a decadent capitalist development, can ponder the fact that the Marxist system, which removes from the price-rationing system many goods and services, is even worse in this regard than the capitalist system. At least under capitalism lots of things cannot be obtained by bribery, since they are sold in open markets. Under the Marxist system, there are still more things rationed by compassionate bureaucrats, and still more artificial scarcities created. Hence the corruption potential is still higher. A country such as India, which has a large component of Marxism in its new system, has many problems more capitalistic countries do not have, since there is so much more possibility for corruption.

You might ponder this whole problem the next time you have to slip a tip to a customs agent, or pay off a local inspector to get your plumbing repairs okayed. We have created a weird system, where in theory everything is noble, kind, compassionate, and fair—but which in practice is rotten and corrupt. We end up with the worst of all possible worlds, because we haven't the guts to figure out what is really going on, as compared to what we wished were going on. Poor countries, ever eager to be ethical, noble, fair—and rich—eagerly adopt our customs. We find that it is easy to bust up their older ideas about what is proper—but we are not too sure we like the results.

· ·

The Model T Ford and the Missed Development Bus

Detroit: The Ford Motor Company is considering a new simple car for Asian countries, it was reported today. The car will have a plywood body and light engine, and be designed specifically for Asian conditions and manufacture. The estimated cost is around $800. Ford officials noted that a vast new potential market exists for such a vehicle in countries where as yet modern, expensive cars and trucks cannot be manufactured, and where incomes preclude large purchases.

The final decision about proceeding with the project will be made later, but preliminary studies indicate excellent potential.

Not long ago, I attended a farm auction in mid-America. An estate was being settled, and the owner hadn't thrown anything away in forty years. As we watched the antique hunters fight over old tobacco tins and canning jars, we chatted about what was going on around the state. My friend was a typical Hoosier—he ran a garage, voted Republican, had a kid at Indiana University, and was worried about pot, acid, and the younger generation.

I kicked a bit of rusty metal. "What's that?"

229

"A 1923 top bow for a Model T Ford," my friend replied.
"Too bad the rest of the top isn't here—it would bring
maybe forty dollars if it was. As is, it will only bring about
ten." (It went for $9.75. He was more accurate on his other
guesses.)

He pushed the rusty piece with his foot. "A great car, the
T—I learned a lot when I was young, fixing them."

It turned out he was a grade-school dropout—seems his
dad needed him on the farm, and in the twenties, when he
was a boy, no one went to high school. Now he ran his own
garage, making maybe $10,000 or $15,000 a year. He kept
going right up the learning curve from the Model T to the
As to the flat head V-8s, on into automatic transmissions,
power steering, electronic ignitions, and diesel equipment.

So there he stood, kicking rusty bits of old machinery,
talking about the kids, worrying about the younger generation, teaching me all sorts of things about old cars I never
knew in spite of my degrees and academic pretensions. His
boy would have a future, by God, and he would finish college and make something of himself. Not like his old man,
who never really got much of an education, and who never
really was able to learn very much.

What nonsense! My mind drifted back to Ahmed, my
Saudi Arabian mechanic, who had come in off the desert just
a few years before. These fellows had a lot in common—they
both were uneducated, both intelligent, both with a natural
curiosity about mechanical things, both worried about their
children. And I remembered Ahmed scratching his head as
he looked at the first alternator he had ever seen. It had
stopped operating a week after the car had arrived, and we
were trying to figure out what made it tick. Of course we
didn't have an instruction manual (it would come six
months later). As it happened, Ahmed never did get the alternator fixed. Its inner electronic logic was just too much
for a man who could barely read. The engineers who had
worked it out knew more about solid-state physics, diode

properties, and other mysterious things than any untutored man could ever know.

There's a theory in development economics called the theory of the missed bus. According to it there may be only one development bus, and if you don't get on, you may never see another one coming by. Thus, a country may have a chance to start a school system, invest in its first electric power plants, or start light manufacturing facilities. Such opportunities were common in the late nineteenth and early twentieth centuries. And country or culture could have started then, as most of Western Europe and Japan, along with the United States, started at that time. In that almost fogotten, unsophisticated world, any group who wanted to get in the game could.

But for one reason or another, many countries decided "no." Perhaps they were so far away they hadn't yet heard the word about the new wonders; perhaps they were colonial states at the time. So while workers and technicians in the countries that took the bus began the arduous and often decades-long process of learning how new things worked, others stayed right where they were, relearning in each generation the same pastoral and agricultural skills their ancestors knew. Every year the bus riders learned new tricks, new ideas, new technologies, as one thing led to another. Steam engines led to gasoline and on to diesels; electric power went on to electronics and ever more complex systems. And finally, when those who missed the first bus decided to get in on the game, the bus was too far ahead for them to catch it. Instead of just a few minor things to learn, whole countries found they had decades to cover in a few years. Very possibly, they could never really catch up.

My Hoosier friend had seen his bus coming (the Model T Ford), and had swung right aboard. He's been riding it ever since, and the ride has been fine. But Ahmed's father missed the bus, sitting out in the desert, fingering his prayer beads, worrying about who owned the next waterhole. And there

was Ahmed, running behind the steadily accelerating bus,
never quite able to get a foothold. He made maybe $50 a
month, and was probably overpaid in terms of the work he
actually did. My $1,000-a-month Hoosier was probably un-
derpaid, in terms of what he could and did do.

On the way home, I did some thinking. Something seemed
wrong for all our friends in the less-developed countries.
Somehow they were short-changed. It was as if we had
cruelly, though probably not deliberately, placed them in a
situation where far too many Ahmeds would never get the
chance that my Indiana friend had casually seized so many
years ago. What went wrong?

The Certification Psychosis

As one looks around the less-developed countries (LDC), it
becomes clear most are deeply in the grip of the certification
psychosis—the idea that no one can do anything unless he
went to a formal school, and come out with the proper diploma in hand. What you know is irrelevant—what matters
is your degree. If you are properly certified at the proper
level, then getting the job done comes naturally. In part,
this psychosis is our fault. People from poorer countries, observing developed countries, could not help but see that the
number of degree holders at all levels was going up fast. So
was GNP. Ergo, the more degrees, the higher the GNP.

But another factor was the rapid shift from genetic sort
systems to something else. In traditional societies, roles are
limited, and sons inherit the job. We all know who is going
to be doctor, lawyer, or merchant chief, by asking whose son
is who. As modernization sets in, and as many new and mysterious roles develop, how can we fill them? Who becomes
the chief water engineer for the new irrigation project, when
nothing like this has ever been seen before? The obvious answer was to choose the fellow who had the right diploma. He

might not know what to do, but the probability of his doing something right was higher than random selection.

Developed countries are much farther down the road to professional certification. They have more or less figured out the professional competence required for various kinds of highly skilled work. They also have schools to match up with certifications. If we want an electrical engineer, or a doctor, the man with the right diploma will have the right qualifications. The reason is we have been at it long enough to have some feel for what any given professional should do. This development is so recent that we still, even in the United States, have vestiges of the older system. Men still alive can remember when self-taught characters designed trucks, for better or worse; and when anyone willing to read lawbooks in some backwater county seat could practice the law. But these are vestiges—M.D.s, lawyers, and engineers are judged by professional competence, not by family background.

In poorer countries creeping professionalism had not occurred. There had been no long period of learning what professionals do, and it is not at all clear what is required to get a task done. Hence, on a new project, people look for visible signs of who might do it. One obvious sign is that the person who does it has the right of diploma—most hang them on the wall, for all to see. Hence, the secret of success must be there, in the diploma on the wall, not in what, if anything, the fellow knows.

People are not stupid, and perceptive LDC parents, seeing this happen, begin to push their children toward the right degree. An illiterate could hope for his son to get a primary certificate, which might make him a useful postman. An old aristocrat, seeing the handwriting on the wall, would send his sons to the United States or France for an engineering degree. And on and on—until the whole culture was wrapped in a new mystique of diplomas instead of birthrights.

I remember helping to send home a young Asian man who had bought his electrical engineering degree from a local direct-mail peddler. He had been to high school, and he spoke passable English, but he was in a graduate program in the States for electrical engineers. The young man was very indignant. He had the right diploma, didn't he? Ergo, he was entitled to the special training. The idea that knowing something went along with the degree had simply never occurred to him. The others who did finish the course and received a Master's degree all went home. One is now practicing his profession; all the rest are government officials in administration. The young man was probably right—he might well have stayed and finished the course, for all the good the technical training would have done him. Given his entrepreneurial talents, he probably would have been a better bureaucrat than the engineers who got the jobs because they did have the right diploma.

The strong white-collar orientation of many LDC cultures reinforces this idea as well: People who think are always better off than people who work—thinkers need diplomas. The end of the line in this situation is a country where everyone pushes hard for more and more diplomas, leaving the dregs to do any useful work. India, for example, appears to be in this situation. Anyone who is good at academic games goes on to college; others are stuck with manual labor. One result is huge unemployment rates among white-collar types, with equally large shortages of technical labor. Even where the diploma certifies one to do technical labor, as in engineering, few degree-holders would dream of actually doing any physical labor—better to leave this to the peasants, while degree-holders sit in offices and think about problems.

A further factor pushing for certification in the LDCs is their typically elitist orientation. Most LDCs are much more interested in a small elite than in the masses. Elitists go to universities. These are very expensive—but the country willingly pays the bill. For the price of one or two college graduates, perhaps fifty persons could attend grade school, but most countries, if faced with such choices, will opt for the elitists, rather than push for more general education. Contributing to this pressure, most foreigners who wander around the LDCs have college degrees. If local persons are to meet these people on their own terms, they also must have the coveted diplomas.

Once one accepts the idea that only diplomas will do, much follows, including many billions of dollars to build schools that probably aren't really necessary. And of course all formal schooling is time-oriented. You have to pace the students through the years, waiting for young men and women to move along to the end of the line. If you want electrical engineers in a semiliterate country, invest $40 million and wait twenty years. Something useful may emerge. Fellows like Ahmed, my Saudi mechanic, are out of this game before it begins. No one wants a man who learned it all himself—how can he prove that he knows? Besides, what prestige is there in just doing the job right? A diploma to hang on the wall looks so much nicer and the neighbors are properly impressed. Too, it is hard to evaluate these self-educated fellows. You have to invent tests, try them out, find out if they can really do the job. Thus, harassed bureaucrats everywhere find it much easier to require a "diploma." It keeps out the peasants. Incidentally, the LDCs are not the only guilty ones. How many American companies require high school diplomas for jobs which require the intelligence of a five-year-old, or college degrees for clerks? Such policies do keep out the peasants, but they also cause more real trouble than most of us realize.

The Black-Box Mania

The second threat is the move to mysterious black boxes that only high-powered scientists and engineers can understand. Instead of doing the job with lever or pushbutton, electronic gadgetry is designed which is elegant in the tech-

nical sense, but pure hell for the servicemen who will have
to fix it. Even when the black boxes work well, Ahmed is
out of the game. It costs money to change bearings and lu-
bricate them—okay, let's put in a lubeless bearing which
will last the life of the equipment. Now there is nothing for
Ahmed to do—if it works; there is no way for him to learn.
So he doesn't. And some place else in his economy, where
such training is badly needed, the AID engineers wonder
why we never seem able to find anyone who can do the job.
Of course, when the new technical school is finished, in
1979, we will get our people, but in the meantime. . . .

My Hoosier friend grew up among things which needed
fixing often. But it was simple enough so any reasonably
bright young men with some mechanical sense could learn
the job. And parts were cheap, too. In 1927 you could buy a
spindle-arm bushing for your T for three cents. If you
jammed it or got it in backward, all you lost was time. (Price
out one for your 1971 Super Eight and see the difference.)

The reason we get those black boxes stems from the way
Americans educate their technical people. Consider the
eighteen-year-old just off to engineering school. Various IQ
tests have shown he will be in the top 5 percent of his age
bracket. He probably has already rebuilt a few cars, shot
some rockets, or operated a ham radio station. And since he's
so bright, he will have been at the top of his high school
class. The world is his oyster—at least for a few weeks. After
his first midterm examinations, the classic engineering inferiority complex sets in. He gets Cs—the first in his life. Instead of coasting through his courses, he has to study hard,
even on weekends. And instead of being number one or two
in the class, he's maybe number 462 out of 528. In short, he
is learning to live his future inferior life. Four years later, he
graduates. He has moved up to number 34 in the class but,
of course, he knows that 33 of his counterparts are smarter
than he is. And his professors are smarter than any of his
peers. His B-minus average doesn't look too good to him,
but some kindly company is willing to give him a break and
a job.

In mechanical design, young engineers get the detailed work. Job one is that black box on the generator the company is putting out. As our young engineer works through the design, he will do his best. He thinks that it's not very good, but then he's not very good. And, of course, in the field it will be maintained by men who are, at worse, about as good as he is. So, no need to worry about being too simple. Besides, his boss will be checking it, and he's *really* smart. Meanwhile, out in the field, in some distant foreign country, the foreman is struggling with his maintenance crew. And what a crew! With luck, one or two of the twenty got through grade school. If he's really lucky, a few of them can read enough English to puzzle through the maintenance manuals. In most less-developed countries, no one ever took apart a car, shot off a rocket, played with an old alarm clock, or came near any electronics gear. The subtle mechanical logic that boys learn in a Western culture is totally lacking. Anyone who's been abroad knows the rest of the story. Maintenance gets done badly, if at all, in most non-Western countries.

The LDCs set up elaborate technical training programs to correct such problems, but they always run at least ten years behind those foreign engineers. By the time the country turns out people who understand what's going on now, Cal Tech and Purdue will have generated another group of frighteningly bright young engineers. So, when they finally get to the job, they will design some new product which is even more subtle, complex, neat. Most American companies still are thinking about the domestic market, which compounds this confusion. Even in the rare cases where engineers do think about the average man, they are thinking about the average American maintenance technician—and these fellows are way above the world average. Not only have they had much more basic education and experience, they often have attended special institutes, colleges, training courses, and what not. They also have the great advantage of friendly dealers on every corner, plus telephones that work to call the man who really knows. Very few American design engineers have any feel at all for the kinds of personnel who will struggle with their equipment in far-off lands. Once again, the "average" turns out to be too high. The "average" Western engineer is in the top 1 or 2 percent of his generation in intelligence, and further up than that in terms of education, training, and attitudes. Yet he designs for the "average" man, just like himself. Until we figure out how to get through to our engineers to make them feel superior, we're in trouble. If we could make them feel superior, we could get them to look down on the rest of us and design something the *really* average man could fix.

All of these points essentially relate to a management rule; which is simply that everyone looks up all the time—never sideways or down. Since organizations are organized as hierarchies, anyone in the system will tend to look up to see what his boss is doing, rather than glance downward. Any man knows he is good enough to be where he is. The key point is whether or not he is good enough to move up. So he spends most of his time either impressing his boss or trying to gain the skills and knowledge necessary to get ahead. He sees all sorts of men around him who are as good as he is (or nearly so), which leads to the strange notion that the "average" man is about like him. The engineer or technical writer has long since forgotten those below him. The mechanics, draftsmen, machinists, clerks and laborers aren't really worth discussing. But since the organization is a pyramid, there are always more below than above. If the one always impresses the fellows up there, we tend to get exactly the kinds of problems I am writing about.

When you move out in the field, to the users of whatever your company is turning out, virtually everybody is below this strange corporate average. After all, most modern companies are extremely good at cornering talent of all sorts, while users may not be so lucky, particularly in developing countries where talented people are always in short supply. And even if the customer is as good a firm as the supplier, maintenance tends to get built in far enough below the top to lead to lesser souls doing the job.

Maintenance Learning Curves

The learning curve idea is simple enough. If a person gets enough practice at something, he will become good at it. The first time anyone fixes something, or builds something, it takes a long time, since he doesn't quite know what is happening. He has to fumble around as he does it. By the tenth time, however, he is pretty good at the job. After a while, there is no gain, because the person has learned as much as he will ever know.

Now, what did Model T Fords have and what will the new Asian Ford have (I hope)—and what difference would it make to the LDCs and maybe even contractors?

The T was simple: Anybody with a small kit of tools could get it apart and maybe even back together again. Even the few special tools needed were cheap.

The T was highly visible: When the engine was torn down, you could see what went where, and why, even if you never went to school at all.

The T needed fixing all the time: The result was that lots of mechanics learned fast, because they had lots of practice. Before you went a thousand miles something needed fixing, and within the first year, you could get to be an expert mechanic. As educators tell us, repetition gets us up the learning curve fast.

There were few critical parts: A fellow with some old cans, bailing wire, and a few chunks of steel could patch a T up and get to the next town. Many repairs were done by blacksmiths, right at the village forge. If it didn't quite come out right, the thing still ran. If you find a blacksmith, try your new car on him—it's fun.

The result: Several million Americans got a real mechanical and maintenance education on simple things that any reasonably bright man could figure out. But LDCs these days do not have this advantage, and as we all know, one result is that most equipment doesn't work too well most of

the time, if it works at all. Another unnoted effect is that
countries spend billions creating formal education systems to
do what we Americans got for nothing a long time ago. If
you need a B.S. in electrical engineering before you can take
the maintenance course for the next black box, don't expect
poorer countries, with their huge educational deficiencies, to
get anything done.

Putting It All Together for the LDCs

We face, as all planners realize, horrible educational deficiencies, which, no matter how hard we try, will not be rec-
tified in this generation. We also face the problem of what to
do with all the bright Ahmeds who will never get that coveted diploma. Do we really have to condemn those people to
subsistence-level poverty for the rest of their lives? Perhaps
not. We could do some low-cost things which might even
work. Like these:

First, recognize the learning value of high maintenance,
simple machinery. The gains are even higher if the equipment is something that someone wants to work, like a radio
or car or truck. Nothing beats a nagging wife and kids for
motivating; and if taxi or truck income is lost because they
won't run, they tend to be fixed fast—if it's at all possible.
As most machinery and equipment is designed in the developed countries by high-powered engineers, high maintenance simplicity will never get built in, unless the LDCs
themselves demand it. Which is highly unlikely, because
Model T Fords and such are seen as rejects from advanced
cultures. Better in the sticks to have a new Olds that doesn't
run than five chugging T's.

Second, get rid of the black boxes and the complex electronics, which only high-powered specialists can understand.
These things have their place, but there are few everyday
things in any culture which cannot be back-designed to simplicity and high maintenance.

Third, get rid of esoteric metallurgy and high-tensile-strength parts. When they break, you wait six months for spares. Better to have a two-inch slab of ordinary steel as a brace than a quarter-inch piece that is beautifully engineered, but can't be found locally—and if it can, cannot be hammered into shape or machined right.

Fourth, get rid of high-tolerance stuff. Keep all critical dimensions to plus or minus a thousandth, instead of going to dimensions so tight only a modern factory with million-dollar machine tools and skilled specialists can work them out. If this is done, things will break—which is what we want!

Fifth, it might pay to structure simple, cheap foreign aid designed as a learning experience for the maximum number of people. Our present aid programs are big, mainstream things, full of power plants and similar large projects. Why not just buy some junk cars (or get the big city police departments to give them to AID) and dump them on some beach in Bangladesh, the Philippines, or India? Anyone who could figure out how to use them would get whatever advantages he could out of them.* The idea would be to give the common citizen a chance to do some learning by messing around with what we call junk, but which would be considered very valuable assets in really poor countries. Learning to take apart junk cars can be a real learning experience, and there is more of value in one of them, particularly when labor costs are very low, than most Americans realize. The cost of such a program would be extremely low by modern standards—to say nothing of solving a problem for Americans which they as yet haven't solved.

The idea behind these suggestions is simple enough—we badly need to use everything we have to educate a few bil-

---

* A Philippine friend, in discussing this point, noted that if the Americans would do this, the junkers would all be running within a month or two in his country. The current quality of Philippine mechanics and tinkerers is very high, and such a program could double the numbers of cars and trucks in the country within a year, at no cost to the country. But the Philippine Government would never accept the idea—who wants someone else's junk?

lion people. Americans, used to school where education takes place, have forgotten that much education takes place in work situations. In poorer countries, which won't have enough schools to go around for a hundred years, such non-school education is critical, yet such countries have often forgotten that this is the way the presently affluent countries got rich. Anything that could possibly be used to get presently illiterate or semiliterate working people willing and eager to learn should be used. And in this case of mechanical tinkering, the training received can be a base to move up to repairs of even more complex modern machinery.

Model T Fords may seem a long way from a diesel-powered earth mover, but when you get right down to it, the basic elements are the same. Both units have crankshafts, valve trains, and all the rest. The modern unit is much more complex, but someone who has fooled around with reciprocating engines is going to be easier to train up than someone who has never seen them. Moreover, the kind of fellow who does this tinkering will be interested in learning more. The idea that things can be fixed is the most useful knowledge one gains from such experience. Black boxes give people helpless feelings; simple machinery gives people lots of confidence.

The reaction in most circles to this suggestion is so negative as to be beyond belief. I was once involved with working out an electrical system for some LDC villages to get them a bit of electric power. The idea was to use rebuilt (in the country) auto generators, batteries, and old electrical systems, scavenged from our numerous junked cars, to build a small power system. It met every one of the above criteria, including, most specifically, lots of maintenance. You could carry the system in on your back to the most remote village, put it together with a windmill or water wheel powering the generator, and get something better than nothing for maybe $100. The technical experts were polite but negative. It seems the kilowatt-hour costs were high, and besides, how could we plan or control backyard shops busily rebuilding generators? Better to wait for the new $127-million hydro scheme, which would do the job right—cheap, low cost, high power and noneducational. It would only be a few more years.

One place where we proposed to do this was supposed to get its hydro power in 1971. I saw recently that the scheme has been postponed to *1978*. There is a shortage of technicians, engineers, managers, financial planners, and so on in the country, and of course capital is very expensive and hard to get. Those villages can wait another ten or fifteen years until they turn on the lights. They will be just as illiterate and ignorant then as now, so it won't really matter much. And of course they won't be able to afford the power anyhow, since they don't have the income to electrify their houses. You see, they just don't seem to be able to build schools fast enough to get the people educated and get those income-producing diplomas.

As a matter of fact, our LDC friends were equally dubious. Nice idea, but do you want us to sit around with a couple of jury-rigged auto headlights, using a one-channel TV set? Far better to wait until we can get our modern power, our color TVs, our high-horsepower electric latches, and all the rest you already have. "Do you think we are a bunch of second-class citizens? Look how you live!"

Our planning friends were the most dubious of all. How could you measure what's happening? If your scheme worked, what would happen to all the carefully drawn plans? What, for that matter, would the planners have to do? Why the peasants might even develop themselves! This is really a *horrible* thought. If they do it themselves, then what do we do with all those "diploma" people who now do all the real thinking in the country?

The illiterate villagers are still sitting around in their huts using no lights, with nothing but animal power for economic use. Per-capita income is still around $80 and it will still be in 1978, or even in 1995, for all that.

My Hoosier friend's son dropped in the office to chat the

other day. His dad told him I was in the business school, and he felt he should come in and say hello. He's a nice kid —going to be an accountant, and maybe make $12,000 a year or so on his first job. As I chatted with this young man, I kept seeing that missed bus careening down some road Ahmed will never quite know. Somehow we messed it up, not because evil men sat down and figured it out this way, but because we did not build into our development equations the simple, obvious things: Model T Fords, Atwater-Kent radios, 1926 washing machines, and all sorts of other odds and ends. Somehow we got ourselves educated by the millions, and no one even knew it was happening. And somehow, our friends in poorer countries will never have the chances we or our fathers had, to get on the development bus and see where it goes.

I wonder what Ahmed's sons are up to these days?

CHAPTER **X V I I**

· ·

The Threat System and
the "Nice-Guys" Hypothesis

In the end, everything gets down to manipulating human behavior. The typical peasant, nomad, or illiterate urban slum dweller in a poor country has behavioral patterns (to say nothing of lack of education) which guarantee that he will not be a very productive citizen in a modern affluent state. The country, firm, and other organizations will have to figure out how to get him working the way he should in a modern situation. Since the typical thrust in many countries is to have big, complex organizations, full of personal inter-actions, careful advance planning, and the like, the need to change behavior is critical. If all the citizens in poor coun-tries behaved and acted like citizens in rich countries, this book wouldn't be necessary.

We are talking about the behavioral change of millions, or even hundreds of millions, of people, not just a handful of the elite. Countries far behind have to accomplish this be-havioral change job in a hurry, not over the next fifty or one hundred years. If the job could be stretched out, we could all go home, since it is quite likely that if we wait long enough, the hoped-for changes will occur—they did in the presently affluent countries without anyone paying much attention. It is the time problem which is critical. How do you change people fast and dramatically by the millions in a hurry? And worse, how do you do it cheaply, since no one has enough money or resources to spare?

Here the poor countries have problems, since most consideration of behavioral change comes from the wealthy countries, and as is typical of such things, is locked into the cultural and behavioral patterns of the affluent countries. The ways to get the behavioral and educational jobs done, like machine tools, are imported from places with quite different backgrounds and values from those of the poor country. And, as usual, it is difficult to make an easy shift of such techniques.

A country serious about shifting its masses into more productive patterns typical in the affluent East or West has to consider first exactly what kinds of changes it wants. Here everyone gets hung up on his own value system. The virtues of home and motherhood, or whatever equivalent values are considered desirable, are quite different from place to place. Of course we want fervent belief in *my* country, right or wrong—and if this interferes with good engineering, or something, then engineering goes down the drain. We want firm support for the local religious values—and if these interfere with proper work habits, well, the work habits will suffer. We want the right kinds of education in the virtues of God and country—and if our views of God and country differ from views needed to get some production out, then production will suffer. A key value, enthusiastically adopted from the West in poor countries, is that no one should interfere with or criticize someone else's critical ethical values.

At this point, we quickly get back to square one, since the reason poor countries are poor is because they have values, beliefs, and behavioral patterns which *are* inconsistent with high economic efficiency. So something has to change, and quickly. If we were serious about it, what would the changes be?

Examination of now-affluent countries does suggest that

certain behavioral patterns are very useful. First and fore-most, education is needed. A country's people starts with basic literacy and mathematical skills, then moves to more advanced technical kinds of education. The very acquiring of such skills is a change agent in itself—people who can read do, and often not the technical manuals we wish that they would. Vocational trainees have to learn to think scien-tifically, even if such thinking might lead them to dangerous religious thoughts. But no wealthy country has been able to get rich without extensive educational activities.

So, off to the educational wars—and our first hitch ap-pears. Educational systems are borrowed more or less intact from affluent countries, mainly America or Europe, and these systems are now set up to serve children of the in-dustrial age. They are also set up to perform, at considerable cost, all sorts of socializing functions, such as learning to love one's country, getting the rich cultural heritage of one's past, and generally locking kids into whatever behavioral patterns seem useful. In most countries, including the United States, the primary and secondary educational systems are staffed by well-trained, college-educated persons who have deep com-mitments to the good life for the kids. And the kids can get it—even the most deprived ghetto school kids in the worst cities in the United States have living standards which would seem upper middle class in most poor countries.

So our poor country borrows the school system whole—and promptly gets into trouble. The personnel are not very skilled, maybe not even committed. After all, poor countries definitionally don't have one well-trained adult for every thirty kids. One overlooked reason why is that nowadays, poor countries have a lot more kids per capita than the afflu-ent countries—that is the result of high net reproduction rates. If population gains are 3 percent per year, within fif-teen to twenty years, half the population will be under fif-teen years old, and no poor country has the money or re-sources to build enough American-style buildings or find enough good administrators to cover all the bases. So typically, only a few kids are covered in the affluent American way.

There are more troubles. Increasingly, because we like it philosophically, and because we think we have the resources to do it, our school systems are getting more high-skill labor-intensive. That is, we are using more and more very well-trained people to work more intensively with fewer children to get them developed into the kinds of people we want. This is not only fun, but humane, since a highly trained person can be a really nice fellow to his charges. Instead of applying various threats and beatings, he can take the time to figure out what's wrong, to work with the child's problems in a personal way. Where we live, the teachers have conferences with parents—report cards are a thing of the past, I guess. Conferences take time, but they are more interesting and maybe even more effective than an F on the report card of a bewildered third-grader.

And of course we now have school psychologists, therapists, special physical-education trainers, assistants to help with the gifted and the handicapped, and all the rest. What we are doing is making a bigger educational investment in the children in a nice-guy way, because we can afford it. The system tries to be humane, fair, and kind as it brainwashes young students into the behavioral patterns desired by society. Most states have laws against beatings, and irate parents can sue teachers or school boards who would resort to historical methods of learning persuasion. The problem is to work with the complete child and get him or her plugged into the social system as productively as possible. Who would want it otherwise? Anyone taking enough time to examine a modern, middle-class elementary American school is pleased and delighted at what is going on. The kids seem very happy; the teachers and administrators are dedicated, and the old image of school as a forbidding place where you prod recalcitrant pupils to learn is fast disappearing.

Now, transfer this delightful image to a poor country (or, for that matter, an American ghetto). Somehow, things come unstuck. There is never enough manpower to do the job right, since lots of kids have real problems, including home situations which are about as far from the American middle class as it is possible to get. Hence the labor-intensive education falls apart. Middle-class parents, worried about their kids, take time to attend the teacher conferences; poor parents, working hard, do not. Because resources are so limited, the wonderful facilities which the schools have are absent, so the children cannot get the training they need. Or, if they exist, they are out of order. Electronic devices for correcting speech defects are fine—until they break. Then no one can fix them. That's what being poor is all about—the country or area lacks the necessary skills.

Like modern American factories, full of labor-saving devices, and stressing high-skill labor for the work to be done, the American school fits well the middle-class-American life pattern. But when it gets stuck abroad, like the factory, it never seems to work right, or more likely, it can only be afforded for a small percentage of the total population affected. Nothing much happens, because the system just doesn't match the environment in which it operates. So, back to square one—How do you get ten or fifteen million kids literate in the next two years with virtually no cash or trained labor on hand? Those who have pondered this problem either go back to the American-style middle-class system, in effect ignoring the problem, or throw up their hands in despair. We in the affluent countries don't know much about this problem, so we can't give much useful advice. Hell, we can't even figure out how to do it in our own poverty areas, let alone in some completely poor country abroad.

Examining the behavioral patterns of the work force also leads to the need for major behavioral change. People ought to have a close-time orientation, in terms of showing up for work when they should, planning ahead to get jobs done right, and being aware of the costs of time. They should be disciplined, in the sense of behaving toward their bosses, wanting to do a good job, and being willing to work until the task is finished. They should also have a high tolerance for boredom, if the job is a repetitious assembly-line activity. They should be change-oriented, willing to take a close look at new things, adopting them where necessary to get things done better. They should be scientifically oriented, well aware of cause/effect reasoning, so that when the machine needs oiling, it gets oiled, thus avoiding costly breakdowns and repairs. They should be team players, cooperating with many others in their tasks, so that the total job gets done with a minimum of effort. In short, they should behave about as we were urged to behave in innumerable Presbyterian church sermons in the late nineteenth century. If people acted like uptight, structured Calvinists of the old school, a lot of our problems would be gone.

If you don't like this image, consider the one common in modern communist countries, where the workers' paradise reigns supreme. What kinds of behavior should workers exhibit? Well, they should have a close-time orientation, in terms of showing up for work when they should, planning ahead to get jobs done right, and being aware of the costs of time. They should be disciplined, in the sense of behaving toward their bosses, wanting to do a good job, and being willing to work until the task is finished. They should also have a high tolerance for boredom. The more one looks at the modern industrial system, in many countries, the more it looks the same. Mr. Castro and Mr. Allende have more in common with the Calvinist preachers of yore than they ever would dream.

In modern America, we get this sort of behavior in a rather pleasant way. Those dedicated teachers work intensively with middle-class youngsters, indoctrinating them into the proper patterns of behavior. It's expensive, but it's fun, and we have the money. We send the kids to college for further indoctrination and training, and there we teach them a lot about concepts of excellence, discipline, and all the rest. And when they go to work in spotless offices or factories, we expect, and usually get, the kinds of behavior noted above.

No one punches a clock, because we expect that people will be disciplined. The boss doesn't have to yell or threaten, because skilled people doing interesting things generally will work well without the fuss. Treat people like nice guys, and they will treat you the same.

Historically it wasn't quite this easy. When the United States was poor, the system was tough. The boss did yell, and the teachers did threaten and flunk kids. People did punch time clocks, because you couldn't trust them otherwise. Workers were fired because they didn't obey orders. It was a rough, crude world, a kind of world that no one really likes, least of all a dedicated planner in a modern poor country. He, and his ancestors, have seen plenty of the threat systems in force, when the country was a colony of some arrogant European power, and if there is any other way to do the job, then he is for it. And along come the American theorists, with their nice-guy systems, their pleasant, work-together educational methods, and the idealistic notion that if we all treat each other well we will be highly productive. All ethical and religious systems point this way, and here are serious pedagogues and managers telling you that it really works. And, if you visit one of the primary schools in the right part of Bloomington, Indiana, or watch skilled technicians at a modern, highly productive American firm, you can see that it works. Why not take it home with you? It's the only way!

But in the organization's back rooms, something else is going on that no one likes to talk about. The finance department doesn't run this way—anyone who has been around more than five minutes knows that if we treat the people who handle cash like nice guys, the company will be broke within a week. Somehow, when the ultimate liquid asset is handled, the nice-guy idea breaks down. Any financial official who assumes anything but that everyone is either a crook or a potential crook is incompetent.

And in the ghetto, even in the factory itself, the time clocks are still there, and nice guys who try to operate find out to their dismay that nothing much works as it should.

You treat a guy right, and he turns around and takes advantage of you. You try to be kind to some poor fellow, and he kicks your teeth in. American cops are very dubious about nice-guy theories, because they so rarely see a nice guy. After all, the police have to grab the not-so-nice people out there.

Moreover, when the nice pleasant middle-class schools are transferred to the ghetto, nothing much works out the way it should. The nice-guy idea works well when the parents are pushing for you, but when the cultural situation is different, somehow things come unstuck. And back at the plant, if the janitor says he's going to his grandmother's funeral, you'd better check it, because you can't really trust him. But if the pleasant professional scientist with his Ph.D. says so, let him go—he can be trusted.

Somewhere around 1940, America began to shift from the older idea of people are no damn good to the more modern concept of people are really very nice guys. Since the top third of the population is pretty nice, including all the theorists and thinkers about human behavior and education, the experiments in trying nice-guy techniques worked out pretty well. There are thousands of reports on efforts to try nice-guy techniques with highly skilled and disciplined people that worked—and thinkers and planners in poor countries can read too. Take a group of highly skilled engineers who are being treated like cattle, put them in a nice-guy environment, where they can behave like the responsible professionals that they are, and output soars. Put some researchers in an environment where they can be more creative and individualistic, and the system operates beautifully. But—put a group of money-changers in the position where they are responsible for the money without supervision, and your company goes broke. This last is the one which is conveniently ignored, since it is not in tune with our present views of what man is, or more importantly, should be.

Since most people who talk, think, and write about organizing humans for production tasks are very nice guys, highly disciplined and able to handle their own affairs, the stress for thirty years has been on the nice-guy routine. And since most of us rather like the idea of being treated well, we find such ideas appealing. And since the poor-country thinkers and planner wants nothing but the best and latest, so does he. Besides, his ethics and values are at least as good as ours! The only problem is that the nice-guy structure doesn't work too well in poor countries. Love-and-kindness routines are fine for highly disciplined, well-trained professionals, but they don't work anywhere with underdeveloped people, which is of course what poor countries have in abundance. So, people don't get changed fast enough, or they don't get changed at all.

It can be put another way. One order a boss cannot give is, "Be creative!" Creative workers are creative if they feel like it. If they are working in a highly structured, authoritarian situation, they may get upset, and use all their creativity to get rid of the boss or sabotage the operation. Any college professor knows all about this technique, as do engineers, medical doctors, lawyers, and other professionals. But illiterate, unskilled ex-peasants rarely can be very creative, and acting as if they were leads to some disastrous results.

So, how does a poor country shape up its rather inept troops? Well, history in the affluent countries shows a precedent. Those dark satanic mills of the nineteenth century were systems to do the job. If the bosses kick the workers in the teeth, apply iron discipline, and structure the reward-punishment system so that one gets a low reward for being good, and a high punishment for being bad, then perhaps in twenty years you can do the job. If your primary schools look like the grimy cheap brick piles in 1900 America, many students will fail, but some will succeed. If you use piece-work to reward the producers, and low minimum wages for the rest, you can get some results. It's a cruel system, but it works—as every currently affluent country knows. And the communists aren't any better. They have their dark satanic mills too, and they push the workers around just as badly as any capitalist country ever did. They have to, to get results, since they too have to change behavior. To get economic development you need hard work and capital, and the only place the capital can be found is where production is happening. And the producers have to be squeezed viciously if they are to save—since they are far too poor to do it voluntarily. The United States did it this way; England did, Germany did; the Soviet Union did; and so will everyone else who wants to get in the game.

In modern America, anyone who advocates a return to the dim, cruel days of early industrialization is not likely to win popularity contests, nor is any politician in a poor country who seriously suggests this strategy. But what else is there? Already the love-and-kindness routines have brought down the death rates so there is a population explosion; if output doesn't go up, the country will fall apart anyhow. If we knew how to do the job with love-and-kindness routines, we would have, right in our own ghettos, a long time ago—but we don't.

Here we run into a common pattern in modern liberal thinking, which is absolutist. If a program is suggested which might benefit five hundred, but hurt ten, then don't do it. All must benefit. Military people know all about the other kind of thinking—minimize your losses to win, even if those losses are human lives. But military thinking is very unpopular these days. The same pattern of thinking is very evident in poor countries. After all, they got it from us. Don't do anything which might be considered inhumane. Yet the usual results, if one seriously tries to adopt such a policy operationally, is that more people are hurt through inaction, incompetence, and just plain inability to get anything done than ever were hurt through application of the older threat system.

Let's go back to the American ghetto to see how this works out. Because it is impossible to use tough threat systems in education, few get educated. So the whole generation goes down the drain, instead of the few that might really get hurt by a tough system. Because all people have to have the best possible housing, or none at all, we end up with none at all—since we can't find the talent or resources to house every poor person simultaneously. Because we can't or won't try threat systems to get workers on the job, and to fire them if they don't behave, we have high unemployment rates. Because it is immoral to get rid of garbage and rats on a piece-work system, we have lots of garbage and more rats than anyone would like. Because it is unethical and immoral to force people to change, they don't change—and they stay poor. It's the same in poor countries, except that the whole country operates like one of our most dreary ghettos. Meanwhile, out in the minute, 1 percent part of the society which faintly resembles the affluent West, the same love-and-kindness routines are earnestly practiced with some success—but they don't change very much. The poor stay poor, and the population keeps on growing to eventual disaster.

We've been hooked good on the narcotic of good people doing good things. Worse, we've sold the idea completely to countries that don't have a prayer of getting as far with the idea as we can get. Maybe, though, there is a somewhat better way to get the job done than the miserable, cruel, tough way most affluent countries did the job. But any options which will work would take more hard-nosed thinking than most countries (except a few communist dictatorships) are willing to do.

It could work out this way: The trick is to pay for what you want done, and don't pay for negative behavior. This is not exactly a new principle, but it is one which is non-U in the United States today. If you want people to learn to read and do basic arithmetic, then don't have a clumsy school system, full of expensive ideas about God and motherhood—pay off those who pass the examinations, and don't worry too much about how they managed to learn. A variation on this theme is to pay the fellow who taught them to read, too —in short, have a free enterprise, profit-making primary educational system.

This idea appalls educators, since it isn't what school is

supposed to do, but the meaningful and realistic option is to have a lot of illiterates around. When you have perhaps 80 percent adult illiteracy in a really poor country, no amount of hand-wringing and wishful thinking will ever get the job done in a realistic time period. Since everyone is diploma-oriented, it would be nice to have a beautiful sheepskin to go with the test-passing, complete with gold seal. If the diploma becomes a passport to simple jobs involving literacy skills (such as a postman), your problem is likely to be getting enough honest examiners, not finding people willing to take the tests.

This idea could be pushed up to all kinds of needed vocational education and skills—anyone who has worked in a poor country knows how desperately short such places are of good typists, file clerks, parts-changing mechanics, and so on. Where simple skills can be tested for competence, pay off people who are willing to invest their time and money in learning them.

Ivan Illich has argued that school systems in very poor countries are a fraud—they do not lead to equality or even provide education, but rather make for class discrimination and elitist creation of the worst sort. When he notes that a country like Chile (which isn't even very poor) has only about 2 percent completing high school and 1 percent college, you can see what he means. This elite, which most likely hasn't learned much that is useful anyhow, runs the country. The other 98 percent are out of the game before they begin. No wonder they have a Marxist government *and* economic stagnation. The egalitarian promise of a free public education just doesn't work out that way in practice. So dump the system (or more realistically, allow the school system to stagnate) and get out and pay off poor people to learn what needs to be learned.

You rich Americans that are reading this (and if your income is over a thousand dollars a year, you're stinking rich by the standards of the poor people being talked about in this book) may think that money won't work, because it isn't everything. But poor people respond very well to money incentives, if they understand the game, because they just happen to need money. That's what poverty is all about. So pay off for peanuts to get the job done. If there is money in it, the hustlers will figure out how to teach fast, and the poor will figure out how to learn fast, too.

Teachers also dislike this idea intensely because if you're good you get rich. If you can't teach, you starve. If you want egalitarianism and not much education, do it the old way— if you really want people to learn by the millions, figure out how. This suggestion will work, if the structure is properly meshed with the poor country's economy and society. I haven't figured out a better way. Can you?

Another similar tack is to go back to piece work and reward systems which work very fast and which pay to do the right things. We have talked about rat bounties and similar payoffs in the American ghetto. The same kinds of things could be used in factories, in transportation, and in services. And the payoff has to be quick, since the time horizon of the poor is so very short. We sometimes paid day laborers in Arabia piecework rates daily—if we did it weekly, they lost interest by the second day. Moreover, they had a bad habit of not showing up for a week or so with all that money in their pocket.

Businessmen of course know all about this sort of thing, and they like it because it gets the job done. Others find the system painful, unethical, and evil. Well, get the job done some other way, then. The hang-up, to repeat, is that not everyone out there is a nice guy like you. The poor are kind of nasty people—they are sick, unreliable, cheaters, and con men. That's why they're poor. But examination of any now-rich country shows that you can push a lot of poor people into the middle class with this technique. And then their kids go to school, and all of a sudden (like, forty years) you don't have so many poor people around any more. A guy who gets locked into a piecework, reward-oriented system gets used to it after a while. He learns skills, develops pride in his work—and then, to everyone's surprise, the boss finds out that he doesn't need the time clocks and the threat system any more. He's got a nice guy on his hands.

My dad came out of the New Mexico hills in 1910, when he was sixteen, to take his apprenticeship with the railroad. The apprentices worked seven days a week, ten hours a day, for four years (in the last two years, they got an occasional Sunday off). If you missed a day, you were fired; if you didn't obey the boss, you got canned; if you were dumb enough to think you had any rights, they got rid of you. Since they were working with semiliterate peasants, and since the world was like that way back when, this was how guys were hammered into shape.

Dad sits back and laughs all the way to the bank these days, enjoying his retirement. He saved his money, minded the boss, obeyed orders, learned his machinist's trade well, suffered a lot, and got hammered into shape. And he sent his kids all the way to college and beyond. If dad had been treated as we treat, or try to treat, the ghetto kids these days, I'd be out on some cruddy New Mexico farm, wondering why, with the lousy eighth-grade education I had, I couldn't get ahead. Like everything else in this world, there's no easy way to do the job, though most modern thinkers appear to believe that there is. Good luck, but it just won't work too well in most places around the world.

CHAPTER **XVIII**

. . . .

Calvinists, Shintoists, and Other Uptight Super-Achievers

The workers and peasants may have to get pushed around a bit to get the job done, but there is another dimension to human behavior which is very important. This is the way managers and entrepreneurs act as they plot their organizations' development and expansion. In the end, some manager or owner has to figure out what to do next—which market to expand into, which new facilities to build (if any), where to go to get the necessary capital to do the job, and how to get their company structured into the whole economy better and more effectively. Such decisions, lots of folklore to the contrary, don't just happen—normally they are the result of much creative thinking about what to do next. The American historical landscape is littered with firms, large and small, which could not carry out this adjustment process well enough. Abroad, half-finished factories, publicly owned firms generating huge losses, and ineffectual companies dot the various countries.

So what kinds of people should be the managers? We want, of course, highly educated and trained men and women, who know what is to be done, and who can generate enthusiasm in their subordinates to do it. We want people

259

who can correctly forecast what is needed, when, and why. We want people who can work with government agencies, who can persuasively argue their case for improvement where necessary. We want them to be hard-working, dynamic types who will stay with the job until it is finished. We want scientifically oriented people, who know all about cause-and-effect reasoning. We may even want people who will respond very well to whatever reward system there is, be it money, prestige, a knighthood, or power. And we want people who get the job done, who will drive forward across obstacles to win, at whatever cost to themselves. In short, we want an uptight super-achiever.

Such people are rarely very pleasant individuals, but as lots of firms have discovered to their sorrow, the nice guys usually finish last. The manager or owner who puts his workers' welfare above getting something done won't be around long, as his firm goes broke. Paradoxically, the hard-driving guy who does the job first and worries about his workers second will give them more in the end—they will have the well-paying, productive jobs, and won't be looking for work because their boss tried to be a nice guy. The publicly owned firm which drifts along will have the very high costs and low output. Not so the firm that acts tough and gets the job done with a minimum of time, machines, and labor.

Economic growth, moreover, calls for more than just cycling the existing system. As soon as the company gets organized and productive, it should be out there trying something new, unsettling markets, productive techniques, and workers. As soon as a worker learns his job well, he should be pushed into something new and more productive. The more of this you get, if it's done right, the more productive and faster growing the country will be. Few of us really like change of this sort—we would rather cycle ourselves in a much more relaxed way. The idea of constantly getting restructured and being forced to learn new tricks leads to problems. But our entrepreneurs and managers should be prodding us this way all the time. Here again is why such people, if they do this successfully, are not ordinarily seen as nice guys. They are just too pushy for the rest of us. Hence they tend to get a bad press wherever they operate. The historical fact that the way they got rewarded was with money, and some of them made huge piles of it, did not help either— who likes billionaires? And the unpleasant habit many of the plutocrats had of conspicuously consuming while the masses starved was not an exactly appealing trait.

The American Way

Nineteenth-century America was full of uptight super-achievers, and the times were ripe for them. The country was open to the west, and the eastern elites could not control very tightly land wealth, which in other countries has had a very stabilizing and antigrowth effect. Those interested in achieving could always bail out westward. Social feelings were also right—any man could achieve anything, without much opposition from the state. Taxes were minimal, and if workers or farmers got had, it was too bad. They were supposed to be able to take care of themselves. And new technologies were coming in in a rush, with intoxicating profit opportunities for those clever enough to take advantage of them. So we got the robber barons, and anyone going to even small libraries can find lots of history about their vast fortunes, their political and business intrigues, and their wild living habits. Their expertise in squashing the working man and farmer is also very well documented.

Not so well documented are the achievements. Somehow, the robber barons managed to figure out how to get thousands of not very skilled workmen organized to accomplish such difficult tasks as running railroads or refining petroleum. Somehow they managed to get subordinate managers to do the work for them. No one manages ten or fifteen thousand men by himself. Somehow the moguls managed to get output up every year, and somehow others' incomes went up too. If a few guys were smashed in the struggle, well, that's the way it was. Moreover, the huge incomes of the super-rich typically went right back into productive investment. What did Carnegie do with his money? Typically, he used it to build some more steel mills. Rockefeller expanded his oil complex, the Vanderbilts built more railroads. To say that a man has $50 million often seems to be interpreted as his having a lot of ten-thousand-dollar bills in his safe. More often, it means he owns productive assets in that amount— and as his wealth goes up, so do the assets. And those assets are exactly what economic growth is all about.

Through the years things became different. Taxes went up; the corporation (so cleverly exploited by the early robber barons) became something run by professional (and uptight) managers, rather than owners; and the wealth grew so large that even the greatest of the robber barons could not finance it all. Public indignation about the worst of the labor practices led to social-security legislation and fair-employment-practices acts. Gradually, the American society calmed down, and the gaps between rich and poor got a bit smaller. Moreover, the rise of the professionals meant that lots more people could have a nice, comfortable income, instead of sweating it out in some smoky factory. The uptight, hard-working types are still around, but they are likely to be professional managers, medical doctors, lawyers, or maybe even professors, not entrepreneurs. The days when any young fellow with $200 could start a business and be a millionaire by age forty seem far away. (Minor point— hundreds of Americans still do it every decade in the old way, but what's a million these days? They work quietly, and without much fuss in putting together the new ventures. But the economy is now so big that they are lost in the shuffle.) The fact remains that we all are riding the backs of the plutocrats and robber barons, to say nothing of the exploited workers in their dingy factories. These people from our own dim past are the ones that worked, saved, and invested, so that the industrial base could be created. After this was done, and the self-sustaining system got going, we were able to ride it all the way to now. They successfully innovated, broke up the agrarian culture, and started us off on the trip we are now taking.

Meanwhile, in Japan

The Japanese did it a bit differently. With the Meiji restoration in the 1870s, the leaders realized that they had to go through the industrial process if they were to maintain their power and prestige. Beating the West became a game the Japanese still play. The leaders were fortunate—not only did they have a group of well-educated ex-warriors to work with, but they also had a homogeneous culture, afraid of the West, confident of their own destiny, certain that they could do the job. The early industrial pattern was for the state to start something, get it going, and then pass it on to one of Japan's big industrial combines, based on family ties, and full of uptight, super-achieving Shintoists. These talented men worked hard, saved the company's money to invest in new enterprises, actively pursued the latest scientific and technical knowledge available in the West, and reached 1941 with an empire built and the ability to challenge the West on its own terms. Unfortunately for us, and fortunately for Japan, they couldn't quite pull off their dream of world empire. After the war they still had all of the uptight types around and opportunity beckoned. World trade was just beginning its incredible postwar expansion, and a group of promoters and salesmen who could provide cheap goods to the rest of the world was a welcome addition to the world's economic base.

Japan, of course, had the advantage of winning World War II. Their military defeat was total—most of industry was in ruins, and production was back at the subsistence level or below in 1945. And after the war, the Americans insisted that the Japanese stay out of military and diplomatic affairs. In a very real sense, there was nothing to do but commit suicide or go back to work creating a nonmilitary, nonimperialistic system, which the Japanese did. The United States, bemused like everyone else by military and political power, thought it was crushing Japan. It turned out very differently. All the creative, uptight, hard-working Japanese had to go to work in industry and commerce—there were no real alternatives. This meant that all creative Japanese now had to succeed in business. A good engineer in the United States would probably be working on some nonproductive military system; a similarly good Japanese engineer had to design a better tape recorder for Sony. Americans seem baffled that Japanese technology is so good, even though American education is so much more extensive. Why not? The Japanese technicians work where the market is— and the market is what income growth is all about.

Another key point was the total destruction of Japanese industry. All the hard-working types had to build new factories—which not only utilized the best technology, but also were placed properly to utilize the lowest-cost raw materials from abroad. Having "won" the war, Japan had no need or ability to utilize second-best local raw materials— the country simple imported high-grade goods from wherever they could be obtained cheaply. Meanwhile, American firms payed high energy costs, because the country has oil import quotas to protect local firms. English and French firms have to figure out how to use high-cost local coal, which of course must be protected. And if a steel mill tries to get away from the high-cost state-owned railway system, it can't. The Japanese, freed from these constraints, simply outproduced everyone with their new, low-cost, well-located plant run by the best people in the country.

Japan also became an open economy, because it had to. On the import side, it was able to avoid imports of both capital and competitive goods, because it was too poor to do otherwise—and so far, Japanese leaders have made this practice stick. On the export side, the problem was to produce what the world wanted, not what some Japanese thought was a good idea. Hence the country became market-oriented. If you want it, we'll provide it, became the watchword. Americans, used to exporting as a sideline, have watched market after market fall to clever Japanese salesmen. So have other countries.

No foreigners told the Japanese to get into steel, machinery, shipbuilding, electronics, or autos. These decisions were made cooperatively by Japanese government officials (another uptight, hard-working bunch) and Japanese managers. Once the basic decisions were made, however, a lot of creative work had to be done. The equipment had to be designed properly, with world markets in mind; the engineers and technicians had to do the design and tooling work; the markets had to be analyzed and covered with salesmen; and all the rest. Such things don't just happen—but they can occur if a group of hard-working managers, supported by equally disciplined and hard-working technicians and workers, are willing to put out.

In Japan, you get the right combination of government-labor-firm cooperation, lots of hard work, and everyone willing to work for the cause. You also get a 30 percent saving rate by consumers, which is about four times the American rate. And those savings are invested, to build more plants and machines to raise output more. It's a nice game, if you can match it. No other country has.

In both Japan and the United States, history presents us with a group of almost fanatical industrial leaders, men who wanted something and went out to get it, no matter what the consequences. One key result was that society was changed for good, upward. No one will argue that such people were exactly nice guys, but most would agree that they changed things—including the poor peasants and workmen who got in their way. By the time society got around to stopping them (and one doubts that the Japanese have got this far yet), they had already launched the country onto new paths, for better or worse. The negative results led to reform, criticism, and intensive study. By now, such activities are not seen as "nice," and elites in poor countries read and study Western books and documents too. Somehow the whole process seems cruel, unfair, and degrading. Maybe it was— but it also was wealth-creating.

The State as Entrepreneur

In poor countries, the usual modern game is to have the state act as entrepreneur. Instead of vulgar capitalists (except, perhaps, for some Americans or Europeans in the guise of multinational firms), the country has state corporations, with various sectors of the economy staked out. Thus we find a state steel company, a state railroad and airline, a state bus system, a state port and docks company, and so on. This is not a radical concept; in both Western Europe and the United States similar companies are found. But unlike the affluent countries, where such activities are only a small part of the modern economic sector, it is likely that the state companies in poor countries are the bulk, if not all, of the modern, expensive productive sector. How well do such companies operate? Badly, in most cases. The men at the top are the most talented to be found; the technicians and engineers are usually superior to those found in the private sector; and workers are usually better paid as well. But somehow such firms have trouble getting off the ground.

One key reason has been discussed. Private firms, with simple, single-minded goal systems, can usually do better than public firms with somewhat nebulous goal systems. Another reason for inept performances lies in the nature of the state entrepreneur as compared to the usual private one. The state man, like most of his affluent country counterparts, is some type of civil servant, politician, or military man. He got as far as he did by being pretty well educated, and adept at ducking really sticky political questions. In the civil service, order and stability are the rule, and the man who is good enough to run a sedate, quiet department without too much fuss may well be the man who is considered for bigger and better things. If, in most countries, he comes from the right kind of family, with the right kinds of friends, so much the better. But we rarely see a wild-eyed type win big in the civil service. The man may well be a brilliant organizer, but he is not likely to be willing to take big risks.

The politician is used to compromise—that's what his game is all about. When he gets the top managerial job in the state company, his natural instinct is to put together an unbeatable coalition, including anyone around (such as labor) who might be interested in the problem. The name of the game is power—getting more and keeping what you have—so the managerial style is likely to be coalition power-oriented, and hang the output. His counterpart, the military man, has one advantage; he knows that there is only one goal—to win. But he may well have his hang-ups too. In most countries, the military is a part of the political power system, so the military man may well go the route of the politician. If he does not, he may go the route of the civil servant, since order, effective organization of the troops, and routinized behavior are also a part of his peacetime game.

An occasional oddball, such as a scholar or ex-private businessman, gets into the game from time to time. The scholars are pretty bad, since they always want more data before doing anything; the ex-private businessmen usually get people so annoyed in a year or so that they gratefully return to private life.

The usual pattern of state firms in noncommunist countries is to have a separate corporation reporting to a cabinet minister. When problems arise, the minister has to defend or explain his corporation. The board of directors is typically appointed from the elites—military men, civil servants, politicians, and so on. Now, the heat goes on really fast if any public corporation gets in a spot where costs have to be

cut—which happens sooner or later. My costs are your income—so those who are hurt scream. Workers being laid
off send delegates to the parliament, and opposition politicians, smelling a nice issue, press embarrassing questions.
Private firms whose contracts were cut back also yelp.
Within a short time, if the manager is wise, he quietly makes
a deal for the state to cover his losses, while his costs stay
high. If he is really astute, he never gets into this public spot
in the first place. The deal is made in advance. Of course, no
government is willing to give any manager a really high payoff for success. His salary will be high by local standards, but
not excessive—to do otherwise would subject the government to searching criticism and inquiry. And there are no
juicy stock options, bonuses, or other tangible symbols of
success either. Like other government employment, this state
managerial job is well paid, but not exactly exciting.

On the other hand, if you make a mistake, you are removed
—this is one major reason why the state firm is a separate corporation, away from civil service. The game is structured so that a manager can't win big, but may lose
everything. Moreover, you can lose if any of your clientele
gets upset—labor, suppliers, the general public, consumers, your ministry, or your own junior managers. Since
doing anything positive is bound to upset someone, the odds
on your being blown out of the saddle for doing much of
anything are high. Low costs are incompatible with high
wages; rapid product-mix changes may satisfy consumers, but
upset your own junior managers; making key components
yourself may upset key suppliers; and so on. The best strategy is to do as little as possible and look forward to retirement. Only when ministerial heat is very high should you do
anything, and even then do it cautiously.

Another common problem occurs when two state firms
collide. If you start expanding, you may get in another firm's
way. A railroad which begins air services may find that its
competitor is another firm—and trouble is certain.
So, even if the airline is doing a dreadful job, and even if

airplanes are better than trains in a given situation, better not to move—it's safer and less troublesome all around. If you are using state coal from another company for your power generation, and you know that natural gas would be a better and cheaper fuel, forget it—it could cost you your job to change. Americans who have to live with the New York Port Authority, the Chicago Transit Authority, or the Los Angeles Transit Authority, know something about this point. It is not that the problems of state-owned firms are hopeless—it is that they have such great difficulty in getting their jobs done, given the structure they work with, plus their nebulous, ill-structured goal systems. He who tries to please everybody ends up pleasing nobody—and to boot, he ends up doing very little innovating either, unless the general political consensus is so great as to force change. Occasionally we find such consensus, but it seems rare in this complex world.

Meanwhile, in the Poor Country's Private Sector

One of the ironies of development is that a country which proudly proclaims itself as socialist (e.g., India) has less public enterprise and government activity than the United States. The bulk of economic activity in any poor country is in the private sector, concentrated mainly in such areas as peasant agriculture, petty services such as small-scale retailing, and a bit of light manufacturing. Like small firms everywhere, these activities are very profit-oriented, but typically they are so small that no one cares about them. A major reason why they are private is that the typical poor-country government does not have the organizational expertise to control them. Even in communist countries much petty private-firm activity goes merrily along.

The entrepreneurs in these small firms are typically crafty, smart, and shrewd—but often very badly educated. Frequently, they are pariahs—not of the dominant religion or ethnic stock. This is because commerce and trade have long been considered vulgar, crude, and not really the sort of thing nice people will do. Given a choice, the smart young man goes into government or the military for a career, or perhaps even the ministry. But minorities are excluded from lucrative and prestigious careers, so they are stuck with business. Americans think that their own racial and sometimes religious problems are serious, but they haven't seen real hatred. This happens in poor countries where detested, and totally discriminated against minorities struggle along. Even when they grow rich, the minorities are still detested. Anyone coming up with a government program to help out such persons would be out of power in a couple of days. This is one major reason, incidentally, why state ownership is so attractive. Not only does it tie in with a country's idea of good careers in government, but it cuts off a lot of bums who don't deserve support.

In poor countries, there typically is one major activity—agriculture, which means that there is one traditional source of wealth—land. The elites in such cultures own land and get income from it. And all the land is owned and has been owned for a thousand years or more. There is no place to go to find riches here, except revolution—which is a major reason why communism and land reform are always such big issues in poorer countries. Unfortunately, a landed gentry rarely generates the type of person who is so common in the United States—the fabled robber barons of yore, who screwed everyone to get what they wanted. Rather, the elites send their sons to the right military schools and foreign universities, to take up sedate and prestigious nonmoney-generating careers that matter. When the pressure mounts for getting into the modern world, the elites will accept state ownership rather than vulgar capitalism. It's the right way to do the job. After all, everyone has a son or cousin in a key position in the right ministries, so the prestigious jobs will go to them, not to a bunch of improbable outcasts peddling groceries down the street. And the one outcast in a million, the fellow who finally does make it big? More often than not, he is absorbed—his daughters marry the local gentry, and his firm gets the key state monopolies, maybe in the third generation. And all is as before— static, nongrowth-oriented, and monopolistic. Since everything in the system is oriented to a static nongrowth situation, there is no particular incentive to have anything happen. It doesn't.

Putting It All Together

We Americans of this generation had it lucky. Most of the dirty work was done by our grandfathers, so we didn't have to go through the mill. We also had a situation where almost everyone around was some sort of outcast, and most of them were very uptight Calvinist types, always striving for the impossible. Even the non-Calvinists (e.g., the Catholics) began to behave that way in large numbers. And still better, there never was a land monopoly for the elites to dominate. Further, we inherited an Anglo-Saxon philosophy of letting things alone—they would work out all right in the end. By the time we tried to do something, it was too late. So, put together a hard-working population, a group of half-mad entrepreneurs without many restrictions, willing to take all sorts of improbable risks, an impotent landed gentry incapable of stopping the process—and here we are.

Those Japanese were lucky too. They had an educated population, an underemployed military elite with no place to go, and a homogeneous population, scared to death of the West and sure that they were the best in the world. To prove it, they copied and outcopied the West to the point where now everybody is more afraid of a Japanese salesman than they ever were of the Japanese generals.

Those West Europeans were also lucky. They had England in the nineteenth century, full of uptight Calvinist types, breaking loose from the feudal shackles, trying to

excel in science and industry—and incidentally, in the
process, getting stinking rich. They also had ancient animosities, wars, and situations where the winner had better have
the best guns science could produce. So they produced them,
and if the landed gentry objected, to hell with them—
look at how we got mauled in the last war! And since most
of the gentry were running the army anyhow, the new society was easy to sell.

The modern poor countries aren't so lucky. They have the
worst of all possible worlds—a population which is non-
Western and not really all that concerned with work, saving,
and all the rest; an elite which thinks that the whole business is a waste of time; a communist threat which really
offers very little different from what they now have; a push,
for all the good reasons in the world, toward a big state-
owned industrial sector; and a group of small businessmen
who are definitionally out of the game and beyond any realistic help. They have a civil-service mentality in exactly the
economic sectors which should be dynamic. And for some
reason, while things do move ahead, they never go as fast as
anyone wants. In attempting to be nice guys and accommodate everyone, they end up not really doing the job for anyone.

I wonder why.

. . . .

The Care and Feeding of Uglies: American, German, Russian, and Japanese Varieties

The ugly American has already reached the stage of mythology—the blundering, ignorant, culture-blind type who wanders around some poor foreign country fouling things up. Not as well known, but just as clumsy, are various other national types. The Russians have as much trouble as the Americans, if not more, in really poor countries; the Germans and other West Europeans also have their problems; and more recently the Japanese are getting into the act. In all cases, the image is the same. The technician arrives to save the culture. Within a few weeks (or even days) he is in deep trouble. Those hanging around the bars frequented by foreigners can hear various horror stories about the ignorant locals, the way they can't seem to get anything straight, and cutting comments about the idiosyncrasies of the local leaders and elites. Harassed technicians from various affluent countries count the days until their contract is up and they can go back to civilization.

On the other side of the fence, the local people are polite but concerned. They accept the foreigners because they have something to offer in the development process—yet, why do they always act so crudely? Why do they consistently and sys-

273

tematically fail to understand what is really going on? They appear to have the skills, knowledge, and technical ability the country so badly needs, but it would be nice if they managed to transmit their skills without being so crummy about it!

What's happening here is cultural confrontation, where a member of a rich and powerful culture is faced with the problem of telling someone from a not-so-rich and rather impotent culture how to get the job done right. The very nature of this confrontation creates lots of problems which relatively few people have been able to get a handle on, largely because everyone is looking at the wrong things. Everyone is equally guilty or innocent in this confrontation, and they will continue to be until someone figures out what the real problem is.

The visitor from a rich country who comes to work in a poor one has certain characteristics which virtually guarantee that he will cause trouble, the most important of which is that he is from a culture that is not only different but interested in warping the poor country's culture its way. In short, he is involved in culture-busting in a major way. Since no one is willing to face up to this fact, everyone gets confused. Here is how the uglies start breaking things up:

Foreigners are rich, so rich as to be almost beyond the dreams of the local peasantry or workers. A welfare mother in Chicago gets as much money as a professor or lawyer in most countries—a good technician or engineer will make perhaps twenty to one hundred times as much as the people he is trying to help. Of course the few local elitists will have ample incomes, but these persons are not those being changed. Few of us like really rich persons, and the sight of a man who may have some abilities, but who makes so much more than we do for mysterious reasons, is not likely to be very popular for this reason alone. His servants, big house, cars, and all the rest will be observed with great care, but not with any particular affection.

The technician who arrives in the poor country is there

because he is a good technician, not because he understands the culture. Good engineers, managers, physicists, agronomists, and all the rest are typically not very sensitive to their cultural differences. Indeed, because their disciplines often are quite scientific, they frequently tend to assume that they are culture-free and value-free—hence whatever might be different in the local culture is probably irrelevant to their jobs. They forget that the very scientific method itself is a value system, and one which is not particularly well known or accepted outside the affluent countries. If it were, the country they are trying to help would not need much help.

This leads quickly to the common complaint that local workers and technicians in the poor country are irrational and don't behave the way they should. Instead of hiring the best engineer, somebody's cousin gets the job. What is happening is a cultural conflict—in societies with extended-family relationships, the cousin is the logical man for the job. The idea that he cannot perform properly by rational criteria is irrelevant. The foreign ugly, seeing this happen, concludes that the peasants in this godforsaken place just don't understand the problem. They just don't behave right— which is a quite correct observation. But the familiar reaction of yelling a lot does not get the job done; it simply leads to more conflicts.

Technicians are also very accustomed to quite elaborate support systems for their work, and they rarely are even aware that these exist. At home clerks can file; typists can type; mail gets delivered; and the electric power system always works. But in the poor country, none of this happens or if it does, it happens badly. The typical result sends a good technician up the wall as he tries to type his own letters, run his own lab samples, or find the lost mail. After a few months of this, people start talking to themselves. Instead of doing their jobs, they end up doing everyone else's job. Things taken for granted at home just don't happen that way in the field.

Because technicians come from a meritocratic society, they

also assume that top people know their jobs. If a man at home is a lab manager, he knows what to do. But in a poor country, this is a wild assumption. It is quite likely that local higher-ups don't really have much idea about what is going on. Often they are hopeful that the narrow technician will also take over the administrative or managerial job—which the poor foreign ugly may be unwilling or unable to do. I have seen a lot of narrow technical types running the whole show, not because they wanted to but because they backed into a vacuum. Of course they did not have the authority, which made their task worse, but what else could they do if the job were to be done?

Very importantly, few technical people know much about economics, and they tend to bring with them the same capital output ratios they experience at home. Thus in the United States, capital is cheap and labor is very expensive, so most factories, mines, and other productive systems are designed with the idea of using lots of capital and not much labor. You see this idea in operation every time you take an automatic elevator. Long ago, labor got far too expensive to have elevator girls, so now some small computer does the job —and it isn't too cheap.

So, when a building in the very poor country is built, it has automatic elevators too. Of course they have to be imported—few really poor countries have the skilled labor and technicians to design and manufacture them. Hence, foreign exchange costs and capital costs go up. And of course you need a highly skilled technician to maintain the things, which the poor country doesn't have either. No one, least of all the foreign technician who is helping out, thinks about this problem. All buildings have automatic elevators; it is a fact of life.

But when the elevator fails to operate and can't be fixed, everyone gets upset. Somehow these brilliant foreign technicians goofed—the building can't even be used! Elevators may be trivial, but when manufacturing plants, railways, and other heavy capital installations are designed and built for the poor country, and when nothing works very well because the skills and abilities of the work force just aren't there to keep them going, there is plenty of trouble.

Poor countries don't help much. They want nothing but the best, and any naïve technician who suggested that the country install hand-operated elevators instead of the most modern automatics would be sent home posthaste. Most technicians are very proud of their work, and they are trained to do the best they can. This leads to the most advanced design work being done—and without the back-up support of all the things at home, such as maintenance technicians, skilled workers, and all the rest, the project can come unstuck very easily. When it does, both foreign uglies and local elites can get very upset. Remember, everyone looks up—and foreign uglies, working way out in some poor country, are no exception.

If it makes Americans feel any better, the ugly Russians are much worse than we are on this particular point. Coming from a culture where heavy capital investment has replaced religion, their inclination is to build bigger and more capital intensive than Americans do. And their projects get into exactly the same kinds of trouble, only more so, than the American ones.

Technicians and professionals also tend to be oriented to their profession, not to the poor country. A good engineer looks to other engineers in his specialty for applause, not to some odd local elitist who happens to want something done. Since the foreign ugly has never even seen the country he is working in before, he is not likely to be emotionally involved with it. He simply wants to get the job done and go home. But the locals are passionately involved with the local culture, and everything that happens is interpreted as being good or bad for the country. Debates between these two types on some minor technical point can be enlightening—it is as if two different types of beings were debating. There simply is no room or ground for rational debate, let alone any kind of agreement.

Take one simple example, like digging an irrigation ditch. It can be an exercise in confusion and futility. The engineer knows exactly how to do the job—he has his ditchdiggers, surveyors, and dump trucks all lined up (note the capital intensivity—the right way to do the job in most poor countries would be with some fellows with shovels, but that is not the way you dig ditches in the United States, so the ditchdigging equipment is imported, as is the guy who runs it and the fellows who maintain it). The local elitist, however, has his problems. He has struggled for months or years with his superiors to get this project started, and his local reputation may well hinge on how it works. He needs some local employment to enhance his prestige, and he wants the engineer to put about two hundred relatives and political hangers-on onto the payroll. None are necessary to the technical effort, but all are necessary politically. And all they do to the engineer is get in the way of doing an efficient job. After everybody shouts and cries a lot, perhaps 150 of the boys are put on the job some place, and the engineer has an extra drink that night back at the hotel. Oh, boy, when my contract expires. The local politician sighs as he goes home. If only those crazy foreigners would to the job logically, we would all be better off.

Because technicians are proud of their work, and because they usually do a good professional job, this sort of thing drives them nuts. It also leads them to emphasize subtly, or not so subtly, the inherent superiority of their own culture. "Back in Iowa," the engineer says (where, by implication, people know what they are doing), "we do it this way. . . ." The engineer from the poor country who is working with him grits his teeth and tries to smile. He knows we aren't back in Iowa—we're out here in his country!

The innate superiority of the home culture is expressed in statements like these—clichés all, but heard every few minutes around any poor-country operation where the uglies operate:

"How much is that in American money?"

"Oh, I like it here, but why don't they do something about the bugs?"

"Did you see all those dirty feet when we had to take off our shoes at the mosque today?"

"Why don't they have a few decent supermarkets in this town?"

"I hate to shop in the bazaar—you never know what the prices are."

"Don't drink the local water—you never know. . . ."

"The local peasants are so picturesque!"

Even if true, such comments are a bit strong for the local sensitivities.

Women Go, Too

Good technical people have the habit of getting married, and their wives often come with them on their foreign assignments. At least the men have their work to fret about, and they work long and hard at their tasks. But the women typically have to sit at home and wonder what to do next. There seems to be two types of women in this game. One type wishes fervently that she had never left Kokomo. She hangs around the air-conditioned house, plays bridge with other idle wives, and sometimes drinks more than she should. This type hates the noise, dirt, bugs, people, and everything else about the place—except the numerous servants she can push around. At least that isn't like home! She counts the days until she can get back home.

The other type dives right into the local culture. She starts learning the language, roams the villages and bazaars, and generally gets involved—maybe too involved in cultures where the role of women is quite different from that at home. Of course she assumes that she will be herself—no veil in Muslim countries, and no local strictures along religious or vocational lines. Such gals can do more culture-busting than their husbands, because they seem so harmless.

They chat with local ladies, start or suggest such radical
things as local schools for adult illiterates, well-baby clinics,
and birth-control systems. Why not? Things need to be
done! Sometimes they do get things done. And because they
are working with other local women in informal ways, they
can plant all sorts of revolutionary seeds before the local
people even know what they are up to.

Few technicians marry a girl because she might be one
sort or another overseas. But the kind of wife a fellow has
can make a huge difference in what actually happens out
there. There is an image of the ugly American male—but
the image of the female is quite blurred. No one in poor
countries knows quite how to take the wide variety of American and European women they encounter.

Neo-Imperialism and All That

If the technician is overseas on a government project, quite
likely his country has a vested interest in things other than
the project. Perhaps the Americans are buying some anti-
communist insurance, or perhaps the Soviets are trying to
impress a neutral country. Aid always has some strings, even
though many would prefer to ignore this fact. Aid allows
others to get into the game, such as CIA men (or the equivalent Russians or Germans or Japanese), propaganda experts,
communications specialists whose main job is influence, not
technology, and all the rest. Such people are often extremely
inept—after all, they are culture-bound too. Those who are
really familiar with third-world countries find American efforts along these lines in such places as Vietnam somewhat
humorous and rather sad. It is as if a hot-shot American soap
salesman tried to peddle his wares to the Hottentots. But
such interference can be quite annoying to the local elites
and peasants alike. It is annoying to discover that a fellow
who is supposed to be an expert on rice marketing is really a

bungling secret agent, who may not even be a very good agent, let alone a skilled rice marketer.

On Being Culture-Bound

What all this adds up to is that our technology and management is more culture-bound than most of us realize. Since the culture we affluent types come from happens to be the one which pays off at the economic gate, lots of poor countries would like the same, and they are often eager to get the foreign uglies to come and show them how to accomplish it. But moving something simple like an automatic elevator to a poor country often involves far more cultural change than anyone, least of all the technician, realizes. When you buy death control, you may end up buying it all—and the technician, interested mainly in his own narrow tasks, rarely realizes that he is merely putting one more pressure on some poor culture that is going to blow up all the way.

What to do? We all know that there is another kind of foreign technician, the kind who recognizes quite clearly what he is up to, the fellow who is sensitive to local values and mores. He is the person who tries to learn a bit of the language, empathizes well with his local counterparts and tries to understand what is really going on in his new country. He is the one who will wander out into the villages, instead of hanging around the bar in the capital, trying to see what is really going on. He's the man who will spend a lot of his own time (and often his wife's) working informally with citizens on all sorts of things he knows about. He might even help. He's the fellow who will take some time to think in advance why Ahmed really wants all those useless people on the job, and help him find a politic way out of his dilemma.

We have our images reversed. In the novel *The Ugly American,* the ugly one was the good guy. He was the one

who introduced the long-handled broom, which revolution-
ized housework in his country. He was the man who thought
small and tried to get some leverage in the system. And for
every crude idiot in the field these days, there are perhaps
twenty good guys. But people remember the bad ones, not the
fellows who do the job right.

The Peace Corps is another example of the new thinking.
Take young people with some skills and send them into the
boondocks, not into the capital. Have them teach school, build
simple irrigation works in a village, work with kids on public-health projects. And don't pay them much, to get away
from the image of the vulgar rich American.

The trouble is that there are so very few really qualified
people to do this sort of work, and so many more are
needed. It is easy to say that what we need is compassion,
empathy, sympathy, and understanding, but if you really
need a good electrical engineer, it is hard enough to find
one, let alone one who has all these humanistic characteristics, plus the willingness to work for one-tenth what he could
get at home. We have always been in extremely short supply
of saints and angels, and it is quite likely that we will continue to be for a long time to come. But the job in the poor
countries demands more such people than anyone can supply.

The poor countries are also the culprits. They desperately
want the Western technology, but they want only the specific parts which won't interfere too much with local customs
and sensitivities. And they are surprised to discover that this
requirement is very difficult to meet. So, they are stuck with
the uglies they get, and all they can do is smile, grit their
teeth, and enjoy it. Recognition of what is actually going on
would help. As I have been saying, the problem is cultural
change, not technology. Yet culture is too sensitive to talk
about, while engineering and technology are sanitary and acceptable. As long as we keep on maintaining this polite fic-
tion, the uglies will be around, culture-bound and ignorant,
trying to do something that they cannot accomplish.

If we really wanted to get something done, we might do some very hard thinking about the whole question of technological and managerial transfer. The efforts to impose without modification the whole mix from the affluent West does not work well. What is needed is a new kind of technology, a new kind of management, which would mesh into the educational and behavioral characteristics of the local culture. I have tried to suggest some of these things, but few sophisticated technicians pay much attention, as I pointed out earlier.

The managerial changes needed are big too. Everyone wants the big organization, complete with thousands of workers, structured organizations, and all that, but the things that work best in poor countries are small family-operated firms that mesh well with the extended family and nepotistic tendencies such countries have. For this sort of thing, you don't need highly skilled accountants, top-level executives, and similar types, but rather, persons who have been successful at running one-truck transportation companies and mama-papa stores. But no one is likely to send this sort of person overseas, ever. Too bad—they might just get things moving.

CHAPTER **X X**

. . . .

What Else Have We Got?

Since World War II, the world has been concerned with economic development and progress, and in spite of the somewhat gloomy issues discussed here, we really haven't done all that badly. There are now about 70 percent more people in the world than in 1945, and most of them are doing a bit better economically than their fathers and mothers did. Of course about half of them go to bed hungry, and more than half are extremely poor. But this has always been true. The only difference now is that we worry about such things. In the old days, poverty was the expected condition of man. Now, we have wild, revolutionary ideas about the total abolition of poverty.

If we took a more traditional position, and considered the success of the world in sustaining more human souls at some subsistence level, then we could argue that the past thirty years or so have been quite successful. One way or another, in spite of famine, pestilence, petty wars, population growth, political turmoil, and plans gone astray, the world has managed to do reasonably well in providing for its teeming billions.

It is the expectations revolution that has created the prob-

285

lem more than anything else. Indians, Africans, South
Americans, and others from poorer countries have taken a
close look at the richer countries and decided that they too
could be better off than they now are. And they have decided to do something about it. Wealthier countries and
their citizens have also taken a close look at poverty, both at
home and abroad, compared it to the striking affluence so
common at home, and agreed that it really isn't necessary for
people to be desperately poor.

The magic of industrialization and modern technology has
fed the expectations revolution. If you can eliminate malaria
with a massive countrywide dose of DDT, why not eliminate
other diseases we know how to fight? If the United States can
produce abundance on its farms, why not India? If West
Germany can set up production lines to manufacture the
consumer goods for a comfortable life, why not Brazil? If the
Soviet Union can educate all its citizens, why not Nigeria?
All that is needed is massive doses of technology and science,
properly supervised by reasonably wise men interested in the
welfare of their own country.

So aid was sent lots of places, including in recent years the
American ghetto. And the more that was sent, the less that
seemed to happen. As I have been suggesting, it isn't all that
easy—somehow, economic development involves more than
just some hard currency, machinery, and good will from the
donors. Indeed, what is involved, as we are increasingly beginning to realize, is a culture-busting effort that will restructure the people being helped. The Marshall Plan recipients in Europe didn't need such restructuring—they already
were trained, skilled, and ready to go back to work. Sending
a machine tool to a skilled German machinist whose plant
had been blown up in World War II turned out to be quite
different from sending a machine tool to some illiterate ex-
peasant in ex-colonial Africa. Setting up complex organizations among Europeans used to and able to work with such
systems was a bit different from trying to set up similarly

complex large organizations in previously tribal societies with very strong notions about extended families.

What has happened is that the major thrust of development is legal, political and economic, though the real problems are educational and behavioral. Because it is unsanitary and distasteful to tell someone to behave differently, but all right to give him a machine that will wreck his culture (in the very long run), we give machines, but fail to consider the culture-busting aspects of the problem. Education we do talk about, but the expectations and prestige aspects of the problem hit us once again. Instead of informal education which might work with simple peasants, we have to have the American/European mainstream with expensive schools, diplomas, and everything done in the classroom. And such education, while good as far as it goes, does not work too well in a country which cannot finance it for everyone.

So, given our expectations, the picture is gloomy. We would like to get 20 or 30 percent economic growth per year, which would move a country like India to the present British level by the turn of the century. Instead we get 1 to 3 percent net of population growth, which means that India and similar countries will still be miserably poor in the year 2000. It also means that the annual increase in American (or West European) per-capita income is larger in dollars than the total Indian GNP. The gap widens; it does not narrow. In today's world one song is truer than ever—the rich *do* get richer and the poor *do* get relatively poorer. And because our own humanitarian instincts are what they are, this bothers us.

The problem bothers poor foreigners too. Why should they remain in stinking poverty, while affluent countries use up the world's resources? Why should their populations suffer, while others live off the fat of all lands? Perhaps just one badly made, very dirty atomic bomb, properly placed, could change things. Put a cobalt casing on it, and you can blackmail the world. What have you got to lose?

The pattern is predictable the way things are going. With a bit of luck, most countries will continue to struggle upward at about 2 or 3 percent a year. A few fortunately placed countries will do much better than that, particularly if they discover oil, or if they have a peculiar combination of circumstances. Such countries as South Korea, Singapore, and Taiwan are now among these lucky ones—their growth rates are over 10 percent a year, and they are getting less poor fast. They had the advantage of being open economies, and able to accept large amounts of foreign private investment, mainly from the United States. And their diligent workers make electronic components, toys, and textiles for a lush American market. It may last—and at least their per-capita incomes have more than doubled in the past ten years. Unfortunately, not every country can play this game.

Of course, we could be unlucky. Petty wars could sap the vitality of the poor countries. We already have examples of the Portuguese colonies' rebellions in Africa. India/Pakistan. Nigeria/Biafra, and Israel/Arab states to consider as models. In such cases, every surplus is tossed into the military pot, and no one gets rich. Some may even starve, and we have models from Biafra to remind us of this. We could also have mass famine, although the green revolution may have put this off thirty years or so. Now, and amazingly quickly, countries have adopted the new strains of wheat and rice, and forecasts of mass famine by 1975 in much of the world seem wrong. But wait thirty years. By then, populations will have doubled or more, and there is only so much land.

The green revolution could, of course, lead to political collapse, as peasants are forced off the land by the agri-businessmen. Even communist-oriented countries could have troubles along these lines, since the food will be more needed than the virtues, whatever they may be, of the local peasants. Indeed, political disintegration, caused by mass upheavals of wars, an agricultural revolution, an expectations revolution, a population explosion, and an attempted organizational revolution in production, all put together, is likely. Bangladesh at this writing is the most likely candidate for such a collapse, but there are others that could be in very serious trouble by 1975. If this happens, you may read of the deaths by famine and pestilence of perhaps 10, 15, or even 50 millions in a single year, as a total economy and society come completely unstuck. Deaths of this magnitude cannot be felt—the numbers are too big for anyone to grasp emotionally. But they could come.

There are already countries with zero or slightly negative income-growth per capita. These countries cannot get ahead of their population increases, so the prognosis is for the country to remain a stagnant backwater, with per-capita incomes of below $100 per year forever—or at least into the foreseeable future. Such backwaters may have only one advantage: if the crisis biologists are right, and if the modern industrial societies are themselves doomed, then such a place is the most likely survivor for the next round.

The rich countries could mess things up too. A major atomic war could really foul up most poor countries, as well as the rich ones, if it didn't ruin the entire world. Ecological problems associated with the hydrocarbon-burning energy system we now have could also wreck the whole world, although if it's any consolation, the rich countries would go first. Already thoughtful observers have pointed out that India *can't* be as rich as England now is, ever, under a hydrocarbon energy system—if 500 million (or 700 million or more by the turn of the century) Indians burned as much coal and oil per capita as the English now do, there not only wouldn't be enough fossil fuels to go around, but the atmosphere would collapse.

Ecological Problems

This book has constantly talked about growth—yet, in a finite world, it is clear that in the end, growth has to stop.

The idea of endless economic growth on spaceship earth is at best absurd. Increasingly, ecologists, crisis biologists, and others have pointed this out. In the limit, the world is expected to collapse by 1980, or maybe even earlier, and we have to go back to the peasant ecological cycle of no growth; others perceive that the final end of growth may yet be some time away. The Club of Rome, in its sophisticated examination of the problem, suggests that around the years 2000 to 2050 things will come unstuck, and present living standards will be unsustainable, even in the more affluent countries. Long before that, some of the poor countries we have been talking about will have experienced mass famine, pestilence, and plague.

Such studies have not yet got at the guts of the income-distribution problem. Many argue that world growth should stop, or at least slow down. Fine, but whose? India, with its per-capita income of perhaps $70 to $80? Or the United States, with its per-capita income of $4,100? In less than two years, American income increases more than equal the total income of India—and if pollution and ecological collapse is directly related to income growth, it is clear that the affluent countries should stop now. The poor countries should be given a chance to catch up.

Try this argument on a middle American family with an income of perhaps $9,000 and see how far you get. Try it on young people, who face, if America quits growing, earning the highest income they will ever get the day they leave school. Try it on some Englishmen, trapped in their own stagnant version of the almost, but not quite, affluent society. Never in human history have the strong voluntarily given up to the weak, and it does not seem likely that it will happen in the next decade.

Provincial Americans may well argue for growth-stopping, which would require massive restructuring of American work and the rest of society—to say nothing of the massive confrontations which our society would face if every change had to be taken out of the hide of someone else, instead of being a part of the growth dividend. And rarely do such persons really think about what growth-stopping would mean to the poor countries. Moreover, no one has even begun to evolve any argument (except perhaps the old-fashioned gunboats-and-imperialism route) which would get India and all the rest who are interested in growth to stop. Such countries may well not grow much, as this book has suggested through many pages, but this slow or no growth won't be by choice. Poor countries will fight to maintain growth, and pollution be damned, no matter what the exquisitely trained biologists from the affluent countries are saying.

Actually, if the affluent countries stopped growing, which is at least a possibility, and the poor kept right on growing, the world could get along with its pollution problems for a long time to come. This stems from the fact that the affluent one-third now consumes about 90 percent of all the products in the world—and generates a corresponding amount of pollution. If the bottom two-thirds became modestly affluent, pollution would increase, but not in amounts so large as to cause collapse by the year 2000, or even 3000. The chance of such an outcome is indeed unlikely, given the present inclinations of all affluent countries. They will keep on growing, if they can, and hope for the best.

Discussions of eventual ecological collapse usually involve analysis of perceived trends, which are extended to some future date. The Club of Rome, which has been a lot more sophisticated in its analysis than most, has taken very close looks at energy consumption, both absolute and per capita; raw-materials supplies; population; food supplies; capital investment; and rates of change in pollution as these things increase through time. By structuring precise relationships, and by computerizing the total system, it is possible to forecast a variety of futures, where everything relates to everything else. And, as suggested above, everything looks pretty gloomy.

But such extrapolations do contain one key element, which could change. They make linear projections of technology, while such key variables as population growth and food-supply needs grow exponentially. Hence it is assumed that the extraction of raw materials will continue to be done more efficiently, but only at a linear rate. And they assume that the same raw materials, with minor exceptions, will continue to be used in about the same amounts as before, increasing, of course, as economic growth proceeds. In effect, such studies discount the possible discontinuities which might occur if something really new happens.

Here is the salvation, for both rich and poor. Income growth, at best, ends up being a study of how efficiently energy can be transformed from something around (say coal or oil) into something people can use. A ton of steel is nothing more than some raw materials (ores of various qualities, coal, limestone, etc.) transformed into a usable product. The better we do this, the more efficient the economy is, and the higher its income. If we don't do more than make minor shifts in transformation, then we get more efficient much more slowly. And as ores get poorer and scarcer, and as coal pollutes more as more is used, we have real cost and pollution problems.

But, suppose we discover whole new, and as yet unknown, technologies to make steel? Or perhaps, because steel is getting more expensive, we use something else, which may not even be around yet? World history is full of such examples —indeed, steel in mass use dates only from around 1870, since no one knew how to make it cheaply and in quantity until that time. It was widely forecast in the 1800s that billiards would always be the preserve of the rich, because of the absolute shortage of ivory for making the balls. And if an analyst in 1890 had been given modern transportation requirements, he would have correctly concluded that the modern world would be impossible, since it would drown in the horse manure generated by its transportation system. Something new is always under the sun—the hell of it is that we can never figure out what the new things might be. In this case, some hints are around. New forms of energy conversion might just do the job, with various forms of atomic power (breeder reactors, fusion) being the most likely possibilities. In an absolute sense, there is no problem—there is enough energy in and around the earth (from the sun) to give 100 billion humans all they want in some non-polluting way. But no one yet knows how to do it. With a bit of luck, we might know by 1999.

The nature of the poor-country problem is that most research and development is being done in the rich countries, which, in an absolute sense, don't need it. Indeed, the basic theme of this book is just this. The idea that capital is being misused, because people are thinking about big things when they should be thinking small, is a part of the idea. The notion that people have to get some kind of population controls among the poor, rather than among the rich and affluent, is still another part. And the whole idea of transferability between cultures, where ideas of use to some poor culture can be transferred rapidly from the rich ones that invent them, is still another.

No one really knows if such transferabilities, or even such relevant inventions, can be transferred fast enough, or at all, since this is not a part of the models of the future, which normally suggest gloom and doom. But here are some actually available, or nearly available, things that could make a huge difference in terms of the ecological collapse forecasts, if they could be transferred fast enough:

1. Population controls: If we could get to under 1 percent population growth within ten years on a global basis, much of the gloom and doom would disappear. The population problem is the bomb, and we already have the techniques. Figure out how to sell 2 billion poor people the idea fast, and we're home free.

2. Some nonpolluting source of energy: Atomic fusion and fast-breeding reactors are promising—maybe solar or thermal energy of some sort would work. Note here, as usual, how these developments come from the very sophisticated rich countries, and how seldom anyone worries about

how such things could be usefully applied in poorer countries.

3. Better food production and nutrition: The green revolution is here, and we have a few decades of relief from famine. The poorer countries have enthusiastically adopted this one (perhaps in part because the research was done largely in poorer countries, for their benefit), but we still don't know enough about providing correct diets, as compared to subsistence ones. We need to know more about efficient protein production, along with lots of other things.

Note also that if we could get population under control, solving this problem would be a lot easier. It is a lot simpler to upgrade people's diets than to try frantically to find enough of whatever is cheap to feed growing numbers.

4. Better use of what we've got: We have talked a lot about efficiently meshing the available resources, like trucks and simple capital equipment, with the available populations. Most capital equipment these days, as one example, is designed to be used in rich countries. One byproduct is that it is used very badly in poor countries, so that we need a lot more capital to get desirable results. How can we become more efficient with what we've actually got, as compared with what we wish we had?

5. Some really efficient medical techniques: Perhaps a single universal vaccine for all bacterial and viral diseases would do—and it may be on the way. An often overlooked point is that medical doctors have become much more efficient in the past century, and they continue to become so—consider how many medical service hours used to be devoted to polio treatment or diphtheria to see why. The population explosion itself is really a tribute to fantastically growing efficiencies in medicine. But suppose it could become even more efficient. Maybe then we would have some resources left over for something more useful.

6. Some kinds of mind-benders and behavioral-control drugs: We already have these, but the ethical implications are so dangerous that most people do not even like to talk

about them. Such drugs could make people learn faster; cure mental diseases; get workers structured into the system; and lots, lots more. The trouble is that we have no idea how to handle them—and poorer countries are even less well equipped to utilize such techniques. But they are here, and more are coming. What do we do about it?

Such unanticipated developments could really accelerate the transferability of all the knowledge which needs to be transferred if poor countries are to become rich. But if this happens, of course, the poor will have their cultures torn apart.

The most likely future scenario for this whole pollution problem (and the world in general) seems to be about the same as it has been for the past one hundred years. The rich will continue to grow, since they perceive themselves as poor. If really horrible pollution problems occur, then they will slowly, too slowly, be taken care of, at considerable cost. And by 2000, or 2050, we may well face a real crisis.

The poor will continue to try to develop, too. Fortunately or unfortunately, depending on your ethics, they will not be a key polluting factor for the foreseeable future, mainly because they are such minor creators of pollutants that even massive gains won't matter much. Pollution, like so many other things in this world, is a rich man's disease.

And it is highly probable that some now-unexpected development, some new discontinuity, will make 1984, or 1999, quite different from what we expect. Although anyone's guess is good on what this might be, it would be a strange world indeed where nothing new happened for twenty, thirty, or fifty years. The world we're in just hasn't worked that way for a long time.

So, in the end, or at least for the next fifty years, the poor are stuck with what they have, as always. What they have is growth potential, and they will continue to do what they can. The rich have options, and these will be debated with considerable heat and fury. In the end, perhaps because they have to, the rich may settle for some modest growth, or

maybe even no growth—but don't bet on it. Even if they
did, everything suggested in this book about the poor countries would still be true. Their problems would stay the same.
There will be no gentle greening of India or Pakistan, or
Uganda, although there may well be in Ohio or Tokyo.

Neo-Colonialist Options

The West (and the affluent communist countries as well)
might perhaps resort to some new form of neo-colonialism—
and there already are signs that something of this sort is happening, helped along enthusiastically, and ironically, by the
poor countries themselves. As we suggested, a poor country
taking over its own mineral and oil assets may be the best
way to lose—the rich countries, losing interest in the problem, will treat the poor country at arm's length, and the results may well be worse than if the West (or the communists) were actively in the game. But the scenario, not too far
removed from current reality, might go like this:

A European country (or countries), annoyed at the last
wild act of the Libyans, for instance, simply sends in a small
army and takes the part of the country that counts—namely,
the oilfields and pipelines. Or, if you like other villains, try
the Americans or Russians. Libya was an Italian colony for a
long time—why not make it some sort of colony again? Why
pay off half the huge profits to irresponsible people? They
can have the rest of the desert, what little agriculture there
is, and so on—the single really significant asset should be
run by responsible people like you and me. A few key sei-
zures of this sort, and the poor world could be in very tough
shape. Moreover, they could do very little about it, particularly if the major communist and capitalist affluent powers
agreed in advance to cooperate. Why shouldn't they? As affluent countries, they have a lot to lose.

The name of the game is power, and power comes from
command over resources. Those who have, get—the affluent

now have the power, and anyone who thinks that the poor and feeble of this world are going to come out on top are likely to be wrong. The poor and feeble never have, so it is hard to see why they would in this generation. Which is why the poor countries are so very anxious to develop and grow economically—even Sweden and Switzerland have power, prestige, and income. If you want these things, get rich yourself.

Other Options

All of this grim prognostication is hard to take, especially if you're poor, so there is no shortage of ideas about what to do, ranging from the reasonable to the utopian. One very common suggestion is to go communist, and a number of countries have tried this. The difficulty is that a political change does not change your people—they are still as uneducated as before, and their attitudes change only slowly through time. Countries which have tried this route, such as North Korea, Burma (here, extreme socialism), Cuba, and Albania, have not shown very impressive results. Red China has, but they had the advantage of being the biggest country in the world, plus having a charismatic leader in Mao. Castro served the same function in Cuba, but smaller countries trying to operate closed, tightly controlled and planned economies often come to grief—or at least economic stagnation. It is hard to get frightened by Albania—better to ignore it.

Another suggestion, made more by outsiders, particularly American radicals interested in communes and other social experiments, is not to develop at all. If it is really true that ecological collapse is near, this suggestion makes considerable sense—*if* a country can solve its population problem. But one shark in the pool can wreck the deal. If every poor country went this route, and if one rich country tried to be an imperialist—then the world would have imperialism. As I said before, if you are going to be a noble savage, make sure that you have a nice zookeeper.

This business about weapons and military power being on the side of the wealthy and technologically advanced is constantly underestimated in the vast literature on development, probably because it is not in line with the values of most persons who are interested in such questions. The idea that the name of the game is to get some factories so that the country can make guns is not exactly what most humanists have in mind. But it is exactly what a lot of planners, politicians, thinkers, and power-seekers in many poor countries have in mind.

Various utopian solutions are proposed in various ways. We should all love one another more; we should cooperate; we should help our neighbors; and we should not bother about such vulgar things as income, dollars, and guns. Agreed. But setting up such a utopian system is difficult. Hence a lot of this thinking is probably wasted—unless some wise man (and culture) comes up with a behavioral-control drug system which really works—and which the wise God is willing to use to his own ends. It could happen, but more likely than not, the system will come from the affluent East or West, not from the poor countries.

Another outside possibility is that someone will come up with a major technological breakthrough which is of more value to poor countries than to rich ones. This has happened once in the past few years—the green revolution. But what else might there be? Aside from the ability to do complex industrial things with less capital and less skilled labor, it is hard to think up something precise which might do the job. A low-cost means of making steel; a way of making auto bodies at low costs with unskilled labor for little capital; a cheap system of metal-working—such things could be very useful. But they would be equally useful in the affluent countries, and it is likely that the rich countries would use them first. Then the usual trickle-down theories would apply, as various poor countries took advantage of them.

Actually, little thinking has been done, and still less research, about specific production problems for the poorer countries. Most industrial and agricultural research is done in rich countries, with their labor/capital ratios in mind. This, indeed, is one major reason why it is so hard to develop—it is very difficult to adapt a General Motors idea to a small, poor country, which lacks everything that GM has. Some really effective research about how to do industrial and agricultural activities on the poor-country scale, with the unskilled labor and little capital the poor countries have, could be a major breakthrough. But highly imaginative, skilled scientists doing such research, or any research, are exactly what the less-developed countries do not have. If such work is to be done, it will probably be done in the West. And what pressures are there to get it done?

Other options involve trying to be a pale copy of the affluent West, or East, complete with the big, complex industrial organizations, the heavy industries, the major schools, the complicated bureaucracies, and large mechanized armies, and all the rest of the trappings of the large and powerful in our time. It's fun to dream, but with very limited resources and talents, the poor countries just can't pull it off. India, Pakistan, Brazil, Argentina, among others, have tried this, and all have managed some impressive gains, but as usual, not fast enough to satisfy their own expectant peoples.

Becoming a closed economy and doing it all yourself, ignoring the rest of the world, is an attractive option to an embittered people, keenly aware of their humiliations at the hands of the West, but only a China- or India-sized country can even consider this realistically as an option if it wants to grow economically. As suggested in the discussion about communism, which typically involves a closed, planned system, smaller countries have not done very well going this route. There is just too much to do which a poor country, desperately short of skilled labor, cannot do by itself.

This list of potential options is not very encouraging. Nothing seems to lead to the kinds of growth which we would like to see, to the kinds of developed human beings which are the ultimate end of the whole exercise. Most of

them will provide that 2 or 3 percent growth, net, but it's
not enough.

The Realistic Option

In the end, you get educational and behavioral change as
fast as possible—and the usual mainstream development tactics and strategies don't do this job. Things change, but
slowly. The major reasons why they don't is that too many
people—in both rich and poor cultures—fail to realize just
how culture-bound most technologies, organizations, and
other paraphernalia from the rich countries are. The technology, including the guns, is the easiest thing to see here.
At least with machinery and machine guns it is clear what
has to be done educationally, and sometimes even behaviorally, to get the things to work. So education begins, and
once again the culture-boundness of the West gets into the
act. For a modern Western school system is about as culture-
bound an institution as anything around. Worse, it is very,
very expensive.

Far too often the affluent fall into the trap of thinking
that the charming, educated, and sophisticated persons they
encounter from poorer countries are typical of everyone
there. And because these people seem very much like the
rest of us (and indeed, often went to the same universities),
it is easy to assume that anything we can do, they can do too,
with just a bit of help and education. This isn't so, because
the 1 percent elite is not the rest of the population. A lot of
what I say may sound like an appeal to go back to the 1920s
or even earlier in poor countries, to replicate what America
and Europe did so painfully so long ago. There is a real reason for this tone; in most poor countries today, educational
levels are way below what they were in the United States in
1920, or even 1890, and no one is going to catch up in a few
years. There is just too much human capital, and too much
implicit human capital built into the industrial system of a

rich country, for any poor country to be able to short-circuit
the long process easily and become rich merely by buying
some machinery, or setting up some big new organizations.

What is the feasible option? It is simply to figure out how
to get people educated and behaviorally changed as fast as
possible, in whatever way works for the given culture. Present patterns are not working, so they have to be changed.
The way to do this is not the way it's being done. Some time
bombs have to be planted at the bottom of the society to get
things moving. This is why we have talked about Model T
Fords, bicycles, transistor radios, old washing machines, rat
bounties, junk autos dumped on beaches, and similar simple
things. Such simple things have a habit of starting behavioral change, and they educate as well, in exactly the best
way, which is giving people what they want anyhow. Much
later, when they figure out what has been done to them, they
may not like you too much, but by then it's too late. Thinking small and doing little things on a mass scale might do
the job better than what is now being done. Actually, nothing said here even interferes much with the big-ticket thinking, and it might even help. The man who knows about simple machinery can more easily be trained to work with more
complex items; the man who has organized a one-truck
shipping company just might be able to work better in larger
organizations than someone who has never had that experience.

Another key is to figure out how to educate without
schools. No poor country can afford to duplicate the present
Western school system, yet every poor country is desperately
short of trained minds. So those trained minds, if they are
going to be there, will have to appear out of the woodwork.
And the way to start is to motivate people to want to learn
badly, then provide the means as cheaply as possible.

Another very realistic limitation on present development
processes is that they are thought up, planned, and carried
out by elites. Unfortunately, elites, whether communist, fascist, agrarian, or democratic, are never large enough in the

poorer world to do the job themselves, though they think and act as if they were. This is one major reason why their plans never quite come off as well as we would hope. American elites, operating in ghetto projects, make exactly the same mistake, so there is no reason to sneer at foreigners on this score. We assume that somehow, nice, sweet, intelligent, trained, disciplined people like you and me will appear, capable of running and structuring our new organizations. It won't happen, not here in an American ghetto, nor abroad in some poor country.

Elitist thinking everywhere seems these days to perceive a real need for control. We have to have big organizations, with chains of command running up to the top, with thinkers, planners, and administrators (always wise, compassionate, competent, and hard-working) to make sure that everything goes according to plan. Try the idea of dumping old cars on beaches and leaving on any thinking person any day. Most people are stunned at the thought. And you are quite likely to be dismissed as slightly mad. Who would control the system? How do we know what will happen? Who will measure results? What kinds of data would we be unable to collect? Why, if this were done, something might happen beyond our control!

If being in control is the way the world is going to grow, sit back and brace yourself for the 2-percent-net-growth world. There's no way that the present elites, either here or in a poor country, can control everything. So, back to a handful of big projects that won't really matter very much, because that's all you can get under control.

Try the idea of education without schools on any teacher or school administrator, and you will be seen as some kind of nut. Schools have to be there—how else would we know what was going on? How could we measure progress? How would we control the process? Why, it is impossible! If you want it that way, sit back and brace yourself for an absolute rise in illiteracy all over the world. There aren't enough formal schools, and there won't be in your lifetime, to take care of those who could use them.

So it boils down to behavioral and educational change which is cheap, which does not use up very scarce skilled human talent, and which can be applied very widely in a country to lots and lots of people. Maybe, if such cheap, simple time bombs were tried, they might go off in the wrong place at the wrong time, with the wrong results. So what? There are not too many other options to worry about.

A second theme, which is particularly related to smaller countries, is really the total marketing concept. This concept, developed by American businessmen and scholars, is actually very simple. Find out what you can do for someone else which they need and are willing to pay a good price for, and then do it. If you do it well, you sell a lot and get rich. And of course what you can do for someone else changes through time, as both they and you shift your tastes and capabilities, so this analysis is a never-ending process.

In international trade, this is called comparative advantage, and too often people act as if it weren't true. What you may be good at may not excite you too much. What you wish you were good at is a lot more exciting. If I would dearly love to be the world's greatest actor, but were very poor at the job, I would often go hungry. If I do what I can, teach, I won't get as rich as a top-flight actor, but I'll be a hell of a lot better off than sitting around on some corner dreaming of fame and fortune.

The same principle applies to countries. Too often what a country is good at (say, peasant agriculture, or providing cheap labor) is not the sort of thing the leaders would want —but if they chase rainbows of what might have been instead of what is, they will be, in the end, much poorer, if not wiser. It would be fun if every country could have its IBM and General Motors, but unfortunately, not every small country will be so lucky. So it might settle for second or third best.

Closely connected with this point is the one about leaving your economy relatively open. Not even utopians imagine that any country will not be tempted to mess a bit with currency controls, import tariffs and quotas, export restrictions, and foreign-investment controls, but if the name of the game is learning something fast from foreigners, the wisest course is to see as much of them and their works as possible. This is painful, but necessary. Too often, someone thinks that the essence of something like a computer or a jet aircraft is in the product, and if one sample is brought in, the thing can be duplicated. But such high-technology products are just the tip of the iceberg—what is really important is the organization that puts the thing together. Without keen insights into the way such organizations function, nothing much will happen. Incidentally, very few planners and thinkers in poorer countries really believe this.

Indeed, one dimension of this whole development process is the conflict between producers and marketers. The producers (which, incidentally, includes most of the communist world) think that production is critical. All you have to do is to produce something, and somehow it will be useful. The marketers think that if you have something that is useful, the game is won. So far, the producers are in the majority, but their game plan is not working well. The suggestion here is to find out what is valuable, try to produce it if you can, and learn as much as you can in the process.

The scarcest asset in every poor country is highly skilled manpower, particularly the kinds of managers and administrators that can make big organizations work reasonably well. Yet this is exactly the kind of man they assume that they have in abundance. Everyone assumes that there are lots of intelligent, educated people just like him around to do the job. But there never are. Hence once again, the feasible option is to think small—to figure out how to do all sorts of things with virtually no organization whatsoever. The very few experts will have more than enough to do for fifty years in every poor country, and there is no point in further burdening them with more duties than they can handle.

This may suggest why the poor countries that have grown the fastest have been those that imported this sort of talent from the West. The oil-rich states let multinational companies do the exploitation job; places like Taiwan let American and Japanese firms run the show, using cheap Taiwanese labor. Only, after ten years, the labor is a lot more skilled and well paid, the products much more sophisticated, and there now seem to be lots of Taiwanese managers to do the job themselves. Why not? They watched and learned their lessons from smart men who really knew what they were doing. The equally smart young Indian may still be unable to do the job because he never had a chance to learn from an expert. The experts were far away, because they could not get in.

Now, all of this advice is very painful, and very unpopular in the developing countries. It's also very unpopular in the ghetto economic development agencies at home. I know about both from experience. The big-time thinkers are not the least bit interested in anything which does not come from their own agency; they are not interested in things they cannot control; and they most decidedly are not interested in things which are not prestigious and attractive to outsiders. Hence, such ideas are hastily buried. Hell, all they do is get people developed! What's that got to do with the problem?

I suppose that in the end we are all micro. That is, we look at ourselves in the mirror every morning, aware of our petty prestige, our Brownie points, our one-upsmanship on our colleagues at the office and in other agencies. If the problem cannot be solved to my credit, why bother? And since most of the stuff talked about here is highly unlikely to give any official credit, they are highly unlikely to be seriously considered. Too bad—only a billion lives are at stake.

If anyone really cared about genuine development, it might be possible to start doing some hard thinking about the time bombs and little levers scattered all over the world ready for use at low cost. It might be possible to do some serious thinking in places like the United Nations about what development really is and what it implies. Instead of emoting about the big things, and worrying about how to get yet one more inept big organization into the boondocks, it might be possible to do some little, yet potent, things to fracture cultures and educate people at great speed.

It might also be possible for the rich countries to give aid in ways that work. Instead of financing the big, mechanized armies, the big, complex projects, it just might be possible to initiate some low-cost enterprises which could make a difference. Bemused as we are about a big, efficient organization, we are paralyzed when we confront billions of illiterate, unskilled peasants. Intuitively, we turn to the things which seemed to work for General Motors, forgetting that there is nothing out there remotely resembling what GM had when it was young. Intuitively we reach for the familiar large bureaucratic organization, forgetting that the people we are dealing with are not quite the same kinds of middle-class people you and I are. The amazing thing is that something works at all, not that it works badly. But we could do a hell of a lot better than we are doing. And unless we do, it will be a grim thirty years lying ahead of us.

CHAPTER **XXI**

. . . .

Conclusion

There are 2½ billion poor people in the less-developed countries of the world, whose per-capita incomes are under $500 per year. Most American poor, by comparison, look upper middle class. Poverty is always relative, but by any standards, the foreign poor are *poor*. Anyone who thinks that he can hide under an American bed and ignore this poverty for the next twenty or thirty years is kidding himself—those poor out there want into the game, and they want to get rich just as fast as they can. What this book has been about is to suggest how this getting-rich process can be accelerated, and to indicate what is wrong with present economic development stereotypes.

We had better get going on this problem. By the year 2000, there will be 5 billion people in the now-poor countries, given population growth. Meanwhile, in the affluent countries, where population growth is so much slower, numbers will rise from perhaps 1.0 billion to 1.3 or 1.5 billion. Anyone living comfortably (yet feeling poor) in the United States, Western Europe, Japan, or Australia is being outbred, if nothing else. If the well-to-do solve their problems, and there is a good chance that they can, the world

will still be in catastrophe and turmoil all the time, because
the poor cannot solve theirs. No one escapes. We are all together on spaceship earth.

The affluent countries are on the growth curve, moving
up steadily from 3 to 5 percent per year per capita in real
terms. This means that by the turn of the century, the rich
countries will have more than doubled their per-capita income. A young American college graduate, instead of going
to work for $400 to $900 per month, can look forward to
earning from $800 to $1,800 per month in the year 2000
while his Indian counterpart, who is lucky to begin his
working career at $50 per month now, can think about his
sons starting at perhaps $70 in the year 2000. The rich have
the pollution problems, and they have the agonizing problems of what to do with affluence, but they also have the real
possibility of resolving, for the first time in human history,
the absolute problems of poverty. Everything will still be relative, but if the American poverty line stands at perhaps
$6,000 in 2000, few would argue that this means absolute
deprivation and starvation.

Meanwhile, in India and other less fortunate places, the
population growth curves rise inexorably. Famine, pestilence, and lots of other horrible things are extremely likely.
And there are lots of smart Indians. If, in desperation, they
start thinking about taking on the affluent, say with badly
made, dirty atomic bombs, what then? They have nothing to
lose, and we have lots. What difference will it make to India,
if half its people are literally starving, while the other half
has no real future at all?

There are two ways out of the box we have got ourselves
into. Both have been considered here. The first is to find a
way, somehow, to reduce the population growth rate. In rich
countries we already know how. All of them, including the
affluent communist states, have low population-growth rates.
But we don't know how to transmit this information in a
practical way to poor countries. Various possibilities were
discussed, such as imposed birth control (perhaps as an act of

war), and the idea that perhaps our own brilliant marketing people could give us some insights. But to date, no one knows how to implement birth control—until the man and woman become affluent, thoughtful, structured, disciplined, uptight people like those in the affluent countries. Such persons in poor countries control family size, but there are very few of them in the less-developed countries.

The other side of the coin is to figure out how to grow faster economically. Americans and Europeans can have fun trying to decide whether to grow or not, given the quality of life and our ecological problems. At least such thoughts are technically feasible. But the poor two-thirds of the world has no choice at all, at least until population growth slows down sharply. They grow or died. Present growth strategies, while effective, are not effective enough. What is needed is some new way of looking at the problem, some new insights into how the growth curves can be accelerated. In the end, perhaps not surprisingly, we end up with people.

It gets down to this: In the past thirty years, brilllant men have devised models for economic growth. For a variety of reasons, such models emphasize the economic, technical, and legal-political dimensions of the development process. Since the models are plausible, sanitary, and even work fairly well, they have been enthusiastically adopted, to the point where it is a poor country indeed that does not have its planning ministries, its development centers, its econometric studies, its technology-transfer systems, and all the rest. Political campaigns everywhere (voting or coups) are based on developing the best patterns for economic development. Everyone interested in economic development around the world has his own intellectual tool kit of things to be done to accomplish the growth job.

Unfortunately, the real problem is the educational/behavioral patterns people have. And here lots of countries are mousetrapped in observing the affluent parts of the world. They see technology and copy it, not realizing that the technology is not critical, but rather, the education and attitudes

of those who use it. They see modern Western school systems and eagerly try to build their own just like them, not
realizing that education, like everything else, subtly reflects
all the economic, social, and behavioral attitudes of those
who developed the system in the first place. They frequently
fail to see the managerial and administrative dimensions of
the large organization, which seems so efficient in rich countries, failing to realize that once again, complex organizations reflect *all* of the society from which they came. And
they are baffled, because things which seem so obvious, so
easy, turn out to work so badly, if at all, in their own countries, which desperately need efficient, working organizations that will rapidly generate new wealth.

The inability of the poor countries to make things work
right has now reached the point where the American Congress seriously debates stopping all aid completely; where
other rich countries' gifts, grants, and loans are dropping off
as a relative share of their national incomes; where wise
men, scholars, and even practitioners of development despair, because so many promises have turned to dust. The
needed element is this: Get your investments, your organizations, your technologies, and all the rest meshed in well with
whatever the country has to offer *now*—not what it wished it
had. If there are masses of illiterate peasants, then try to
figure out things to do which illiterate peasants can really do
and which will enable them to learn more while they are
doing. Forget some project which only MIT engineers can
design and operate. If you can only afford very cheap
schools, which work, then have lots of them. Discard the idea
of pale copies of the expensive best in Europe or the United
States. Try to structure organizations that fit the country,
and abandon the crude and farcical copies of General Motors or General Electric, which can't possibly succeed. If you
don't have lots of cash for capital investments, then figure
out what little things can be done with lots of cheap manpower. In short, be realistic about what can and cannot be
done. Ignore the dreamland of the affluent countries, where

everything works well because the countries *are* doing things they can do well and efficiently. It's a simple prescription, but very tough to follow.

Many persons from poorer countries would recoil in horror at such suggestions. Why, you would make us second- or third-rate! You would make us stay poor forevermore, while you rich go on controlling the world! You want us to change our cherished beliefs, religion, and ethics! No, we'll go the sanitary way with large organizations, jet aircraft, mechanized armies, the very latest in capital-intensive technologies borrowed from the West, and all the rest. It's the only way. Great, if it works—but it won't. The sad fact is that this "copy the affluent at any cost" strategy only works for a small fraction of the persons in the countries that try it. The affluent are indeed seductive—who wouldn't want to earn the incomes we rich do, working in air-conditioned offices, with pretty secretaries, relaxed and able colleagues, and all the rest? Who wants to strip old cars, work in some backyard factory in Bombay, or do whatever else is needed to get the development job really done? Moreover, who would want to give up the juicy possibilities of influence-peddling, the ability to put not-so-bright cousins on the payroll, and the corruption potential such big organizations provide for the quick and clever in the poorer countries?

Still worse, who really wants to be manipulated by the system, be made over from the nice person he now is to some crude copy of an uptight Shintoist or Calvinist? Much better to copy technology, rather than behavior—not realizing that these two things in the end are the same. We practice indirect behavioral control by sending some poor country a machine tool or jet aircraft, but so far, neither we nor anyone else talks about how to manipulate people directly. And because in the end the people not the machines count, we end up being very inefficient in our efforts to transfer things Western to poorer countries.

The unpleasant consequences of present development efforts have led many to seek new options. An attractive one is

to become an Albania—withdraw from the world and to
hell with it. But if you do, make sure your neighbors are
compassionate. And remember, you might just become a modern version of the nineteenth-century American Indian if you
miscalculate. Another option is not to get richer, but just to
redistribute income better. This usually leads directly to
some sort of Marxist politics, where the poor take from the
rich. But in a country with only $200 income per capita,
no matter how you divide it, that's all there is. Some may be
rich and some very poor, or all can be very poor—those are
your options. A country can be fascist, democratic, or communist, and still be stinking poor—it really doesn't matter.
Americans, used to the good-guys and bad-guys arguments involving what the country is politcally, may find this bafflling
or ridiculous. Only very slowly are we learning that whether
Chile is Marxist or not makes little difference—and indeed, if it did go communist, it would probably be a break for
our side. Either way, the issue is not critical.

The rich have pollution problems, and since most development analysts are from the wealthy countries, there is a
tendency to relate the world question to this ecological problem which basically involves only the rich. The poor, no
matter how fast they grow, will only marginally influence
world pollution levels, so from their point of view pollution
doesn't matter. If the rich decide to go slow because of pollution and not grow so fast, then the poor can (maybe) benefit
—it will make it that much easier to catch up. But even cur-
sory examination of the problems rich countries who don't
grow much face (try modern Britain as one example) suggest
that growth may be the lesser of many evils. Most poor-country citizens who have looked at the ecological problem have
concluded that this one is irrelevant. If the rich want to mess
with it, fine, but count them out. They will continue to try
to grow as best they can—air, noise or other pollution may
well cost a few lives in rich countries, but no one in the
United States, Western Europe, or Eastern Europe is talking
about perhaps 500 million people literally starving to death

—which is what the poor world's problem is. So, on with pollution, if necessary. When a year of American growth almost equals total Indian output, whatever India does won't really matter anyhow.

When we talk about economic development, in all its delightful complexities, we are really talking about utopias. Someone perceives that things are in tough shape—incomes are low, people go to bed hungry, a country cannot defend itself from its enemies. To solve the problem, we have to do things, like raise income levels. The relatively simple-minded concept of increasing per-capita GNP becomes a surrogate for the complexities of modernization across the board. And this focus on the economic variables may lead us astray, in that in the end it is really behavior we are changing, not technology or financial institutions, or anything else.

Very few utopias in literature say much about economics or organization or technology. The authors create delightful worlds where peace, brotherhood, love, intellectual pursuits, and religious activities are the important factors. Close reading also suggests that most utopias are viciously elitist. If the society ignored its economics and business as thoroughly as the writers imply, there would be just enough income above bare subsistence to support only a small percentage of the population in the style suggested. For the rest, life would be nasty, brutish and short, as they struggled with the animal-powered society, using crude, traditional technology, to get the small surplus the elite might enjoy. And if the utopias were as unscientific as most writers suggest, the population explosion would be no problem—lots of people would die from the traditional plague diseases long before they reached adulthood. Like it or not, modern medical science and technology would have to be plugged into any meaningful utopia—and that implies all sorts of cold-blooded science, research, technology (How can you make a really good scalpel or hypodermic needle without a superb steel industry?). Somehow we drift back to where we are now.

Models of economic development, predicated as they are on what is going on in affluent countries, are subject to violent criticism, both in the rich and the poor countries. Most literary criticism in the United States has been antitechnological, antibusiness, and antimaterialistic for a long, long time—not only do engineers in poor countries read the technical journals, but poets read the literary critiques as well. Hence few intellectuals would be willing to stand up and be counted in a showdown about what the poor countries should do, if the plan is to create some sort of mini-United States.

What this boils down to is that we all have pretty good ideas about how to create partial utopias, but no one has a clue how a total one which is viable might work out. We all know what's wrong with what *is* around the world, but suggestions for reform are blurred and inconsistent. The nature of man's social, economic, and political organizations is still too messy and complicated for us to grasp.

Like everyone else, citizens of poor countries and cultures want it both ways. They want their own delightful culture, with all its local hang-ups, excitement, values, and so on, plus all the West's wealth. They also want the prestige, recognition, and military power that goes with being very affluent. The hang-up is, How can you do this? Since no one knows yet, everyone gets confused. It is easy enough for me to say that you should change, but if you suggest that to me, I suspect your motive. Once again, what else have we to suggest?

Men think linearly, and the world goes merrily on expanding geometrically. Anyone writing about what is happening now is likely to be wrong. Some unexpected discovery, some discontinuity, will pop up at an unexpected time and place, and the result will be that new options, new possibilities, and new rainbows will appear. About the time that the United States seems very tired, very unsure of itself, very aware that its own utopias are not quite what everyone expected them to be, the poor countries are striving mightily to get where we are. Almost any poor country would happily trade its particular miseries for those perceived to be miserable in the United States. Their problems are of a different order of magnitude from ours. Yet we are probably both wrong. There will be things undreamed of in our philosophies, right around the corner, ten years from now, to worry about.

Right now, the options outside the typical mainstream Western ones do not look too good. We have a mess, but all other options look messier. We know what's wrong—and anyone else's utopia would have still more problems than the ones we have. We all hate the vulgar business of making and earning a living, but unless you get this part of your utopia straight, nothing else comes out right. Indeed, nothing comes out at all, and if you are a poor country with an exploding population and the need to expand economic activities, you go back to square one. Sad, but true.

There was a time, not too long ago, when everything seemed very easy, very straightforward. There really was some political utopia out there—all we needed to do was to restructure things a bit politically, so men could be kind to each other. The West (and East) could easily help out by sending some technicians and capital equipment, which would immediately be as productive as that in Detroit, Essen, or Murmansk. And after ten or twenty years, no one would be poor any more, and our world utopia would be upon us. Nothing turned out to be that easy. In fact, it turned out to be so tough that no one at this moment really knows what to do next. Lots of political and economic theories were propounded, and some were tried; lots of technical help and capital were sent abroad, but little worked out the way we wanted it to; lots of serious and competent men and women tried hard to make things go, to make people a bit better off one way or another. But we got swamped with population growth and the dawning realization that about the toughest thing in the world to do is to change any culture in a really significant way. Moving from a static, tradition-ridden peasant or nomadic society to a dynamic, modern, growing, technologically oriented economy is what development is really all about. If we start thinking in these terms, if we discard the ikons of our culture, we will have made the first significant step in a new era.

Bibliography

A steadily expanding literature on economic development and related topics exists. The field was virtually ignored, except by a few specialists, before World War II, but since that date the number of books, articles, pamphlets, government documents, United Nations publications, World Bank materials, and much more has continued to grow.

The following materials are arranged by chapters. Only more generally available works are noted here, but for potential scholars, the footnote trail is laid out. That is, the bibliographical and footnote citations in the materials included in this bibliography will quickly lead you to the specialized literature of the field.

Chapters I and II

Asher, Robert E. *Development Assistance in the Seventies, Alternatives for the U.S.* Washington: Brookings Institution, 1970.

Black, Cyril. *The Transformation of Russian Society.* Cambridge, Mass.: Harvard University Press, 1958.

Campbell, Robert W. *Soviet Economic Power.* Boston: Houghton Mifflin Company, 1960.

Clubb, Edmund. *Twentieth Century China.* New York: Columbia University Press, 1964.

Cohen, Jerome B. *Japan's Postwar Economy.* Bloomington, Indiana: Indiana University Press, 1958.

Columbia Conference on International Economic Development. *The Widening Gap: Development in the 1970's.* Edited by Barbara Ward, J. D. Runnalls and Lenore D'Anjou. New York: Columbia University Press, 1971.

Commission on International Development. *Partners in Development.* Chairman, Lester B. Pearson. New York: Praeger, 1970.

Conference on Tension in Development, Oxford University, 1961. *Restless Nations: A Study of World Tension and Development.* Foreword by Lester B. Pearson. New York: Dodd Mead, 1962.

Dean, Vera M. *Builders of Emerging Nations.* New York: Holt, Rinehart and Winston, 1961.

————. *Nature of the Non-Western World.* New York: New American Library, 1966.

Drucker, Peter Ferdinand. *The Age of Discontinuity.* New York: Harper & Row, 1969.

Farmer, Richard N. and Barry M. Richman. *Comparative Management and Economic Progress.* Bloomington, Indiana: Cedarwood Publishing Co., 1970.

Galbraith, John Kenneth. *The New Industrial State.* Boston: Houghton Mifflin Company, 1967.

Harbison, Frederick and Charles A. Myers. *Education, Manpower and Economic Growth.* New York: McGraw-Hill Book Company, 1964.

Jackson, Barbara (Ward). *The Lop-Sided World.* New York: W. W. Norton, 1968.

Kindleberger, Charles P. *Economic Development.* New York: McGraw-Hill Book Company, 1965.

Kuznet, Simon Smith. *Economic Growth and Structure.* New York: W. W. Norton, 1965.

Levy, Lester Samuel and Roy J. Sampson. *American Economic Development*. Boston: Allyn and Bacon, 1962.

McClelland, David Clarence. *The Achieving Society*. Princeton, N.J.: Van Nostrand, 1961.

McLuhan, Herbert Marshall. *Culture Is Our Business*. New York: McGraw-Hill Book Company, 1970.

McNeill, William H. *The Rise of the West*. New York: New American Library, 1965.

Myrdal, Gunnar. *An International Economy: Problems and Prospects*. New York: Harper & Brothers, 1956.

————. *Asian Drama: An Inquiry into the Poverty of Nations*. New York: Twentieth Century Fund, 1968.

————. *Rich Land and Poor, the Road to World Prosperity*. New York: Harper & Brothers, 1958.

Panikkar, Kavalam M. *Asia and Western Dominance*. New York: John Day Co., 1954.

Rostow, Walt Whitman. *The Stages of Economic Growth: A Non-Communist Manifesto*. Cambridge, Eng.: University Press, 1960.

Turnbull, Colin. *The Lonely African*. New York: Simon and Schuster, 1962.

Chapter III

Appleman, Philip. *The Silent Explosion*. Boston: Beacon Press, 1965.

Chamberlain, Neil W. *Beyond Malthus: Population and Power*. New York: Basic Books, 1970.

Clark, Colin. *Population Growth and Land Use*. New York: St. Martin's Press, 1967.

Farmer, Richard N., J. D. Long, and G. J. Stolnitz. *World Population: The View Ahead*. Bloomington, Indiana: Bureau of Business Research, Graduate School of Business, 1968.

Huxley, Julian. *The Human Crisis*. Seattle: University of Washington Press, 1963.

Leibenstein, Harvey. *A Theory of Economic-Demographic Development*. Princeton: Princeton University Press, 1954.

McCormack, Arthur. *Poverty and Population: The Catholic Doctrine of International Responsibility*. Oxford: Catholic Social Guild, 1964.

Population Crisis Committee. *Foreign Aid for Family Planning: Proposals for Action in the Congress of the U.S.*, Washington, D.C., 1967.

Sax, Karl. *Standing Room Only: The Challenge of Overpopulation*. Boston: Beacon Press, 1955.

Chapters IV and V

Cantor, Norman F. *The History of Popular Culture*. New York: Macmillan, 1968.

Dewey, John. *Freedom and Culture*. New York: G. P. Putman's Sons, 1939.

Ford, Henry. *My Philosophy of Industry*. New York: Coward-McCann, 1929.

Huxley, Aldous Leonard. *Brave New World Revisited*. London: Chatto & Windus, 1959.

McLuhan, Herbert Marshall. *Culture Is Our Business*. New York: McGraw-Hill Book Company, 1970.

Mead, Margaret. *Culture and Commitment: A Study of the Generation Gap*. Garden City, N.Y.: Natural History Press, 1970.

————. *New Lives for Old: Cultural Transformation-Manus, 1928–1953*. New York: Morrow, 1956.

Montagu, Ashley. *Culture: Man's Adaptive Dimension*. New York: Oxford University Press, 1968.

Strayer, Joseph R. *et al. The Mainstream of Civilization*. New York: Harcourt, Brace and World, 1969.

Toynbee, Arnold Joseph. *The World and the West*. New York: Oxford University Press, 1953.

Chapter VI

Bloomberg, Warner and Henry J. Schmandt (eds.). *Urban Poverty, Its Social and Political Dimensions.* Beverly Hills, Calif.: Sage Publications, 1970.

Downs, Anthony. *Urban Problems and Prospects.* Chicago: Markham Publishing Co., 1971.

Etzkowitz, Henry and Gerald M. Schaflander. *Ghetto Crisis: Riots or Reconciliation?* Boston: Little, Brown, 1969.

Meissner, Hanna H. (ed.). *Poverty in the Affluent Society.* New York: Harper & Row, 1966.

Miller, Herman Phillip (ed.). *Poverty American Style.* Belmont, Calif.: Wadsworth Publishing Co., 1966.

Penchef, Ester. *Four Horsemen: Pollution, Poverty, Famine, Violence.* San Francisco: Camfield Press, 1971.

Phelps, Edmund (ed.). *Private Wants and Public Needs.* New York: W. W. Norton, 1965.

Seligman, Ben B. *Poverty as a Public Issue.* New York: The Free Press, 1965.

Sexton, Patricia Cayo. *Spanish Harlem: An Anatomy of Poverty.* New York: Harper & Row, 1965.

Sturdivant, Frederick D. (ed.). *The Ghetto Market Place.* New York: The Free Press, 1969.

Weber, Max. *The City.* New York: The Free Press, 1958.

Will, Robert Erwin and Harold G. Vatter (eds.). *Poverty in Affluence: The Social, Political and Economic Dimensions of Poverty in the U.S.* New York: Harcourt, Brace and World, 1970.

Chapter VII

Goulet, Denis. *The Cruel Choice: A New Concept in the Theory of Development.* New York: Atheneum Publishers, 1971.

Jackson, Barbara (Ward). *Nationalism and Ideology.* New York: W. W. Norton, 1966.
Joshua, Wynfred and Stephen P. Gilbert. *Arms for the Third World: Soviet Military Aid Diplomacy.* Baltimore: Johns Hopkins Press, 1969.
Snyder, Louis Leo. *The New Nationalism.* Ithaca, N.Y.: Cornell University Press, 1968.

Chapter VIII

Aptheker, Herbert (ed.). *Marxism and Alienation.* New York: Humanities Press, 1965.
Campbell, Robert W. *Soviet Economic Power,* Boston: Houghton Mifflin, 1960.
"Communism and the New Left," *U.S. News and World Report.* Washington, 1969.
Communist China's Foreign Trade. Santa Monica, Calif.: Rand Corporation, 1963.
Communist Industry; Its Problems and Difficulties. Taipei, Taiwan: Asian Peoples Anti-Communist League, China, 1964.
Fitzsimmons, Thomas. *USSR, Its People, Its Society, Its Culture.* New Haven: HRAF Press, 1960.
Hague, René. *Marxism in the 20th Century.* London: Collins, 1970.
Monsen, J. *Modern American Capitalism.* Boston: Houghton Mifflin, 1963.
Oxenfeldt, Alfred. *Economic Systems in Action.* New York: Holt, Rinehart and Winston, 1957.
Remer, C. F. (ed.). *International Economics of Communist China.* Ann Arbor: University of Michigan Press, 1959.
Richman, B. M. *Industrial Society in Communist China.* New York: Random House, 1969.
————. *Soviet Management: With Significant American Comparisons.* Englewood Cliffs, N.J.: Prentice-Hall, 1965.

Chapter IX

Blodgett, Ralph M. and Donald L. Kemmeres. *Comparative Economic Development*. New York: McGraw-Hill Book Company, 1956.

Bruckberger, Raymond L., *Image of America*. New York: Viking Press, 1959.

Friedman, Milton. *Capitalism and Freedom*. Chicago: University of Chicago Press, 1962.

Galbraith, John Kenneth. *American Capitalism*. Boston: Houghton Mifflin, 1952.

Gorst, Sheila. *Cooperative Organization in Tropical Countries*. Oxford: Basil Blackwell, 1959.

Grudy, Allan G. *Comparative Economic Systems*. Boston: Houghton Mifflin, 1966.

Halm, George N. *Economic Systems—A Comparative Analysis*. New York: Holt, Rinehart and Winston, 1960.

Prybyla, Jan S. *Comparative Economic Systems*. New York: Appleton-Century-Crofts, 1969.

Schnitzer, Martin C. and James W. Nordyke. *Comparative Economic Systems*. Cincinnati: Southwestern Publishing Co., 1971.

Chapter X

Burgess, Ernest Waton. *Urban Community*. Chicago: University of Chicago Press, 1926.

Duhl, Leonard J. *The Urban Condition*. New York: Basic Books, 1963.

Etzkowitz, Henry and Gerald M. Schaflander. *Ghetto Crisis: Riots or Reconciliation?* Boston: Little, Brown, 1969.

Robson, Brian Turnbull. *Urban Analysis*. London: Cambridge University Press, 1969.

Rose, Peter Isaac. *The Ghetto and Beyond*. New York: Random House, 1969.

Sturdivant, Frederick D. (ed.). *The Ghetto Market Place*. New York: The Free Press, 1969.

U.S. Mutual Security Mission to China. *Urban and Industrial Taiwan*. Taipei: Foreign Operations Administration, 1954.

Chapter XI

Bevenuti, Bruno. *Farming in Cultural Change*. Netherlands: Van Gorcum, 1962.

Fox, Karl August. *Farming, Farmers and Markets for Farm Goods*. New York: Committee for Economic Development, 1962.

Griswold, Alfred Whitney. *Farming and Democracy*. New York: Harcourt, Brace, 1948.

Higbee, Edward Gunselman. *Farms and Farmers in an Urban Age*. New York: Twentieth Century Fund, 1963.

McKee, Alexander. *Farming the Sea*. London: Souvenir Press, 1967.

Chapter XII

Friedman, Samy. *Expropriation in International Law*. London: Stevens and Sons, 1953.

Gaither, Roscoe Bradley. *Expropriation in Mexico*. New York: W. Morrow, 1940.

Gordon, Wendell Chaffee. *The Expropriation of Foreign-owned Property*. Washington, D.C.: American Council on Public Affairs.

Wortley, Ben Atkinson. *Expropriation in Public International Law*. Cambridge, Eng.: University Press, 1959.

Chapters XIII, XVII, XX

Agarwala, Amar Narain. *Education for Business in a Developing Society*. East Lansing, Mich.: Michigan State University Press, 1969.

Allport, Gordon W. *Cultural Groups and Human Relations.*
New York: Columbia University Press, 1951.

Basile, Joseph. *The Cultural Development of Managers, Executives and Professionals.* Baltimore: Helicon, 1968.

Broomfield, J. H. *Elite Conflict in a Plural Society.* Berkeley, Calif.: Univeristy of California Press, 1968.

Cultural Affairs and Foreign Relations. Englewood Cliffs,
N.J.: Prentice-Hall, 1963.

Cultural Life of the Chinese Workers. Peking: Foreign Lan-
guages Press, 1962.

Élites et Responsabilités. Série régionale du Sud-Ouest.
Paris, 1955/56.

Evans, Rupert Nelson. *Education for Employment.* Ann
Arbor, Mich.: University of Michigan Press, 1969.

Girvetz, Harry K. *Elitism.* New York: Charles Scribner's
Sons, 1967.

Hunter, Guy. *Education for a Developing Region.* London:
Allen and Unwin, 1963.

Kluckhohn, Clyde. *Culture and Behavior.* New York: The
Free Press, 1962.

Lasswell, Harold Dwight. *Elites.* Stanford, Calif.: Stanford
University Press, 1952.

Leach, Edmund and S. N. Mukherjee. *Elites in South Asia,*
Cambridge, Eng.: University Press, 1970.

Lipset, Seymour Martin, *Culture and Social Character.* New
York: The Free Press, 1961.

―――. *Elites in Latin America.* New York: Oxford University Press, 1967.

Lorimer, Frank. *Culture and Human Fertility.* Paris:
UNESCO, 1954.

Mead, Margaret (ed.), *Cultural Patterns and Technical
Change.* New York: New American Library, 1961.

―――. *Culture and Commitment.* Garden City, N.Y.: Natural History Press, 1970.

Neo-colonialism. Djakarta, Indonesia: Government of the
Republic of Indonesia, 1964.

Nkrumah, Kwame. *Neo-colonialism.* London: Nebson, 1965.

Oliver, Robert Tarbell. *Culture and Communication.* Springfield, Ill.: Thomas Publishing Co., 1962.

Ray, Verne F. (ed.). *Cultural Stability and Cultural Change.* Seattle: University of Washington Press, 1969.

Robinson, Mary Electa. *Education for Social Change.* Washington: Brookings Institution, 1961.

Ulric, John. *Cultural Foundations of Industrial Civilization.* Cambridge, Eng.: University Press, 1958.

Valentine, Charles A. *Culture and Poverty.* Chicago: University of Chicago Press, 1968.

Webber, Ross A. *Culture and Management.* Homewood, Ill.: Richard D. Irwin, 1969.

Chapter XVI

Buchanan, Robert Angus. *Technology and Social Progress.* New York: Pergamon Press, 1965.

Cappon, Daniel. *Technology and Perception.* Springfield, Ill.: Thomas Publishing Co., 1971.

Carleton, William Groves. *Technology and Humanism.* Nashville, Tenn.: Vanderbilt University Press, 1970.

George, Roy Edwin. *Technological Redundancy in a Small Isolated Society.* Toronto, Canada: McGill University Press, 1969.

Gouldner, Alvin Ward. *Technology and the Moral Order.* Indianapolis, Ind.: Bobbs-Merrill, 1962.

Jackson, Sir Willis. *Technology and the Developing Countries.* London: London University Press, 1966.

Mesthene, Emmanuel G. *Technological Change: Its Impact on Man and Society.* Boston: Harvard University Press, 1970.

Mohan, Robert Paul. *Technology and Christian Culture.* Washington: Catholic University of America Press, 1960.

Morse, Dean and Aaron W. Warner. *Technological Innovation and Society.* New York: Columbia University Press, 1966.

Mueller, Eva. *Technological Advance in an Expanding Economy*. Ann Arbor: University of Michigan Press, 1969.

Nelson, Richard R. *The Technology Gap*. Santa Monica, Calif.: Rand Corporation, 1967.

Prasad, Kedarnath. *Technological Choice Under Developmental Planning*. Bombay, India: Popular Prakashar, 1963.

Rosenbloom, Richard S. *Technology Transfer*. Washington, D.C.: National Planning Association, 1965.

Strassmann, W. Paul. *Technological Change and Economic Development*. Ithaca, N.Y.: Cornell University Press, 1968.

Technological Change and Human Development. International Conference on Technological Change and Human Development. Hebrew University Press, 1969.

Technology and Human Values. Symposium on the Technological Society. Santa Barbara, Calif.: Center for the Study of Democratic Institutions, 1966.

Chapter XVIII

Fujisawa, Chikao. *Shinto Influence on Japanese Life*. Tokyo, Japan: The Foreign Affairs Association of Japan, 1960.

Kiyohora, Sadao. *Shintoshe* (Shinto History). Tokyo, Japan, 1940.

Mosse, George Lachmann. *Calvinism: Authoritarian or Democratic?* New York: Holt, Rinehart and Winston, 1961.

Ross, Floyd Hiatt. *Shinto, the Way of Japan*. Boston: Beacon Press, 1965.

Van Til, Henry R. *The Calvinistic Concept of Culture*. Grand Rapids, Mich.: Buke Book House, 1959.

Index

INDEX

RICHARD N. FARMER is Chairman of the Department of International Business at Indiana University. In addition to teaching economics at various American educational institutions, he has taught business administration in Beirut, Lebanon. Professor Farmer worked briefly in export shipping and interrupted his academic career to be general manager of a construction-transportation company located in Saudi Arabia. He had full responsibility for overall managerial, financial, and operational results.

Professor Farmer received his Ph.D. from the University of California at Berkeley. He is married and has four children. He maintains several antique automobiles in mint condition, claiming he does his best thinking while tinkering.